Ultimate Blockchain Security Handbook

Advanced Cybersecurity Techniques and Strategies for Risk Management, Threat Modeling, Pen Testing, and Smart Contract Defense for Blockchain

Taha Sajid
M.Sc., CISSP

Orangeava.com

First published: October 2023

Published by: Orange Education Pvt Ltd, AVA™

Address: 9, Daryaganj, Delhi, 110002

ISBN: 978-93-90475-98-8

www.orangeava.com

Dedicated to

My beloved parents:

Sajid Qayyum

Sajida Khanum

and

My wife **Ayesha** *and my kids* **Mustafa**, **Ibrahim**, *and* **Aizah**

Forewords

Tommy Cooksey
Cloud & Blockchain Architect and Instructor

Having collaborated with Taha since 2019, I can attest to his unparalleled knowledge and expertise in blockchain, 5G networks, project management, and security. His book serves as a comprehensive guide for anyone navigating the complex landscape of blockchain technology. Taha's dedication to educating and advancing the community is evident in his YouTube channel and online courses. His contributions to the field have earned him international recognition, and I wholeheartedly recommend this book as a valuable resource for professionals and enthusiasts alike. Taha Sajid is undeniably a proven winner in the world of emerging technologies

Samson Williams
Adjunct Professor, UNH School of Law, Cofounder
Co-founder, Milkyway Economy, Space Economy Think Tank
Co-Author, Blockchain & The Space Economy

We both reside on a tiny blue marble that hangs in an infinity of darkness. The name of this infinity of darkness isSpace. We just call it what it is, as so vast are the distances between the points of light that are the stars in this part of the Milky Way Galaxy and the entirety of the known universe. The reason I start this forward in a book about cybersecurity waxing on about Space is simple because the fifth Industrial Revolution is the development and maturation of The Space Economy. What does cybersecurity and blockchain have to do with The Space Economy? Everything.

Space is a purely digital ecosystem. Yes, we send hardware and metal carapaces into orbit. But these satellites are simply the mediums by which we capture, collect, and transmit back down into the gravity well of Earth the most valuable thing in the known universe, Data.

You have probably heard that data is the new oil of the Fourth Industrial Revolution. However, in the fifth Industrial Revolution, which is not only the establishment of permanent human settlements on the Moon, Mars, and beyond, data is not oil. Data is not a thing to be simply collected, refined, and burned. In microgravity, data does not function as oil. Rather, in orbit, data is gold. Data is the currency of Space. Data is the money upon which the businesses of the Fifth Industrial Revolution are being built.

That is of course if you can secure that record of debt. What is currently the best method to secure a digital record of debts, transactions, ownership, orbits, and data from the stars and beyond?

In the fifth Industrial Revolution, mastering blockchain security isnot just a novel idea. Rather than a necessity of the financial and economic infrastructure upon which Humanity will secure its future amongst the stars, this book is the steppingstone for that.

Jamiel Sheikh

CEO Scifn, adjunct professor Zicklin Business School

Blockchain, the mothership of the decentralized promise, stands juxtaposed against the intrinsic challenges of security. Within this transformative digital paradigm lies an Achilles' heel, bridging human design and the adaptive arms race of cybersecurity. As the author delves into the intricate realms of zero-knowledge proofs and more, we're reminded that security is an evolving equilibrium, essential for blockchain's fruition. The nexus of blockchain and security, both nascent and paramount, demands our immediate attention. This book provides not just vast knowledge, but a compass for our shared digital journey, emphasizing the intertwined fate of trust, security, and decentralized progress. I am happy to see the book on the market now because Taha fills this gap and market demand.

About the Author

Taha Sajid is a Principal Security Architect and a 5G Security Lead at Comcast. He is responsible for security design and architecture, vulnerability management and security operations for the end-to-end 5G wireless network. He is also focused on driving Data Privacy controls and security standards of 5G for the 3GPP SA3 group aimed towards Zero Trust Security policy.

He has over 15 years of experience in telecommunication and cybersecurity design and operations. Prior to Comcast, he worked for organizations like Huawei, STC, Mobily, Ericsson and Ufone as a technology leader and has supported over a dozen enterprises, financial institutions, and startups as a cybersecurity advisor for Blockchain and digital currency solutions.

Taha is also a principal cybersecurity advisor at a digital currency think tank advising central banks and financial institutions on security architecture and design. Taha serves as a co-chair of the IEEE FNTC Webinar Series, also an active member of working groups for the ATIS 5G Zero Trust and IEEE Future Networks for Data Security and Privacy. He also runs a YouTube channel to educate the community, where he publishes technical design and cybersecurity content timely for 5G and Blockchain.

Taha has also authored online courses on cybersecurity for blockchain, Defi and Fintech, which are used by thousands of professionals, having a 5-star rating.

Taha is a Certified Information Systems Security Professional (CISSP), Project Management Professional (PMP), holds an MSc in Digital Currency from University of Nicosia and a BS in Telecom from FAST-NU.

Due to his valuable contributions globally and several publications on emerging technology and pressing IT topics, he has received several international awards and featured/interviewed by the media/ newspapers.

LinkedIn profile: **https://www.linkedin.com/in/taha-sajid**
Website: **www.tahasajid.com**,
YouTube channel: **https://www.youtube.com/@TahaSajid**

About the Reviewer

Waqar Ahmed has a distinguished career with over a decade of experience as a cybersecurity professional.He has led the charge in fortifying global enterprise cybersecurity programs, showcasing his analytical acumen through revamping policies and procedures, gap analyses, penetration tests, and developing and deploying cutting-edge security tools. His experiences include working with government agencies, financial institutions, and global companies in different countries, including the UK, Singapore, Qatar, and the UAE.

Holding an MSc in Network Security from Queen Mary University of London, Waqar combines academic excellence with real-world experience. Hiseducational journey has instilled a disciplined and structured mindset, a trait that shines through in hismeticulously crafted book reviews. This solid academic foundation equips Waqar with the analytical skills required to delve into the intricate layers of technical corrections and literary improvements.

Furthermore, Waqar has garnered a formidable array of certifications, including OSCP, CEH, CISSP, ECIH, ISO27001, Certified Blockchain Security Engineer, and API Security Architect. These certifications not only underscore Waqar's dedication to continuous learning but also enhance hisability to critically assess environments and tools. Waqar's certifications in cybersecurity serve as a testament to hiscommitment to excellence and attention to detail, qualities that extend seamlessly to the realm of critique.

In addition to hisacademic achievements and certifications, Waqar has also shared hisexpertise as a speaker at SANS HackFest. Here, Waqar addressed a captivated audience on the intricate topic of smart contract security—a testament to hisability to communicate complex ideas with clarity and authority.

In essence, Waqar brings a unique blend of academic rigor, real-world cybersecurity experience, and a passion for literature to the art of book reviewing. With exceptional qualifications and an innate ability to dissect and analyze, Waqar boasts a rich academic background and a portfolio of certifications, which have been instrumental in shaping hisinsightful approach to book reviewing.

Acknowledgement

There are a few people I want to thank for the continued and ongoing support they have given me during the writing of this book. First and foremost, I would like to thank my family for continuously encouraging me to write the book — I could have never completed this book without their support.

Thank you, Mom and Dad, this is for you. Dad, for keeping me motivated and for your timely follow-ups. Mom, for your tireless prayers for getting me through this journey smoothly.

I am grateful to my awesome wife, Ayesha, from taking care of our kids to serving delicious biryani, and keeping the home in peace so I can concentrate, "Thank you so much, dear."

Next, I want to acknowledge and thank my University of Nicosia alumni and colleagues, my blockchain network, LinkedIn family in general who always appreciated my efforts whenever I was presenting and posting, and being there with me when I didn't know much. It motivated me to always strive for an extra mile, and this is where I thought of coming up with a book.

I also highly regard the technical reviewers for my book, Waqar Ahmed and Hasshi Sudler for their thoughtful comments and actionable feedback and ensuring that I convey the right message.

My gratitude also goes to the Orange AVA team, especially the editors Sonali and Shubha for keeping everything on track and making sure the book is up to scratch.

Preface

Blockchain technology is being tested and used in several fields right now. Central banks from many countries are also looking into how blockchain and distributed ledger technology can be used to solve problems that have been around for a long time. From production to banking services. Retail and telecommunication are some of the other industries that are starting to try out possible uses.

It's more important than ever to talk about blockchain security because if this isn't fixed, it will become a problem for every household soon. There's no reason to leave it up to chance or hire a security audit company, even though we think blockchain is already safe because it uses cryptography. Everyone involved in the business and technology of blockchain should work together to make sure the design is safe, from the code to the user's wallet and all the way to the bottom of the infrastructure. There is a strong possibility that an attack or breakdown of blockchain protocols to have effects that put economies, financial markets, and enterprises at greater risk.

This book is divided into 6 chapters. They will cover Public and private blockchain security design, inherent security capabilities and vulnerabilities. The chapters touched upon blockchain risk identification, classifying methods and tools, and how those risks can be further analyzed and exploited. The latter half of the book provided remediations and security solutions. Interestingly, in one of the chapters, the author discussed strategies on how to avoid a crypto scam and guidelines for the victims on how they can trace and recover their funds.

The details of each chapter are listed as follows:

Chapter 1 will start with the fundamentals of blockchain, types of blockchain, blockchain use cases and benefits, then it covers the technical design of bitcoin, in which transactions chaining, mining and authenticity are explained. The last section covers Bitcoin security with consideration on decentralization and handling of wallet and cryptographic keys.

Chapter 2 will cover types of blockchain and will explain Ethereum architecture, Smart contracts, and EVM design. Then it covers an in-depth security review of EVM nodes, smart contracts vulnerabilities with root cause analysis and security recommendations. The last topic covers hype ledger fabric architecture and security design review and security best design practices for private blockchain secure development. The discussion points revolve around chain code exploits, MSP downtime considerations, key management, governance, and cloud deployment principles with examples and case studies.

Chapter 3 will covers blockchain risk management and top security risks in blockchain applications. Then it covers Blockchain risk identification methods and risk analysis, and we discuss classification scenarios in depth, where a threat modeling tool is introduced and explained with a use case of how it can be applied to a wallet application. The chapter also highlights mitigation strategies as a risk response, addressing threat modeling attack vectors with examples and lab work recommendations.

Chapter 4 will cover techniques and tools to exploit blockchain applications. It starts with blockchain penetration testing explaining different phases, and touches upon vulnerability scanning tools like Nessus, OpenVAS, and smart bugs framework to analyze solidity, bytecode, and runtime code in depth. Then the chapter explains the exploitation phase by digging deep into injection attacks and the CVE analysis of overflow attacks. We also discuss the last phase, where the attacker maintains access with the APT progress matrix with security measures. The latter half of the chapter shows an example of how smart contracts can be hacked, where the vulnerable code is discussed in depth. The chapter ends with suggestions on Best Security Practices and tools to secure Smart Contracts.

Chapter 5 will cover different tools and techniques for how you can audit your blockchain application. It starts with explaining different methods of smart contract testing like automated, unit, testing frameworks, integration testing, and manual testing procedures. It then explains the formal verification procedure of smart contracts, K frameworks, and their application with code examples. It also explains how to define EVM specification, with a case study example of Open Zeppelin's contract. The chapter ends with an explanation of the bug bounty program, which can be useful in the public verification of smart contracts.

Chapter 6 will cover blockchain security solutions from Zero knowledge proof to identity and access management, public key infrastructure and security logging and monitoring of a blockchain solution. While explaining the usability of these security controls, examples, design and architecture principles are explained with case studies to show how security hardening can be done for a blockchain solution against cyber hacks.

Downloading the code bundles and colored images

Please follow the link to download the
Code Bundles of the book:

https://github.com/OrangeAVA/Ultimate-Blockchain-Security-Handbook

The code bundles and images of the book are also hosted on
https://rebrand.ly/ldey32r

In case there's an update to the code, it will be updated on the existing GitHub repository.

Errata

We take immense pride in our work at **Orange Education Pvt Ltd,** and follow best practices to ensure the accuracy of our content to provide an indulging reading experience to our subscribers. Our readers are our mirrors, and we use their inputs to reflect and improve upon human errors, if any, that may have occurred during the publishing processes involved. To let us maintain the quality and help us reach out to any readers who might be having difficulties due to any unforeseen errors, please write to us at :

errata@orangeava.com

Your support, suggestions, and feedback are highly appreciated.

DID YOU KNOW

Did you know that Orange Education Pvt Ltd offers eBook versions of every book published, with PDF and ePub files available? You can upgrade to the eBook version at **www.orangeava.com** and as a print book customer, you are entitled to a discount on the eBook copy. Get in touch with us at: **info@orangeava.com** for more details.

At **www.orangeava.com**, you can also read a collection of free technical articles, sign up for a range of free newsletters, and receive exclusive discounts and offers on AVA™ Books and eBooks.

PIRACY

If you come across any illegal copies of our works in any form on the internet, we would be grateful if you would provide us with the location address or website name. Please contact us at **info@orangeava.com** with a link to the material.

ARE YOU INTERESTED IN AUTHORING WITH US?

If there is a topic that you have expertise in, and you are interested in either writing or contributing to a book, please write to us at **business@orangeava.com**. We are on a journey to help developers and tech professionals to gain insights on the present technological advancements and innovations happening across the globe and build a community that believes Knowledge is best acquired by sharing and learning with others. Please reach out to us to learn what our audience demands and how you can be part of this educational reform. We also welcome ideas from tech experts and help them build learning and development content for their domains.

REVIEWS

Please leave a review. Once you have read and used this book, why not leave a review on the site that you purchased it from? Potential readers can then see and use your unbiased opinion to make purchase decisions. We at Orange Education would love to know what you think about our products, and our authors can learn from your feedback. Thank you!

For more information about Orange Education, please visit **www.orangeava.com**.

Table of Contents

Chapter 1
Blockchain Security Overview

Introduction

If you browse the internet to search on blockchain, you must be hearing news about several use cases for blockchain technology, the **benefits** it provides, people looking into opportunities to switch careers to blockchain, and investment opportunities that can reach 10x. On the other hand, you also heard about hackings of exchanges, Ponzi schemes, inflation around bitcoin prices, regulators cracking down on start-ups, founders going to jail, and whatnot. The result of all of this can leave anyone confused; this is what's really going on: there is a lot of information, but there is not a clear and safer direction around blockchain technology that a professional can take, and this book provides exactly that. So, congrats on choosing the journey with me to go through this book.

To emphasize my point even more, if Blockchain is truly revolutionary, solves real-world problems, and attracts a lot of attention, why isn't it being used more widely? Secondly, why is it a convenient target for hackers, even though it has been developed ever since its inception? We are talking about more than $100 billion across more than 100 incidents worldwide. The Binance Blockchain Hit, which resulted in the theft of $570 million, was one significant cyberattack that made headlines recently. In addition to the loss of money and sleep, these cyber incidents also result in a lack of confidence. If these hacks continue, people will eventually lose faith in blockchain technology.

What exactly is the source of these attacks? A few examples to ponder could include software bugs, security breaches brought on by poor architectural design, the absence of backups, improperly configured security controls, or simply a lack of due care and diligence. The fact of the matter is, there could be a combination of these reasons or even more, but if you think deep down, security has never been a priority, always been an afterthought, and it's a rat race where one has to be just in the blockchain game, whether getting crypto coins or just getting done with a blockchain app for point scoring inside the organization to compete or resume building.

In addition, Blockchain solutions are difficult to architect and design due to the complexity of protocols and interdependency of chains and assets, and with the lack of resources and knowledge available in the market, you get stuck in just playing with what you have, leaving the door locks open.

Do not worry now! Not only will this book provide you with a simplified understanding of Blockchain in a fun way, but also in-depth concepts across various layers and protocols. Most importantly, it will equip you with the right tools you need to identify attack vectors and design and architect security solutions. With real-world case studies, interactive questions, and practical attack scenarios with prevention techniques, we will keep this journey a fun experience for you.

There is absolutely no free lunch for the attackers, and the good news is, even if you are just beginning your blockchain journey, this is the book you need to have!

Let's get right to the chapter scope without further delay.

Structure

In this chapter, we will cover the following topics:

- Fundamentals of blockchain
- Blockchain security overview
- Exploring Blockchain security benefits
- Inherent security capabilities of Bitcoin

Fundamentals of blockchain

Everywhere you look in the news, there will be headlines about blockchain, usually about cryptocurrencies rising or falling. However, the what, why, and how of blockchain can quickly become confusing if you read beyond the headlines.

Imagine a Super Mario LEGO game, where to complete the structure, you need to fit the pieces in a specified order, following the rules of the manual.

I'll walk you through the fundamentals of how blockchain technology works on this topic by giving you a heads-up and then explaining the pieces through the analogy. Why is this important? As they say, if you want to protect your house, you have to know the functions inside your house, such as the entry and exit, the safe location, etc. You can put the right locks on the right door, if you know the fundamentals, your foundation will be built, which will support your future learning.

Blockchain is a database made up of chunks of data. Each chunk of data is piled up into a block. As additional chunks of related data are added, they are piled into new blocks and linked to the previous ones to create a chain. How does it sound, easy right? Let's visualize this.

Consider a row of three interconnected boxes. Inside these boxes are the plans for the office improvement project you're currently working on. The plans for your cafeteria are in the first box, those for your conference room are in the second box, and those for your employee cabins are in the third box.

Blockchain technology keeps blueprints secure by assigning each block a unique alphanumeric code related to the data inside. This code is known as a hash. The hash for each block is linked to the hash of the next block in the chain. So, the box of your cafeteria blueprints is labeled with the hash 01CAFE, then the box of your Conference room blueprints gets both the hashes 01CAFE and 02CONF, and finally, the box of your employee cabin blueprints is assigned the hashes 02CONF and 03CABIN.

You employ a group of skilled craftspeople to carry out the work on your Office improvement project to guarantee its success. You don't hire a contractor to supervise them on purpose because you want everyone working in your home to be treated equally. A carpenter with an axe to grind ruining the wood in your cafeteria and preventing the plumber and electrician from doing their jobs is an example of how decentralizing the workers' power prevents any one worker from ruining the entire project. Having multiple artisans with shared responsibilities enables everyone to stay on task and under control.

These construction professionals are known as the miners or participants in your network, with each one first looking to make sure the hashes labeled on the boxes correspond to the blueprints inside. So, if the craftspeople peek into box 01CAFE and see the Cafeteria blueprints, they'd validate the block and use it to start the chain. Since this is the first block, it is called a Genesis block. Then they'd repeat the process for boxes 02CONF and 03CABIN, checking that they have the Conference room and Cabin area blueprints, respectively.

Note

What do you think would be in the blueprint? If you are thinking that the blueprints are validation rules, or in the blockchain language, mining rules, or simply how blocks need to be mined, you are absolutely right. I will add more light to it later in the chapter.

After they're validated, these hashes become the glue that binds the boxes together. Your blueprints, or data, are secure because if someone tampered with the contents of any single box from the chain, the hashes would change and the boxes would no longer be glued together. This would cause the whole blockchain to fall apart, and your office improvement project plans would become an indecipherable pile of rubble.

To help make the home improvement process smoother, you can add an automated feature to the project's workflow. Along with the blueprints in the boxes, there's also a contract that specifies when and how the craftspeople get paid. For example, in box 01CAFE with the data for the CAFE, the contract states that *If carpenter builds counters and plumber installs sink and electrician adds lights, then each worker gets a direct deposit as payment in their bank accounts.* This is a smart contract, in this case, services were exchanged for money, with a digital bank or computer handling the whole transaction. It helps keep your OFFICE improvement project moving forward because the craftspeople don't have to wait for you to hand them cash after they complete their work.

Highlight the terms Decentralization, miners, Smart contract, Hashes, and of course immutability (block is linked) in the preceding context.

It is merely an illustration of blockchain in its physical form. However, blockchains in the real world are only digital, so allow me to demonstrate how this might actually function with a Bitcoin transaction.

Say John sends 10 Bitcoins to their friend Tina. First, a block is created containing a record of the transaction and is assigned a unique hash. While Bitcoin hashes are actually 256 alphanumeric characters long, for simplicity's sake, let us say this transaction's hash is JOHN2TINA10.

Next, the record is checked by the network. The computers owned by the workers in the network – the participants or miners – inspect the details of the trade to make sure it is valid. For example, they'd make sure that John wasn't also sending the same 10 Bitcoins to someone else at the same time. Is the transaction signed by John's private key, the math game AKA Proof of Work?

Don't worry; I will come back to the private key and math game AKA proof of work part later. For now, just consider it as part of the blueprint process.

After the record is accepted, the block is finally added to the blockchain. The hashcode of a previous transaction - ALX2JOHN10 - from when Alex sent 10 Bitcoin to JOHN would be added to and referenced in this one, connecting the blocks together in a specific order. This provides security because if someone tries to change the record of the transactions within the blocks, they would cause the whole chain to fall apart.

Now that you can visualize the fundamental parts of a blockchain, keep this picture in mind the next time you read about this novel technology in the news.

Blockchain security overview

Is the blockchain actually safe? How can millions of people trust a technology with their hard-earned money, without knowing its creator, without anybody controlling the governance like in a traditional organization? What has made it so trustworthy that even countries are adopting it as a legal tender for their public?

Let's dissect it by getting to know the security features it relies on. Blockchain security principles like immutability, decentralization, cryptography, and consensus algorithms have been discussed, but how do they actually operate and where do they apply? You need to acquire a solid understanding of such security principles to conduct a thorough investigation into its security, identify areas where vulnerabilities exist, and determine the additional layers you can employ to strengthen it.

A process known as *minting or mining* a new block of data adds new transactions to the blockchain. A few characteristics are shared by all block-minting systems. Let us first learn about the security concept, and then see how it applies to blockchain.

Every security attack, control, and mitigation revolves around these basic security principles.

- **Confidentiality**: The protection of data from unauthorized access and disclosure, as well as methods for safeguarding personal privacy and proprietary information, is referred to as data confidentiality.

  Example: Any data that does not contain any information must be disclosed. It can be phone numbers, names, email addresses, company records, financial transactions, and so on.

  Attack scenario: John is only sending a file to Peter, and he doesn't want anyone else to see it. However, Henry intercepted the message and read it.

- **Integrity:** The accuracy, completeness, and consistency of the data as a whole constitute data integrity.

  Example: A specific *employee number* and their name should be the primary keys in a database of employees. In simple words, if John is sending an X file to Peter with Y contents, Peter should not receive a Y file with X contents.

  Attack scenario: A file is accessed without authorization and altered to reflect information other than what authorized users intend. For instance, John is sending an X file only to Peter because he does not want anyone to alter or change the file's content. However, Henry intercepted the file and changed the file's content from X to Y.

- **Availability:** The frequency with which your data can be utilized by either your own organization or one of your partners is known as data availability. It would be ideal for your data to be accessible round-the-clock, 365 days a year, allowing your business to continue uninterrupted.

  Example: A customer-serving application's data processing server is up and running without interruption. Availability guarantees that users can access systems, applications, and data at any time.

  Attack Scenario: John's laptop's operating system has crashed due to ransomware and is no longer accessible or usable, so he is unable to send any data to Peter.

- **Traceability:** Any data event that occurs on your server or in a network can be identified by its subject, whether a human or a non-human user. It's the capacity to locate the source of a particular piece of content or message.

  Example: To keep track of all data accesses and modifications, data traceability follows the lifecycle of the data providing audit trails to the legal and quality assurance teams.

  Attack Scenario: Peter receives a message from John, but he is unable to determine whether the message is from John. Tracing gives us the data we need in real-time to detect and stop attacks.

Now, let us take a look at how it all makes sense in the context of security attributes in the blockchain. We need to see if the Blockchain security ecosystem protects users under the CIAT umbrella. Let us take a look in the context of *Public blockchains*.

Confidentiality in Blockchain

A transaction's counterparties should not be identifiable by an unauthorized third party in a blockchain until their counterparties reveal that information.

Second, unless the parties to the transaction do not disclose their information, the details of the transaction must not be visible to anyone who is not a party to it.

Within a blockchain network, there is no middleman involved, meaning that if John is sending the transaction to Peter with no intentions of withdrawing it to the bank account, he just needs to have a wallet. There is no bank or financial intermediary like a payment gateway that will facilitate the transaction. With this, no personal information between the sender and receiver will be shared. The distribution network sits in between John and Peter, does the validation for that transaction with signature to public key mapping and performing the math equation.

Instead, a string of alphanumeric characters known as a public key is the only way to identify transactions on the blockchain. This key renders transactions in Bitcoin pseudo-anonymous. This means that even though other people can look at your holdings and transactions, they can't figure out who the real person behind the public key is. While knowing the public key, allows you to see all the transaction history, the fact that the actual identity, such as the name and address, is unknown, doesn't raise any concerns.

There are two main concerns about the confidentiality of a public blockchain network. The first is the point where anyone goes to third parties, such as wallet providers and centralized exchanges, to store or transact cryptos. They can consume personal information in the shape of account sign-ups.

Second, miners of the network, who actually process the blocks can see how much money the public key holder has. However, due to the economic factor of rewards, the fair play rule, downplays any misuse of exploiting the block information.

Data Integrity in Blockchain

It ought to guarantee that the data written to the blockchain is accurate and cannot be altered in the future. Additionally, blockchain only allows authorized parties to add transactions, and once a transaction is committed, it cannot be denied later.

Since every transaction is immutable, editing it after it has been completed is difficult. There is no way to reverse or cancel any transaction.

Data Integrity is achieved in blockchain in the following ways.

- In the blockchain mining process, each block is represented by a hash value. Any alteration of data would result in a different hash.
- Excluding the genesis block, every block represents a hash of its neighboring block. So, any changes to any block's data would break the chain.
- Consistency is maintained due to the distribution of nodes. In a blockchain network, the nodes are peer-to-peer distributed, and the addition of any new block means that every participant in a network will have to update their records. Think of this like a WhatsApp group: any new message in the group reaches every group member, and everyone will have a copy on their phones.

Data Availability in Blockchain

The capacity of blockchain systems to withstand outages and attacks is referred to as their availability. In blockchain, data should always be accessible to all participating nodes. This is inherent in the distributed nature of blockchain technologies. The main concern in the availability domain is the chance of pulling up a Denial of Service or a Distributed denial of service attack. However, given the millions of nodes involved in the validation process, any chance of a few numbers of nodes crashing down will not make any difference, the mining process would still continue.

However, if you look at the endpoints where the user operates, like wallets, APIs, and exchanges, any network entity that is part of the ecosystem can be exploited. There is a lot to talk about regarding the availability aspect while discussing private blockchains.

Traceability in Blockchain

Traceability is also referred to as the non-repudiation principle. In simple words, a person cannot deny receiving or sending it; the transaction should be able to trace back to the sender without tampering. Lastly, the receiver of the message can only read it, and nobody else in the network can view it until the block data is updated on the chain. Let us dissect all this magic into two categories.

Firstly, the blocks are immutable through hashing reference code, meaning data cannot be changed or altered, a topic we covered earlier. So, whatever information has been stored in a block, let's say block 1, can be visible and tracked down even if you have reached up to 1 million blocks of information in your chain. From a security standpoint, this gives better control and visibility in case you have to reverse engineer up to some point to extract information for a compliance use case or auditing purposes.

Secondly, sender authentication in the process involves validation of the sender by the miner, the encrypted flow of the data across the chain, and the sender being able to decrypt the message. All this happens with the help of cryptography.

If you think about the exact features of cryptography, blockchain inherits the use of hashing for data integrity use cases, the use of public and private keys for the sender's address, unlocking the funds, and finally digital signature for non-repudiation and authenticity and encrypting the data in transit as it leaves the wallet to travel across the chain.

Digital signatures are similar to proof that a user provides to the recipient and other network nodes to demonstrate that the node is a legitimate one for carrying out transactions. The user must first use a special algorithm to combine the transaction data with the user's private key to create a unique digital signature before initiating a transaction with other nodes in the blockchain network. Both the integrity of the data and the authenticity of the node will be guaranteed by this procedure.

Now that you have understood the key security principles of blockchain, let's take a look at the overview of blockchain architecture to understand how these controls are in place in the stack.

Blockchain Security ecosystem

Blockchain, like most modern technologies, is not a single entity. It has several distinct layers, each with its own advantages and security concerns. An understanding of the system as a whole requires an understanding of how each level functions and the security assumptions it makes.

In *Figure 1.1*, you can see the layered structure of a blockchain stack. When people discuss blockchain, they usually discuss only a few layers, such as smart contracts and consensus algorithms. Data, network, and infrastructure layers are often missed. When designing a security architecture of the stack, understanding each layer is important. It's like if you want to protect your house worth $$$$$$, you don't just lock the main doors; you lock cupboards, safe vaults, install security cameras, fences, etc. If you don't know what you are protecting, a good view of the inventory, the chance of missing some valuable entry points is high, and leaving back doors open is high.

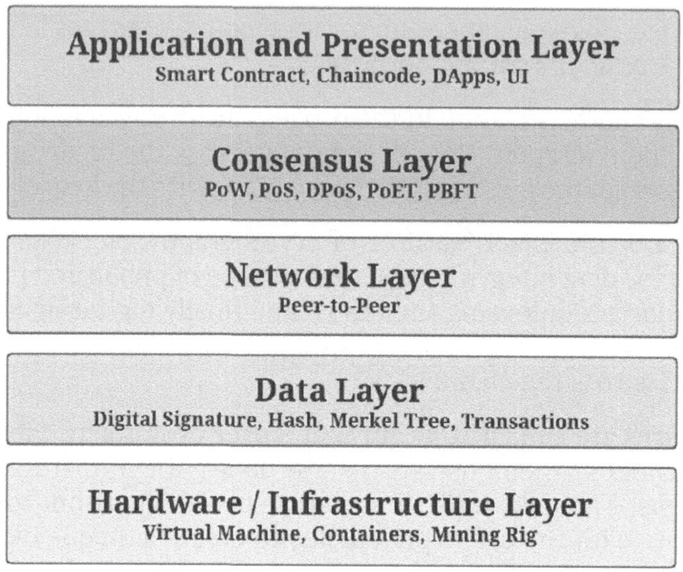

Figure 1.1: *Layered view of the blockchain stack*

Now let us take a look at each layer from the conceptual as well as from the security risk standpoint.

Application Layer

The application layer is made up of chain code, smart contracts, and decentralized applications (DApps). The protocols in the application layer are further broken down into the application and execution layers. The applications that end-users use to communicate with the blockchain network are included in the application layer. It includes user interfaces, frameworks, application programming interfaces (APIs), and scripts.

Smart contract platforms, like Ethereum, are designed to enable the creation of Turing-complete programs that run on the blockchain. These programs are associated with accounts on the blockchain network and are called via transactions that contain code to be executed. Each node in the blockchain network executes the same code and updates the state of the blockchain in the same way, maintaining consistency across the network.

The addition of programs that run on top of the blockchain network introduces new potential security risks to the blockchain. These programs run on virtual machines, which may have security flaws. Secure coding practices and a secure software development lifecycle need to be adopted to ensure the security of an application layer.

Consensus Algorithm Layer

Getting everyone into an agreement is such a difficult task. The capacity to implement a digital ledger that is completely decentralized is one of the main advantages of blockchain technology. For this to be possible, there needs to be a way to make sure that everyone agrees on the current state of the ledger, which is the transactions in each block.

Blockchain consensus algorithms take on this responsibility. It is the mechanism in which participant in a distributed network, validates the truthfulness of a transaction before it gets added on the chain (This is covered in more detail under Bitcoin Overview topic). Security is mapped to economic principles such as supply and demand, and no consensus algorithm is perfect. These principles generally shield blockchains from attack; however, there is a point where the security of consensus algorithms breaks down. The most frequently used consensus algorithms have flaws that can be exploited by an attacker, giving them a slight advantage when trying to take over a blockchain network.

Please visit ***https://cointelegraph.com/news/what-is-a-51-attack-and-how-to-detect-it****, for an example of an attack targeting the consensus algorithm layer. We will cover all of this in greater detail later in the book.*

Network Layer

The theory of blockchain technology is hammered out in the first two layers of the blockchain stack. A blockchain platform can theoretically operate over any communication medium, such as routers and computers that are used to build up the network. Basically, the network is implemented on computers, the internet, and private corporate networks in practice.

A variety of conventional cyberattacks can target a blockchain network because it is essentially software running on a collection of computers connected by peer-to-peer networks. Malware or phishing attacks directed at a computer running the software, or a **node**, have the potential to compromise a user's account and impact the network as a whole. An attacker can also target the network infrastructure of a blockchain network, which can have an impact on the blockchain's functionality and security guarantees.

Data layer

Blockchain technology is made up of cryptographic algorithms and data structures at the base. Blockchain's **blocks** are made to store data, including the actual transactions themselves and additional metadata. Cryptographic hashes are used to connect blocks in the blockchain's **chains**, making it much harder to change them later.

At this point, the security of a blockchain depends on the safety of its cryptographic algorithms. The use of prime numbers, the length of the key, the bits in the hashing algorithm, and other factors can have a significant impact on the strength of public-key cryptography and blockchain. These need to be rigorously tested with threat modeling taking into account both internal and external threat actors. We are in charge of the risk.

Note

*The hardening of the cryptographic algorithm and how strong it is depends upon what ingredients are used in its formation. If you want to learn more about prime numbers, key formation, and length in developing a safe crypto algorithm, please visit **https://www.baeldung.com/cs/prime-numbers-cryptography**.*

Infrastructure and Virtualization Layer

The blockchain's content is stored on a server in a data center somewhere on this lovely globe. Clients request content or data from application servers while browsing the web or utilizing any apps, which is known as the client-server architecture. This consists of virtual machines, containers, services, and messaging. Infrastructure can be on-premise using bare metal or private cloud setups. In addition, blockchain can also be deployed in the public cloud. The security of this layer comes down to how many security controls you have used in Session, TCP, IP, and data switch layers if you have an on-premise setup. Whereas, in the case of a public cloud, service-level agreement in contractual agreements with cloud providers plays a pivotal role.

Exploring blockchain security benefits

Just to recap what we know about the blockchain rules:

- Blockchains are decentralized, so there's no single source of data to hack, and there's no need to bring in third-party suppliers—who may also be hacked—to process transactions.

- Blockchains are encrypted with a private key to provide an extra layer of security and ensure data doesn't fall into the wrong hands.
- All changes are made in real time across all nodes, which adds transparency and trust in the ledger and ensures there's no single point of failure.
- Blockchains are virtually tamper-proof because changing a record would invalidate its file signature and raise a massive red flag.
- The consensus process requires members of the network to solve a mathematical puzzle that requires strong computational power. For example, you have to come up with a nonce value to match the difficulty level, and if the miner gets that right, the result is broadcast to the network for validation. The longest chain rule, which checks the work done (how long the chain is, how much effort is put in place to build the chain) before the network accepts any transaction, like building a spoofed chain that is longer/more powerful than the real chain for the network to agree, as shown in *Figure 1.2*.

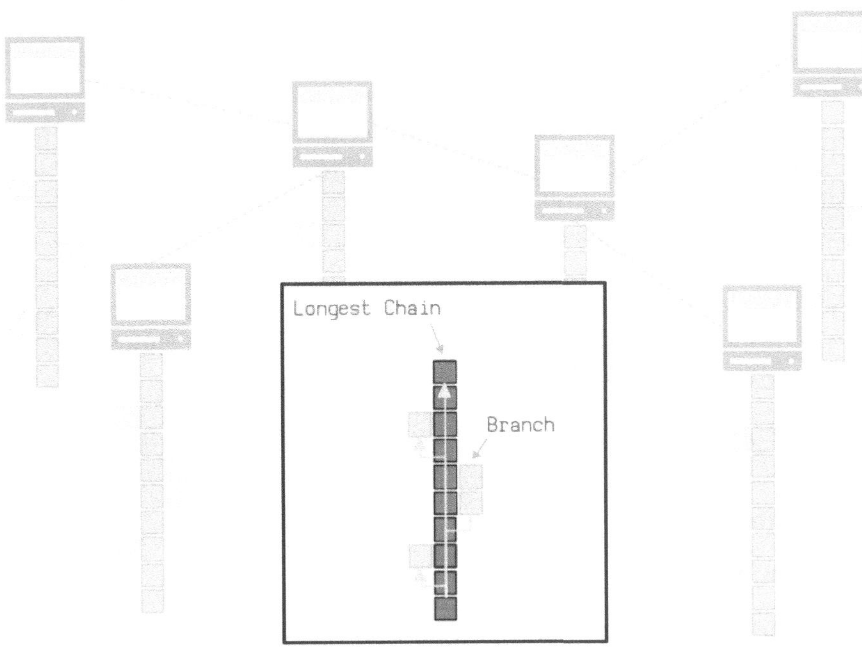

Figure 1.2: *Longest chains illustration in a blockchain network*

Just to explain my point about the longest chain and with the most effort, consider the following example; if the chain has more blocks but the difficulty level is less, it will not be accepted by the network (refer to *Figure 1.3*).

The blockchain that has required the most energy to construct is referred to as the *longest chain*. Typically, this is the chain with the most blocks or, more accurately, the chain with the most work in it.

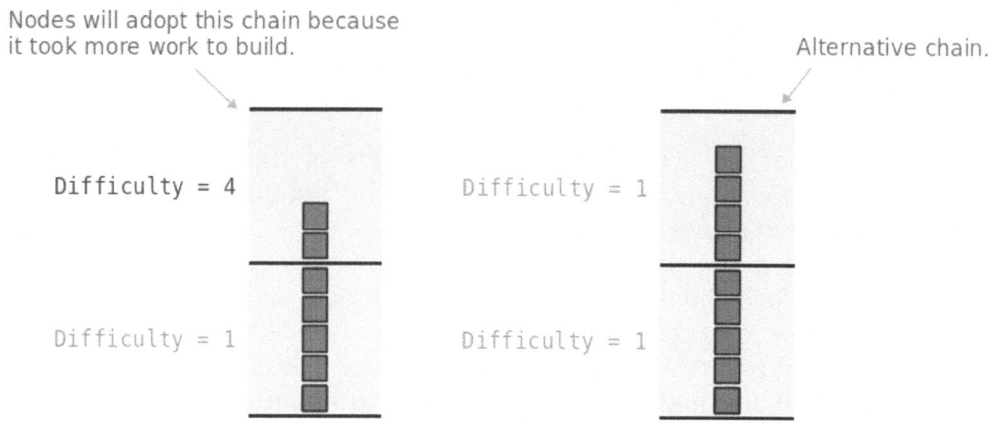

Figure 1.3: *Longest Chain acceptance criteria*

Note

Please visit ***https://learnmeabitcoin.com/technical/longest-chain*** *to learn more. It is recommended to develop a good understanding of how long the chain is calculated, chain work formulas and results.*

If you have to spoof a chain, meaning to create a duplicate similar chain but with more work done, more blocks, and broadcast the block faster than any other miner in the network, you need to have developed a supercomputer, which is technically and economically not feasible for such gains.

Economic incentives are given to miners who are part of the validation process, with the current reward fee being 6.25 bitcoins.

Any block contains the following data:

- **Version:** current version of the block.
- **Previous block header hash:** reference hash of a block's parent block.
- **Merkel root hash:** cryptographic hash of all the transactions present in the block.
- **Time:** when a block is created.
- **nBits:** the encoded form of the target threshold and the current difficulty of the block.

- **Nonce:** an abbreviation for *number used once*, which is a random number added to a block by miners.

When the block is hashed, all the metadata within the block goes to an input to the hashing function, and any change in any of these values produces a different hash.

If you want to pen down the blockchain security benefits, consider the preceding rules and the security features comprising blockchain. So, whatever the benefits these security features bring, blockchain technology has it built in.

We will see how this also comes together while discussing how blockchain empowers security and helps several industries.

Manufacturing

Due to their extensive and intricate supply chains, manufacturers need to ensure that specifications sent from upstream partners can be trusted. At this point, the blockchain's resistance to manipulation comes into its own. The time stamping of blocks provides an additional level of granularity, which further enhances assurance.

Health Care

The anonymity of individual patients who may be a part of the network can be preserved by securely encrypting electronic patient records, preventing them from being hacked, and using blockchain technology. This guarantees that patients, healthcare providers, and clinicians can seamlessly share data without worrying about privacy or security.

Moreover, it is difficult for healthcare organizations to securely share data across platforms. In the end, improved data collaboration between providers may result in more accurate diagnoses, more effective treatments, and cost-effective care.

HealthVerity is one of the players in this space, combining a health data exchange with a blockchain product to manage permissions and access rights.

Crowdfunding

Blockchain technology can help secure crowdfunding by providing an immutable ledger, automating the process through smart contracts, promoting decentralization, and using advanced security measures. These features can help increase transparency, reduce fraud, and improve the overall trustworthiness of the crowdfunding process. With its immutable ledger, transparency and integrity of the crowdfunding process can be achieved, by providing an auditable record of all transactions. Using smart contracts in the process flow, ensures that ensure that funds are only released to project creators once certain conditions have been met, such as reaching a specific funding goal or completing certain project milestones. This helps prevent fraud and ensures that donors' contributions are only used for the intended purpose.

Note

Giveth is a blockchain-based crowdfunding platform that focuses on social impact projects. The platform uses smart contracts to ensure that funds are distributed to the intended recipients and that donors can track the progress of the project.

Binance Launchpad is a blockchain-based crowdfunding platform that helps blockchain startups raise funds through token sales. The platform uses smart contracts to ensure that funds are collected and distributed securely and transparently.

Finance

Blockchain can securely encrypt financial transactions, making it simpler to trace and monitor payments to reduce fraud. These same principles apply to the sharing and storage of private and confidential documents. The use cases in finance go from capital markets to asset management, payments, and remittances, all the way to trade finance.

Elimination of a single point of failure through decentralized utilities in the core area. Other areas include assets and financial instruments that are digitized or tokenized to become programmable and much simpler to trade and manage. Through increased connectivity and the possibility of fractionalized ownership, they expand their market access in token form. As a result, capital costs are reduced and liquidity is increased.

Mastercard's patented blockchain technology allows for the processing of cryptocurrency payments on conventional credit card systems. The business is aware that blockchain-based payments are becoming increasingly popular and wants customers to maintain their anonymity while maintaining the speed of payment infrastructure that is already in place. Using a hybrid payment method, Mastercard also aims to reduce risk and fraud.

Charity

For organizations making charitable contributions, blockchain can track where your donations are going, when they arrive, and whose hands they end up in. The transaction history can be maintained by referencing the public key of the various parties involved.

The BitGive Foundation and other Bitcoin-based charities use a distributed ledger that is safe and transparent to give donors a better view of funds utilization.

Additionally, the company has launched GiveTrack, a multidimensional donation platform based on the blockchain that permits the transfer, tracking, and storage of global charitable financial transactions. Charities can increase donor trust by using GiveTrack.

Automotive

A prime example of how the technology could be used to track ownership with a tamper-proof, neutral, and resilient system is by recording physical assets like auto parts on a blockchain. Blockchains are immutable and have no single entity controlling the ledger, whereas paper records are susceptible to forgery and/or physical degradation, and centralized databases may be vulnerable to hacking, human error, and/or tampering.

Blockchains could be used to identify counterfeit parts in a supply chain and track them. The technology also has significant effects on recalls of automobiles, which will affect approximately 32 million vehicles in 2020. Blockchain could enable targeted recalls by keeping track of where parts have gone, from the supplier to the individual vehicle.

The Mobility Open Blockchain Initiative (MOBI), *a consortium that includes automakers like Ford,* BMW, *Honda, and* GM, *has been working on a vehicle and parts tracking initiative.*

Real estate

A lack of transparency during and after a property transaction, a lot of paperwork, the possibility of fraud, and errors in public records pose significant challenges. Blockchain provides a means to speed up transactions and eliminate the need for paper-based record-keeping, thereby assisting stakeholders in enhancing efficiency and lowering transaction costs on all sides.

Note

Propy is seeking to offer secure home buying through a blockchain-based smart contract platform. All documents are signed and securely stored online, while deeds and other contracts are recorded using blockchain technology as well as on paper.

You must be wondering, if all this information is good, but can we see the real-world benefits of blockchain? What focused area the investors should consider? With blockchain reaching 20 Billion dollars in 2023 and expected to reach 200 billion by 2027 (refer to *Figure 1.4*), let us identify key domains while looking at the results from blockchain case study.

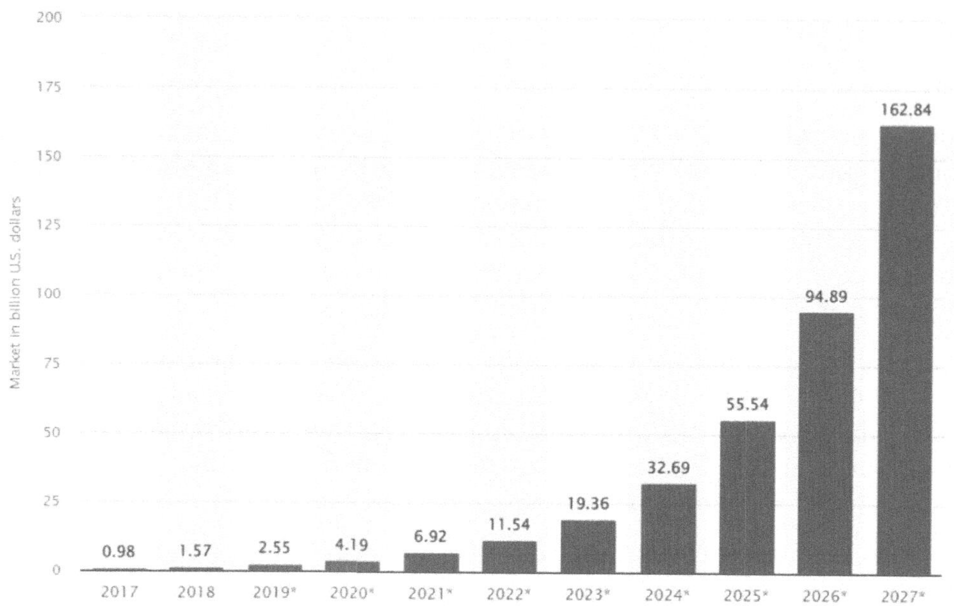

Figure 1.4: *Blockchain market size in billion US dollars*

Source: Statista

Case Study: Procurement and Supply Chain

Blockchain eases supplier master data management: **Trust Your Supplier**

Challenges: When it came to finding and integrating a reputable supplier, 'Trust Your Supplier' saw an opportunity to save time and money. Companies must deal with supply chain disruptions and quality expectations to comply with regulations or stakeholders' environmental and social concerns. Businesses spend a lot of time and money trying to find a good supplier. This is because it's hard to verify and get data from providers, as companies don't want to openly share their data.

Solution: An open-source blockchain platform that allows businesses to securely and effectively share data with permissions third-party partners.

Once the company's data is confirmed, a blockchain-based corporate digital passport is created, allowing:

- Enhanced compliance
- Enhanced risk management
- Reduced onboarding duration of suppliers

The digital password contains the hash output of the data, which gives the data integrity. Third-party verifiers give the view of the P2P network and validate the supplier information, which gives authenticity, and supplier data on the blockchain gives traceability. So, what you see here, as explained earlier, ensures that all security domains are covered when you use blockchain.

Results:

- Reduces the supplier onboarding duration by more than 70%.
- Lessens the cost of data verification to work with a suitable supplier by 50%.
- Improves compliance by almost instantaneously checking international quality certificates of other parties like GRI, ISO, SASB, etc.

Inherent security capabilities of Bitcoin

Bitcoin Overview

A digital money ecosystem is built on the ideas and technologies contained in Bitcoin. Value is stored and transferred among participants in the Bitcoin network using Bitcoin units. It is worth mentioning, there are thousands of cryptocurrencies globally, and bitcoin is the most well-known and widely used. The internet and other transport networks can also be used by Bitcoin users to communicate with one another using the Bitcoin protocol. Open-source software known as the bitcoin protocol stack is compatible with a wide range of computing platforms, including smartphones and laptops, making the technology readily available.

Bitcoin, in contrast to conventional currencies, is entirely virtual. There are neither actual coins nor digital coins. In transactions where value is transferred from one party to another, the coins are implied. The keys that enable Bitcoin users to demonstrate ownership in the Bitcoin network are their own. They can sign transactions with these keys to unlock the value and spend it by giving it to a new owner. Keys are frequently kept in a digital wallet on each user's smartphone or computer. The only requirement to spend Bitcoin is possession of the key that can sign a transaction, giving each user complete control.

We will be going through the concepts repeatedly that we have learned as we unfold Bitcoin. Hold tight, as this will all help you to clear your concepts and allow you to join the missing dots as we march along in this book. In a nutshell, bitcoin consists of:

- A decentralized P2P network (the Bitcoin protocol)
- A public transaction ledger (the blockchain)
- A set of rules for independent transaction validation and currency issuance (consensus rules)
- A mechanism for reaching decentralized global consensus on the valid blockchain (Proof-of-Work algorithm)

Now let's move one step forward and examine how it works and how it protects the users from the lens of confidentiality, integrity, availability, and traceability.

I will try to keep my context on a high level since digging deep into Bitcoin core architecture and its various components is beyond the scope of this book. We will try to cover all the pieces from a security standpoint. Having said that, developing a thorough understanding is equally important, so the reference URLs have been provided for you to explor in parallel.

Bitcoin Working Process Overview

To recap, decentralized trust is the foundation of the Bitcoin system, in contrast to conventional banking and payment methods. In Bitcoin, instead of relying on a single trusted authority, trust emerges naturally from the interactions of various system participants.

By following a single transaction through the Bitcoin system and watching it become *trusted* and accepted by the Bitcoin mechanism of distributed consensus before being recorded on the blockchain, the distributed ledger of all transactions.

We can see in the Bitcoin process overview illustration (refer to *Figure 1.5*) that the Bitcoin system is made up of users who have wallets that contain both public and private keys. Consider a public key like an email address or the identity of a user, while the private key unlocks the spends and signs transactions that are spread across the network. Miners who produce the consensus blockchain, which is the authoritative ledger of all transactions, through competitive computation.

In addition, there are other participants like exchanges, and merchants, which are part of this ecosystem as well. Recall the initial topic of this chapter, where we saw the analogy of an office improvement project; with that in mind, exchanges and merchants are part of the supply chain, which fuels the marketplace.

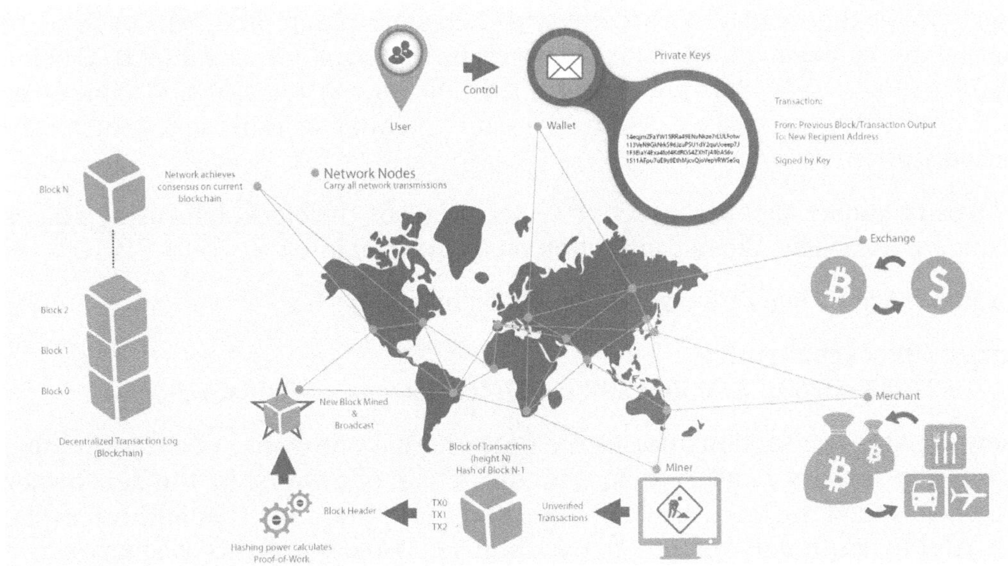

Figure 1.5: *Bitcoin Process Overview*

source: https://cypherpunks-core.github.io/

The example shown here is based on a real-world Bitcoin transaction that simulated Joe, Alice, Bob, and Gopesh's interactions as they moved money from one wallet to another. We will use a blockchain explorer site to visualize each step as we follow a transaction through the Bitcoin network to the blockchain.

Note: In the same way that a bitcoin search engine does, a blockchain explorer is a web application that lets you search for addresses, transactions, and blocks and see how they relate to one another.

Popular blockchain explorers include:

- BlockCypher Explorer
- blockchain.info
- Blockstream Explorer

Using a bitcoin address, transaction hash, block number, or block hash, any of these can be searched to find the relevant information on the Bitcoin network. I will provide a URL for each transaction or block example so that you can examine it in depth yourself.

For coffee lovers, let us see what buying coffee with Bitcoin looks like.

Alice, a coffee lover, is a brand-new user with 0.10 Bitcoin. which she has received from Joe. She will now make her first purchase at Bob's coffee shop in Palo Alto, California, for a cup of coffee.

Alice scans the displayed barcode with her smartphone and selects Send to authorize the payment, which is shown on her smartphone as 0.0150 BTC being paid to Bob's Cafe. Bob sees the transaction on the register and completes it within a few seconds—roughly the same amount of time as a credit card authorization.

You can examine Alice's transaction to Bob's Cafe on the blockchain using a block explorer site (View Alice's transaction on blockchain.info):

Example: View Alice's transaction on blockchain.info

https://blockchain.info/tx/0627052b6f28912f2703066a912ea577f2ce4da4caa5a5fbd8a57286c

Simply put, a transaction informs the network that one owner of a bitcoin value has authorized its transfer to another. In a chain of ownership, the new owner can now spend the bitcoin by initiating another transaction that authorizes the transfer to another owner, and so on. Confused? Hold on, all this will make sense in a while.

Transactions chaining for Authenticity

Just keep in mind that Alice has received BTC from Joe, which she has spent at Bob's café. In her ledger, Alice's receipt from Joe will be an input, and the amount she would have spent on coffee will be an output. As an input, the difference will be returned to her wallet.

Alice's key secured a bitcoin value as a result of the transaction. You see, the new transaction she made with Bob's Café uses the previous one as an input and generates new outputs for paying for the coffee and receiving change. The signature that unlocks those previous transaction outputs is provided by Alice's key, demonstrating to the Bitcoin network that she owns the funds.

All of this creates authenticity and ensures that Alice is only spending what she has, and not sending the same amount to any other person. Figure 1.6 illustrates all of this, and these ledgers pile up in a Bitcoin block. If you add a hashing algorithm and a private key signature on top of all this, this gives security in-depth, meaning that with authenticity, you get data integrity and confidentiality from someone who wishes to tamper.

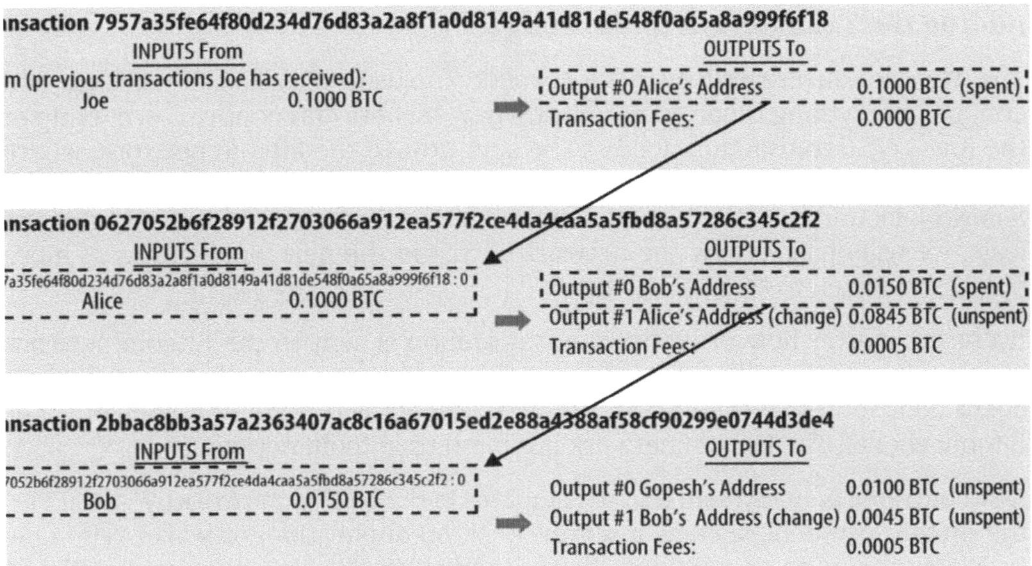

***Figure 1.6**: Bitcoin Transaction Review*

Source: https://cypherpunks-core.github.io/

The resulting transaction can be seen using a blockchain explorer web application, as shown in Alice's transaction to Bob's Cafe (refer to *Figure 1.7*). So, if anybody has a transaction address or an Alice public key, blockchain explorer can be used to view the history.

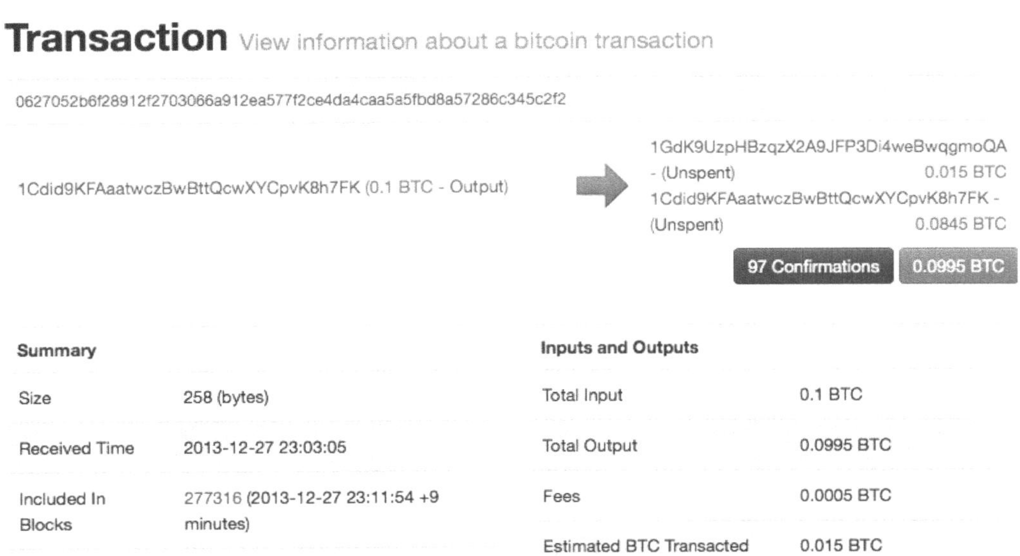

***Figure 1.7**: Alex Transaction to Bob's cafe*

Source: https://cypherpunks-core.github.io/

Adding the Transaction to the Ledger

The transaction created by Alice's wallet application is 258 bytes long and contains everything required to identify new owners and confirm ownership of the funds. The transaction needs to be sent now to the Bitcoin network, where it will be added to the blockchain. We'll see how a transaction becomes a part of a new block and how the block is "mined" in the next section. Last but not the least, we will observe how the network's trust in the new block grows as more blocks are added to the blockchain.

It doesn't matter how or where the transaction is sent to the Bitcoin network because it contains all of the information needed for processing. Each Bitcoin client contributes to the Bitcoin network by connecting to a number of other Bitcoin clients. The Bitcoin network is a peer-to-Bitcoin network.

A Bitcoin node is any system that participates in the Bitcoin network by "speaking" the Bitcoin protocol, such as a server, desktop application, or wallet. The new transaction can be sent to any Bitcoin node that Alice's wallet application is connected to via any connection: mobile, WiFi, wired, etc.

A method of propagation known as flooding occurs when any Bitcoin node that has never seen a valid transaction will immediately forward it to all other connected nodes. As a result, the transaction spreads quickly across the peer-to-peer network, reaching many nodes within a few seconds. This peer-to-peer network offers resilience and availability. And in case a few nodes are down due to a denial of service attack, for instance, the process will not be stopped, it continues as there are thousands of other servers that would be interested in getting this transaction across the mining journey.

Mining of Bitcoin Transactions

From user wallets and other applications, the network is constantly receiving new transactions. These are added to a temporary mining pool of unverified transactions that each Bitcoin network node manages as soon as they see them. Using the mining algorithm (Proof-of-Work), miners attempt to establish the validity of a new block by including unverified transactions from this mining pool into it as they create it.

A mining pool is a joint group of cryptocurrency miners who combine their computational resources over a network to strengthen the probability of finding a block or otherwise successfully mining for cryptocurrency.

The highest-fee transactions and a few other criteria determine the order in which transactions are added to the new block. Knowing that they lost the previous competition, each miner begins mining a new block of transactions as soon as they receive the previous block from the network. The miner immediately starts calculating the Proof-of-Work for the new block and populates it with transactions and the fingerprint of the previous block. Each miner adds a unique transaction to his or her block.

This transaction pays the miner's Bitcoin address the block reward, which is currently equal to 12.5 newly created bitcoins, in addition to the total amount of transaction fees from all of the transactions in the block. The miner"wins" this reward if they solve the problem and validate that block, as their successful block is added to the global blockchain and the included reward transaction can be spent.

The economics of rewards and transaction fees, which go to the miners prevent them from any foul play. In other words, the Bitcoin protocol is designed in a way that the chances of manipulation, double spending, and corruption are practically not possible.

Bitcoin Security Review

Now that you have understood how Bitcoin works in detail and its ecosystem, let us dissect it even further to understand where the vulnerability exists. If you have noticed in all the earlier explanations, it comes down to the core concepts of decentralization, the P2P network, wallet keys, exchanges, bitcoin source code, mining pool operation, and the bitcoin networking nodes that are holding up the chain.

Decentralization Aspect

Decentralization is at the heart of Bitcoin, and it has significant security implications. A decentralized system like Bitcoin gives users control and responsibility. The network's security is based on Proof-of-Work and not access control, so it can be open. Bitcoin Core is essentially an open-source software used to connect to the Bitcoin network and run a node. While anyone can suggest modifications, not all proposed code modifications are incorporated into Bitcoin Core. Instead, each proposed change is thoroughly reviewed and debated by the community before acceptance or rejection is decided, and the security is maintained by the overall community.

If you compare it with a traditional payment system, which contains the user's private identifier (the credit card number), it is open-ended on a traditional payment network like a credit card system. Anyone with access to the identifier can "pull" funds and charge the owner multiple times after the initial charge.

As a result, the payment network must be encrypted from beginning to end to ensure that neither eavesdroppers nor intermediaries can compromise payment traffic while it is in transit or stored (at rest). A bad actor can compromise both existing transactions and payment tokens that can be used to create new ones if he gains access to the system. Worse still, when customer data is compromised, customers are at risk of identity theft and must protect their accounts from fraudulent use.

The decentralized security model of Bitcoin gives users a lot of control. The responsibility to keep the keys secret comes with that authority. This is difficult for the majority of users, particularly on general-purpose computing devices like smartphones and laptops connected to the internet. Although Bitcoin's decentralized model prevents the kind of widespread compromise that occurs with credit cards, many users fail to adequately protect their keys and are hacked one at a time.

Handling of Keys and Transactions

The security of Bitcoin is dependent on miners independently validating transactions and having decentralized control over keys. In order to take advantage of Bitcoin's security, one must adhere to the Bitcoin security model. Simply stated: Users should not be given control over keys, and transactions should not be removed from the blockchain. Avoid giving the custody of your keys to an exchange or a third party. Exercise proper diligence when it comes to key backups.

As a result of always-on internet connections, our computers are constantly exposed to threats from the outside. They frequently possess unrestricted access to the user's files and run thousands of software components from hundreds of authors. Among the many thousands of malicious programs that are installed on your computer, a single piece of malicious software can compromise your keyboard and files, stealing any Bitcoin stored in wallet applications. Only a small percentage of computer users are capable of performing the level of computer maintenance required to maintain viruses and trojan-free computers. So this is one vulnerability area to take care of.

Another common error is to "take transactions off the blockchain" in an erroneous attempt to speed up transaction processing or reduce transaction fees. Transactions will be recorded on an internal, centralized ledger in an "off-blockchain" system, with occasional synchronization to the Bitcoin blockchain. Again, this practice uses a proprietary and centralized method to replace decentralized Bitcoin security. Inadequately secured centralized ledgers can be tampered with during off-chain transactions, causing funds to be diverted and reserves to be depleted without being noticed.

Conclusion

Great job in completing the first chapter! With this knowledge, you can easily comprehend the buzz around blockchain. With the concepts and toolsets you were able to grasp, you will be able to find a use case in your organization where blockchain can be applied. Also, you can advise your peers on how to use bitcoin blockchain securely.

In the next chapter, we will take a look at other public blockchain variants like Ethereum and Solana in detail. We will showcase how private and hybrid blockchains are different from the security and architecture standpoint while exploring the ecosystem of wallets, and exchanges. This will be interesting!

Points to remember

- Blockchain is a suite of technologies; the underlying features like decentralization, peer-to-peer network, cryptography, and immutability are what make blockchain useful.
- Blockchain can be applied in any industry where the information is stored, transmitted, and valued.
- Bitcoin is not a blockchain, but rather an open-source software protocol, composed of source code, client, and cryptographic keys. It is the decentralized nature, economic design, and cryptographic functions which gives security.
- Vulnerability areas of bitcoin are the wallet keys, user terminals, and offline transactions.
- Due diligence is required when it comes to storing wallet keys.

References

- **https://www.baeldung.com/cs/prime-numbers-cryptography.**
- **https://cypherpunks-core.github.io/bitcoinbook/**
- **https://research.aimultiple.com/blockchain-case-studies/**
- **https://learnmeabitcoin.com/technical/longest-chain**
- **https://bitcoin.org/**

Multiple choice questions

1. **What does blockchain comprise?**
   a. Peer-to-peer network
   b. Cryptography
   c. Consensus algorithm
   d. All of the above

2. **What does the block in a blockchain contain?**
   a. Hash
   b. Bitcoins
   c. Nonce value
   d. Transaction ledger
   e. Name and address

3. **Which of the following security principles is provided by hashing?**
   a. Confidentiality
   b. Integrity
   c. Availability
   d. All of the above

4. **Why do we use a private key in a wallet?**
   a. To unlock the unspent transactions
   b. To sign the transaction
   c. To view the transactions
   d. None of the above

5. **What is the purpose of the public key?**
   a. To identify a user
   b. To sign a transaction
   c. To mine a transaction
   d. To store the transactions

Answers

1. d. 2. a, b, c, d 3. b 4. a, b 5. a

CHAPTER 2
Blockchain Security Variations

Introduction

There are numerous use cases for blockchain at the moment: thousands of cryptocurrency projects, hundreds of live blockchain applications, and billions of dollars in market capital flowing into this new technology. I would also add that most of the issues we face in your financial ecosystem—taking out a loan from a bank, sending money to your peers, or just moving and storing data—can be solved by using blockchain. In other words, any issue involving information that needs to be shared or validated can be solved by using blockchain.

At this point you may be wondering, are we talking about the Ethereum blockchain or the Bitcoin blockchain? What about the other blockchains on the market, like the hyper ledger and Solana? Somebody also mentioned Defi, and how they are different. You are correct; things start to get confusing as we dig deep, and it gets difficult to get a hold of it. What happens in a situation like this, is that you happen to apply security controls the same as an IT, and when the reality hits you in the shape of a security incident, then you start to backtrack it and, in most cases, reach out to security consultants.

The question now is, how would you decide which blockchain to use, which one is the best fit for your problem, and, most importantly, how to categorize each from a risk identification and mitigation perspective? We will try to answer these questions in this chapter, taking you to the different blockchain flavors, discussing the use case selection process, from Ethereum to Hyperledger, and Defi, taking a deep dive into the security features each brings, weaknesses, and then closing it with wallets and exchanges.

Structure

In this chapter, we will cover the following topics:

- Types of blockchain
- Security overview of Ethereum
- Ethereum security consideration
- Security overview of Hyperledger fabric
- Private blockchain security considerations

Types of blockchain

There is no question that blockchain has developed a ton somewhat recently. It all started with Bitcoin, which offered the first kind of blockchain, the public blockchain. The Bitcoin blockchain can also be referred to as the first generation of blockchain technology.

Before we have a genuine conversation about blockchain types, we should realize the reason why we want them in any case.

When blockchain technology was first made available to the public, it was a type of public blockchain that was used for cryptocurrencies. Although it is extremely difficult to comprehend the creator's intention, it generally introduced the concept of decentralized ledger technology (DLT). The DLT idea changed how we solve problems in our environment. It enabled organizations to function independently of a centralized body.

While distributed technology eliminates the drawbacks of centralization, it also brought with it a slew of additional challenges when it comes to implementing blockchain technology in various contexts. Proof-of-Work, for instance, was an ineffective consensus algorithm utilized in Bitcoin. It expected the hubs to settle numerical estimations utilizing energy.

It wasn't a problem at first, but as the difficulty grew, so did the amount of time and effort required to solve those mathematical equations. This shortcoming makes it inadequate for an organization to adopt. For instance, banks manage a ton of exchanges consistently. As a result, this particular kind of blockchain is unsuitable, since the bank has to settle x number of transactions each day, and the information does not need to be disclosed.

Additionally, A public blockchain is not appropriate for private companies for data storage use cases. For example, if Amazon or Google put their confidential information on a public blockchain, then this data can be used against them by their competitors. It also doesn't make business sense to use blockchain, just for the sake of using it, not being able to solve a genuine problem which also yields cost benefits. Although, some would argue that putting data on a public blockchain means anybody can view the record, which in turn attracts trust from their customers but such a use case is weak.

Private or federated blockchain was developed to address the aforementioned use cases. Private blockchains provide an entirely private environment in which the organization selects participants. They can take advantage of the features of the blockchain without having to publish everything.

The following figure shows the four major types of blockchain technologies. They mainly fall under permissioned and permissionless, which are further classified into public, private, hybrid, and consortiums.

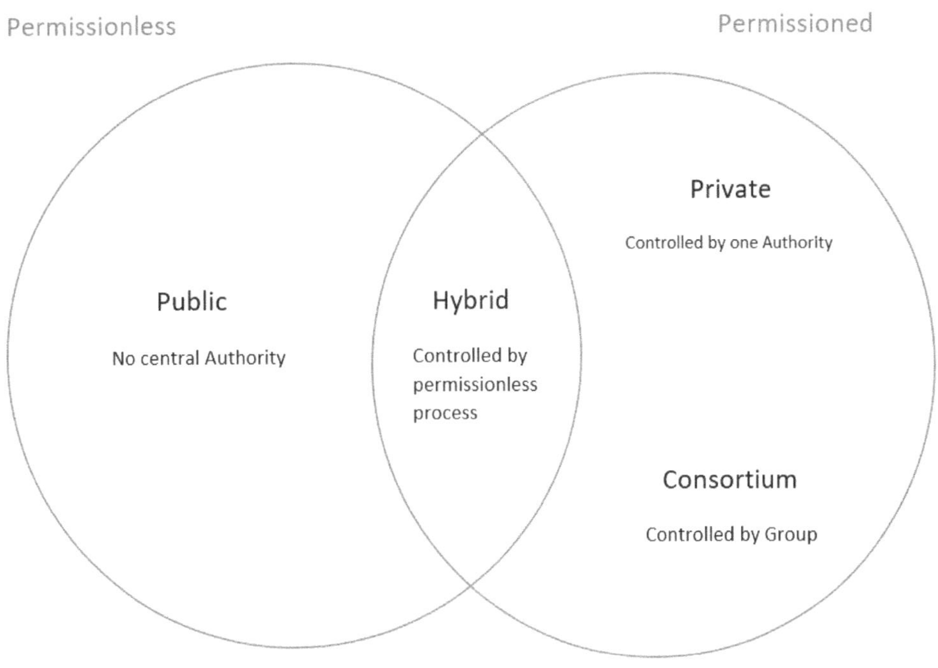

***Figure 2.1**: Types of blockchain technologies*

Let us take a look at each one from features, pros, and cons, as well as from the use case perspective.

Public blockchain

The idea of decentralization is completely supported by these blockchains. Anyone with a computer and access to the internet can join the network—there are no restrictions. This is what we have covered in *Chapter 1: Blockchain Security Review*. We will try to look at this now from the comparative analysis lens, so you can understand the differences.

- It's open to the public because of its name, meaning that no one owns it.
- It allows anyone with access to the internet and a computer with high-quality hardware to participate.

You can verify transactions or records because every computer in the network stores a copy of other nodes or blocks. This can be seen from the following figure, a new node joining the network from anywhere in the world, will also maintain a copy of the transaction.

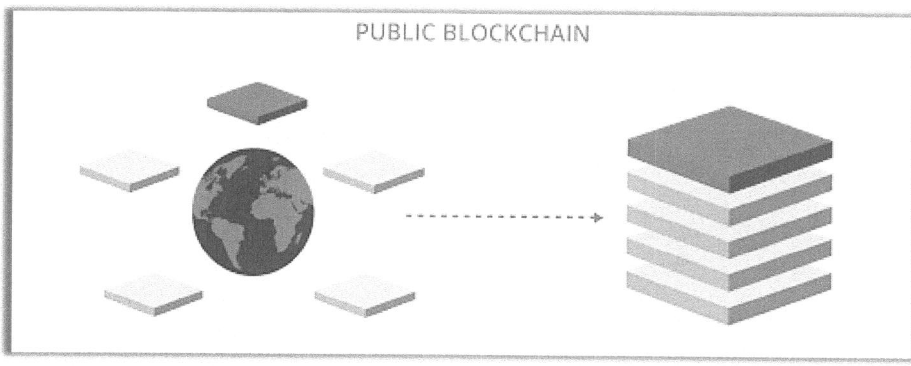

***Figure 2.2**: Public Blockchain type*

So what are the disadvantages, and why do we need to seek out other versions of blockchain? There are a few core problems, such as:

- **Lower TPS:** In a public blockchain, the number of transactions per second is extremely low. This is because it takes time to verify a transaction and perform proof-of-work due to the large network's many nodes.
- **Scalability issues:** It takes a long time to process and complete its transactions. Scalability is harmed by this. Because the network will become slower the more we try to expand its size.
- **High energy consumption:** Because it requires specialized systems (hardware components) to run a particular algorithm, the proof-of-work procedure consumes a significant amount of energy. Both the economic and environmental aspects of it are cause for concern.

- **Case studies:** Because they are protected by proof of work or proof of stake, public blockchains have the potential to replace conventional financial systems. The smart contract that made it possible for this blockchain to support decentralization is the more advanced aspect of this blockchain. Instances of public blockchain are Bitcoin and Ethereum.
- **Voting:** Governments can use a public blockchain to vote, ensuring openness and trust.
- **Fundraising:** Businesses or initiatives can use the public Blockchain to improve transparency and trust.

Private blockchain

Private blockchains are a confined organization of approved hubs. Information exchanged between two nodes can't be accessed by anyone outside the private network. Private blockchains are impressive, but they also have some drawbacks. The following figure is an illustration of a private blockchain, in which if a new node has to participate, it has to be explicitly allowed.

Figure 2.3: *Private Blockchain type*

They differ from public blockchains in their transactions per second (TPS) and scalability:

- **TPS - Speed:** In contrast to a public network, a private network only has a limited number of nodes. This speeds up a transaction's consensus or verification process by all network nodes. Also, new transactions are added to a block quickly. Up to thousands or hundreds of thousands of TPS can be processed at once by private blockchains.
- **Scalability:** Scalability is fairly good with private blockchains. That is, you can decide how big your private blockchain should be based on your requirements. For instance, if an organization only requires 20 nodes, it can easily deploy a blockchain. After expansion, they will have no trouble adding additional nodes.

Every good thing comes at a cost, so what is the trade-off of having fast performance and improved scalability? Trust and centralization aspects directly impact security tolerance. Let us have a look.

- **Trust dependency:** Private blockchains have a decent level of scalability. This means that your needs can dictate the size of your private blockchain. For instance, a blockchain can be easily implemented by an organization with just 20 nodes. They won't have any trouble adding more nodes as a result of the expansion.
- **Tight centralization:** Since they require a central Identity and Access Management (IAM) system for proper operation, private blockchains are restricted. This framework has all the observing and managerial privileges. It grants permission to either select the level of access they have to the data stored in the blockchain or to add a new node to the network. The concept of decentralization, which is one of the pillars of blockchain technology, is in direct opposition to this system as shown below.

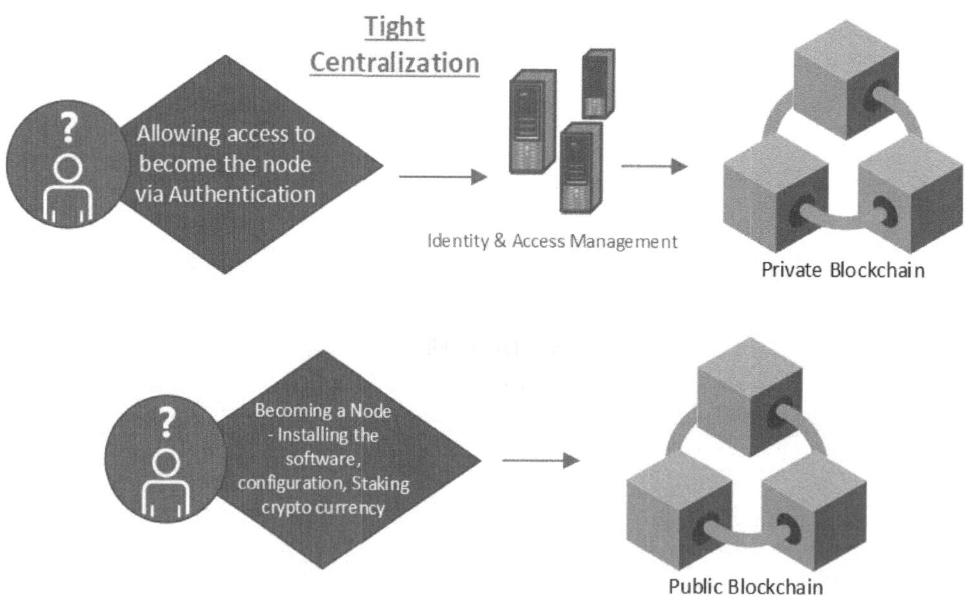

Figure 2.4: *Centralization aspect of Private blockchain as compared to Public Blockchains*

Both aforementioned factors influence the security aspect, such that a private blockchain network is more vulnerable to security breaches because it has fewer participants or nodes. Assuming anybody of the hubs accesses the focal administration framework, it can get close enough to every one of the hubs in the organization. This makes it more straightforward for a hub to hack the whole private blockchain and abuse the data.

Case study: Hyperledger Fabric is a blockchain framework for application development with unique access control and identity management features. Walmart uses a private Hyperledger Fabric-based blockchain system. An illustration of a permissioned blockchain is the Linux Foundation's open-source framework.

It lets Walmart find out where its products came from. The certificates of authenticity are added to the ledger by its suppliers. The business is able to track the origin of their products in seconds rather than days thanks to this.

Hybrid blockchain

It is the mingled content of the private and public blockchains, with some parts under the control of a specific organization and others made public. You can think of an implementation of Ethereum and a Hyperledger fabric. Any industry can be benefitted from such a design, where in some cases, where information can't be shared with the public yet needs to be kept unaltered, and automated with a workflow, you can leverage a private blockchain. Whereas in the same organization, where you want to target public trust and enable P2P transactions, a Bitcoin or an Ethereum can be used.

Case Study: It gives a more noteworthy answer for the medical services industry, government, land, and monetary organizations. It offers a solution when data must be kept private but can be accessed by the public. A good example would be when a patient wants to share medical data with the doctor and health insurance company but also wants to ensure personal privacy and security.

The other good use case would be to use a private payment system on public networks. The following figure is a good illustration to see the difference, you get the best of both Public and Private blockchain types.

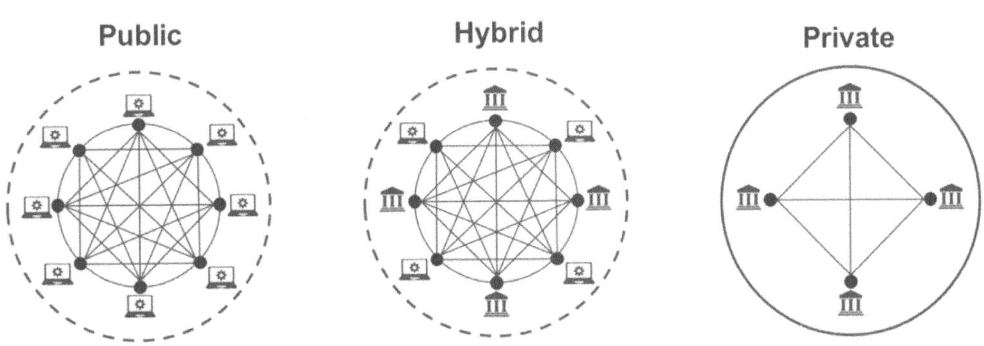

***Figure 2.5**: Hybrid Blockchain type*

Consortium blockchain

Nodes from multiple businesses or organizations govern the network in a consortium blockchain in much greater privacy. Through this platform, they collaborate to share and modify information to maintain workflow, scalability, and accountability. This can be seen from the following figure that consortium blockchain is restricted to the organization that is part of the consortium group.

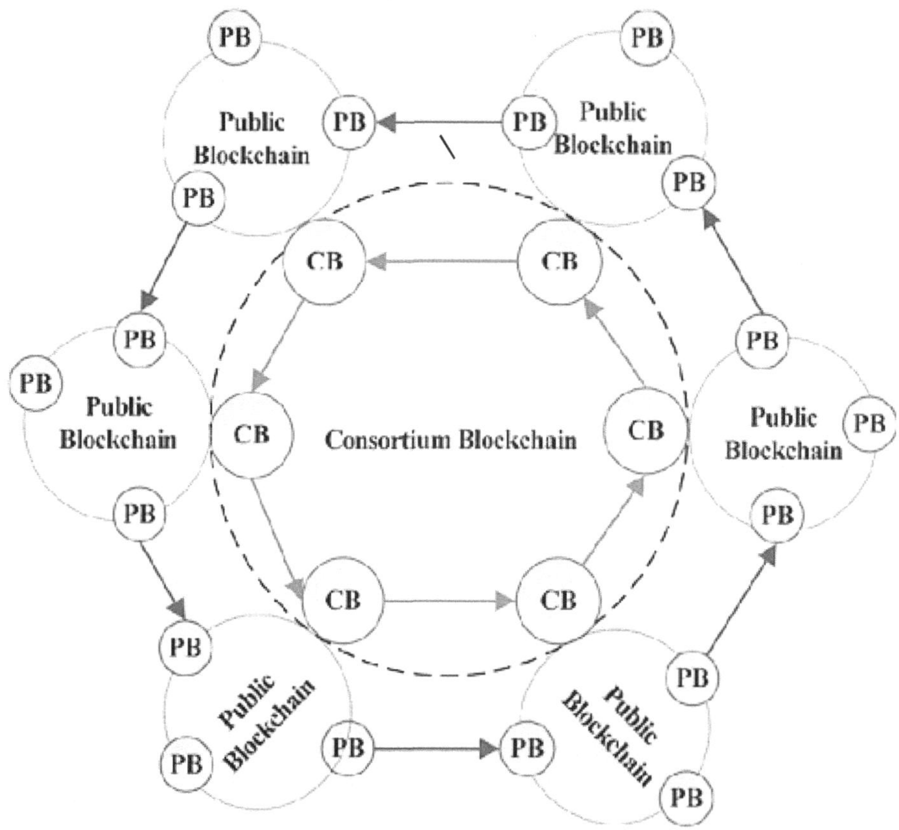

Figure 2.6: *Consortium Blockchain*

The primary objective of a consortium blockchain is to assist institutions in resolving issues and locating applicable solutions through this platform. CORDA and Quorum are two well-known consortium blockchains in which different organizations are involved.

To be clear, and separate it from a Private blockchain, while a consortium blockchain has a few chosen members (for example a few associations), a private blockchain has a member who has sole command over the principles of the blockchain, meaning he can use the same blockchain platform, for example, HL Fabric in a private enterprise setup.

Case Study: In the Financial sector, KYC is a part of the business of issuing and trading assets in this sector. Dataset information is centrally stored by all participating banks in a consortium. This distributed ledger will be there for a bank whenever it needs to verify or access the creditor's information. A detailed analysis reveals that consortium is the best option for implementing cross-sector projects.

Other blockchain implementations can be seen as follows. It extends from healthcare to energy, all the way to technology and media, where common groups combine to solve a specific solution. The following figure gives a good indication of how consortium blockchain implementation is distributed across various sectors, with the financial sector taking the majority of the share.

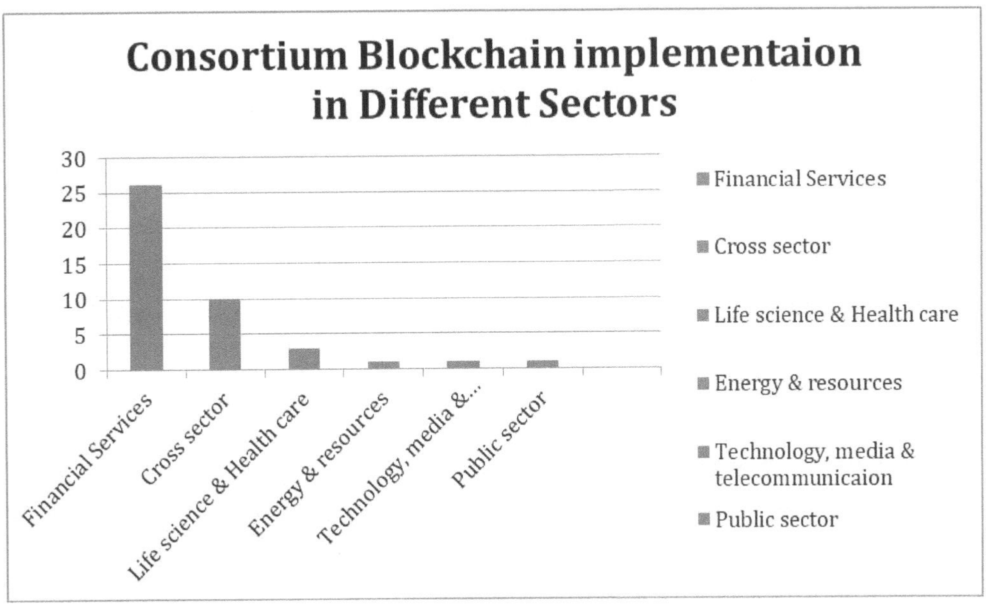

***Figure 2.7**: Consortium Blockchain Sector Distribution*

Ethereum Overview

Before going into its security posture, let us take a moment to review Ethereum.

Introduction to Ethereum

Let us start with the basics. What is Ethereum, how is it different from Bitcoin, and what does the architecture look like? These are all important questions to unfold, before going into deep dive, reviewing the security posture, and then finding ways to exploit and finally secure it.

This also comes under the public blockchain category. You must be wondering why we didn't discuss it in *Chapter 1, Blockchain Security Overview*. One reason is that its architecture is a bit different from the Bitcoin blockchain, in way that it involves smart contact and enables the creation of decentralized application, which can be tuned for a private blockchain as well, so I wanted to open it up after we discussed different types of blockchain, so you don't get confused. Let's start.

Ethereum is a decentralized technology that can be used to build apps and organizations, hold assets, conduct business, and communicate. Ethereum lets you keep control of your own data and what is shared, so you do not have to hand over all of your personal information. Ether, Ethereum's own cryptocurrency, is used to pay for certain network-based activities.

Difference between Ethereum and Bitcoin

Both are public blockchains, which let you use digital money to send without involving centralized payment providers or banks. But Ethereum is programmable, meaning you can build applications on top of its network. Being decentralized, the applications are known as decentralized applications.

Ethereum is more like a marketplace for financial services, games, social networks, and other apps that respect your privacy and cannot censor you than Bitcoin is just a payment network.

The native cryptocurrency of Ethereum is called Ether (ETH). It can be sent instantly to anyone in the world because it is entirely digital. Decentralized and transparent, the supply of ETH is not controlled by any government or business. Only validators (like miners in the POW consensus mechanism), who have staked their coins, and who work to protect the network receive new coins, which are also referred to as tokens.

On the Ethereum network, a certain amount of computational power is required for each action. The payment for this service is made in ether. This means that to use the network, you need at least a small amount of ETH.

Working of Ethereum

There is no single entity in charge of Ethereum. It is only possible because of the community's decentralized participation and cooperation. Nodes, which are computers that store a copy of the Ethereum blockchain's data, are run by volunteers to replace individual cloud and server systems owned by major internet service providers.

Essentially, the Ethereum blockchain is a transaction-based state machine. A machine that reads a series of inputs and changes its state based on those inputs is known as a state machine.

A *genesis state* is where we start with Ethereum's state machine. This is like starting from scratch before any network transactions have taken place. This genesis state changes into a final state when transactions are carried out. This final state is the current state of Ethereum at any given time.

This can be seen in the following figure; it all starts from genesis and then the state changes as the inputs are fed.

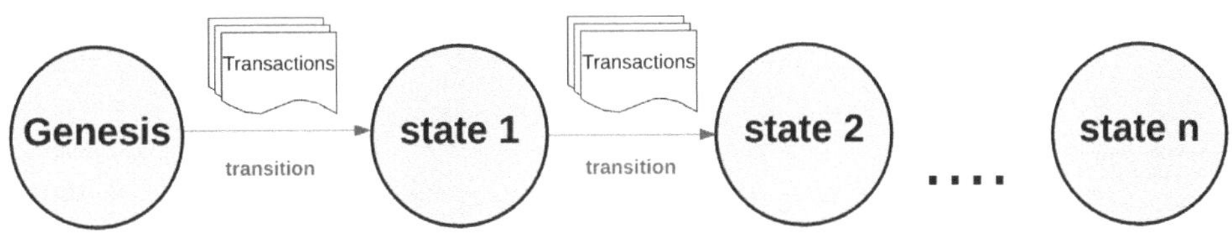

Figure 2.8: *State transition in Ethereum*

There are millions of transactions in the Ethereum state. These exchanges are gathered into "blocks." A block is a collection of transactions, and each block is linked to the one before it. Now that you have understood the fundamental concept, let us take a look at important features such as accounts, states, and gas and payment.

Accounts

Ethereum's global *shared state* is made up of many small objects, or *accounts*, that can communicate with one another using a message-passing framework. A 20-byte address and a state are associated with each account. In Ethereum, any account is identified by a 160-bit identifier known as an address. There are two types of accounts:

- Externally owned: They are controlled by private keys and have no code associated with them.
- Contact accounts: They are controlled by their contract code and have code associated with them.

So, what is the difference between them?

By creating and signing a transaction with its private key, an externally owned account can send messages to other externally owned accounts OR to contract accounts. A message between two externally owned accounts is simply a value transfer. But a message from an externally owned account to a contract account activates the contract account's code, allowing it to perform various actions (for example, transfer tokens, write to internal storage, mint new tokens, perform some calculations, create new contracts, and so on).

Contract accounts, in contrast to accounts owned by third parties, are unable to independently initiate new transactions. Contract accounts, on the other hand, can only initiate transactions in response to other transactions they have received (either from another contract account or an externally owned account). You can conceptualize better with the following figure, where the difference between both account types is shown.

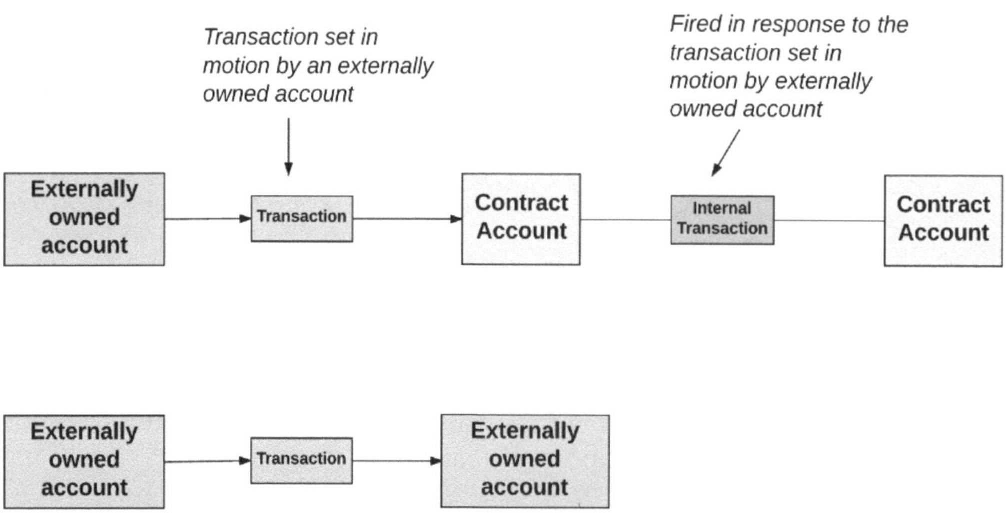

Figure 2.9: *Difference between Externally owned and Contract Accounts*

So, any transactions that you see on the Ethereum blockchain are the ones that are triggered by an externally owned account.

Account state

The account state consists of four components, which are present regardless of the type of account:

- **nonce:** If the account is externally owned, this number represents the number of transactions sent from the account's address. If the account is a contract account, the nonce is the number of contracts created by the account.
- **balance:** The number of Wei owned by this address. There are 1e+18 Wei per Ether.

- **Storage Root:** A hash of the root node of a Merkle Patricia tree (we'll explain Merkle trees later on). This tree encodes the hash of the storage contents of this account and is empty by default.
- **Code Hash:** The hash of the EVM (Ethereum Virtual Machine—more on this later) code of this account. For contract accounts, this is the code that gets hashed and stored as the code Hash. For externally owned accounts, the code Hash field is the hash of the empty string.

The following figure gives a good view of how components are held in each account type.

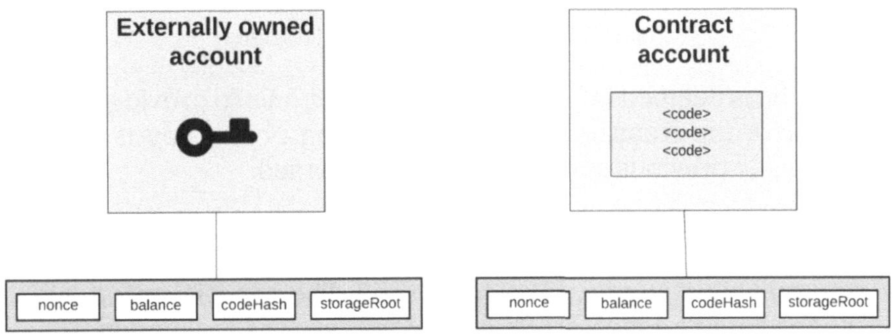

***Figure 2.10**: Components in Account states*

Gas and Payment

No freebie here. There is a fee associated with each computation carried out on the Ethereum network as a result of a transaction.

The currency used to pay this fee is called **gas**. Gas is the unit used to quantify the charges expected for a specific calculation.

A sender sets a gas limit and gas price for each transaction. The maximum amount of Wei that the sender is willing to pay to carry out a transaction is the sum of the gas price and the gas limit.

Let's say, for instance, that the sender specifies a 50,000-gallon gas cap and a 20-gwei gas price. This indicates that the sender is prepared to spend no more than 50,000 x 20 gwei, which equals 1,000,000,000,000,000 Wei, or 0.001 Ether, to carry out the transaction.

Keep in mind that the sender's maximum expenditure for gas is represented by the gas limit. They are good to go if they have enough Ether in their account balance to cover this maximum. At the conclusion of the transaction, the sender receives a refund equal to the original rate for any gas that was not utilized.

In the following figure, you can see how the payment and gas fees are related in a transaction.

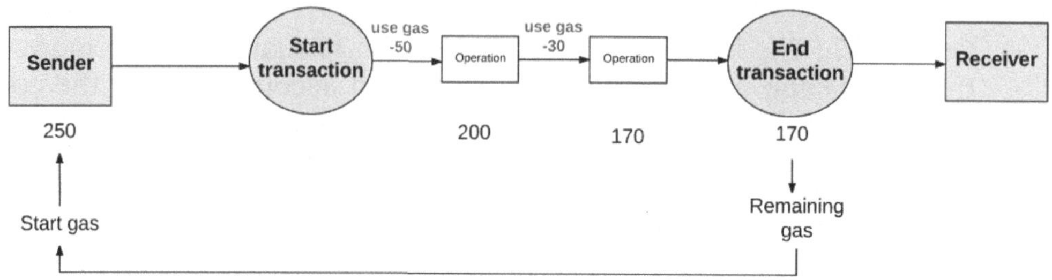

***Figure 2.11**: Payment and GAS relationship*

The transaction is deemed invalid when the sender fails to provide the necessary gas to complete the transaction. The transaction processing is halted in this instance, and any previous state changes are reversed.

Additionally, since the machine had already exerted effort to perform the calculations before running out of gas, it stands to reason that the sender receives no reimbursement for the gas it used. The **beneficiary** address, which is typically the miner's address, receives all the sender's gas money. The concept is illustrated in the following figure.

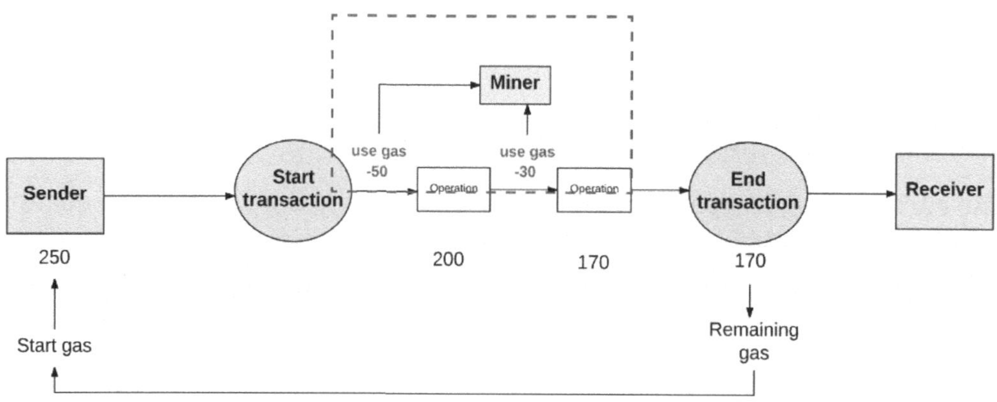

***Figure 2.12**: GAS Money going to Miner account*

Now, it's time to talk about the most talked about feature of blockchain in general, the Smart Contract. Yes, Smart Contracts are Ethereum discoveries.

Ethereum virtual machine

The Ethereum virtual machine (EVM), which is Ethereum's very own virtual machine, is the component of the protocol that takes care of processing the transactions. The architecture view shown in the following figure will help to picture all this as we move along.

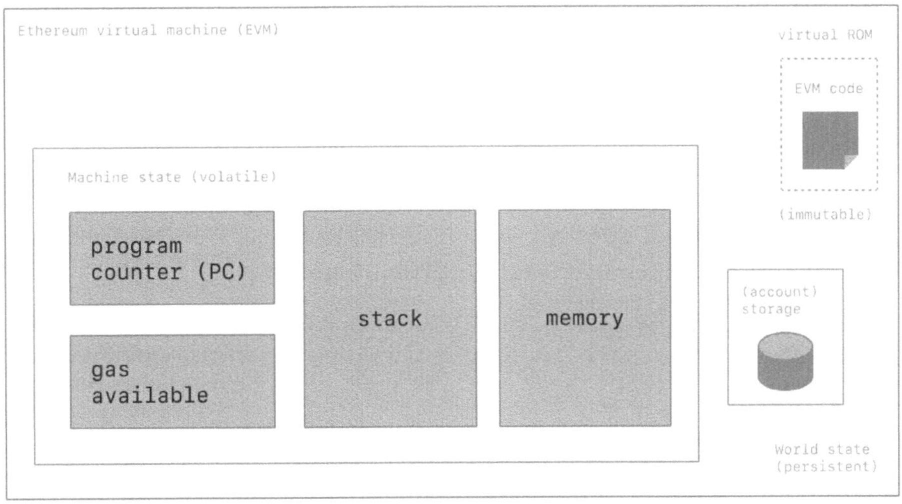

Figure 2.13: *Ethereum Virtual Machine Architecture*

The EVM is a Turing complete virtual machine. Because it is intrinsically bound by gas, the EVM has no limitations that a typical Turing complete machine does not. As a result, the total amount of computation that can be performed is intrinsically constrained by the gas supply.

Items are stored in word-addressed byte arrays in the EVM's memory. Memory is unpredictable, it isn't super durable to mean it that way.

The EVM has storage as well. Storage is non-volatile and is maintained as part of the system state, unlike memory. Program code is stored separately by the EVM in a virtual ROM that can only be accessed by following specific instructions.

Smart contracts

Smart Contracts are nothing more than computer programs or scripts for the blockchain environment. They only take effect when prompted by a user transaction (or another contract). They set Ethereum apart from other cryptocurrencies by making it very adaptable in its capabilities. We now refer to these programs as decentralized apps or dapps.

If a Smart Contract has been published on Ethereum, it will stay live and work as long as Ethereum is around. Even the person who wrote it can't take it down. Since smart contracts are digital, they don't force anyone and are always ready to use. Lending apps, insurance apps, crowdfunding apps, and decentralized trading exchanges are all popular examples of smart contracts.

Did you know, Szabo came up with the term *smart contract* in 1994? He defines *a smart contract as a computerized transaction protocol that executes the terms of a contract* as the definition he uses.

Another important thing to note here is the source code and bytecode differentiation in the Ethereum Smart Contract.

The syntax of Solidity, which is similar to that of JavaScript, is typically used to write the Smart Contract's source code. A Solidity Smart Contract's structure is similar to that of an object-oriented programming class.

The Solidity compiler also produces a bytecode version of the source code, just like the Java compiler does. This bytecode version is run by the Ethereum Virtual Machine (EVM).

The Ethereum bytecode is made up of several low-level commands called opcodes. It is written in a language called assembly. Ethereum only stores the text of a smart contract.

More details on solidity can be found at **https://github.com/ethereum/wiki/wiki/Proof-of-Stake-FAQ**

Here is a sample Solidity Smart Contract code along with a brief description and use case:

```
************************************************************************
pragma solidity ^0.8.0;
contract Voting {
    mapping(address => bool) public hasVoted;
    mapping(bytes32 => uint256) public voteCount;
    function vote(bytes32 candidate) public {
        require(!hasVoted[msg.sender], "You have already voted.");
        voteCount[candidate] += 1;
        hasVoted[msg.sender] = true;
    }
    function getVoteCount(bytes32 candidate) public view returns
(uint256) {
        return voteCount[candidate];
    }
}
************************************************************************
```

Description:

This is a simple Smart Contract that enables users to vote for a candidate by calling the vote function. Each user can only vote once, as the contract keeps track of whether or not a user has already voted. The contract stores the vote count for each candidate in a mapping called voteCount and provides a function to retrieve the vote count for a given candidate called getVoteCount.

The number of votes that users enter is the trigger condition. If the value of vote is more than 1, the result will say *you have already voted.* Trigger to contract can also happen in several other ways also, like time and schedule, event triggers, harvesting yield, minting NFTs, liquidation of loans etc.

No matter how small or big the contract is, from the security standpoint, there should be some important consideration that can be done:

- **Secure Authentication**: The contract should implement strong authentication measures to prevent any un-authorized access, this can be achieved using public, private key pair, controller subjects and resources by policy enforcements, or simply using ACLs at the perimeter level, if you know the ports, source, and destination Ips.
- **Encryption at rest and transit**: The vote count result should be encrypted at rest; confidentiality can be achieved using secure vault like HSM. Also, if the data must be sent outside, the API should have TLS enabled.

More on this and lot more on blockchain security solutions will be discussed in *Chapter 6, Blockchain Security Solution.*

Use case

This smart contract could be used to implement a simple voting system, where users can cast their votes for a candidate in a transparent and secure manner. For example, it could be used in a student government election or a company board member election, where votes need to be tallied and verified in a decentralized and trustworthy manner.

You can learn more about the Ethereum community, and different Dapps at **https://ethereum.org/**

Now that you have understood the fundamentals of Ethereum and smart contracts, let's take a look at the structure of an Ethereum node.

Structure of an Ethereum node

Ethereum can be divided into several layers, the Application layer, consensus layer, data layer, and network layer as shown in the following figure. These are then subdivided into other various types, depending on the design and the use case.

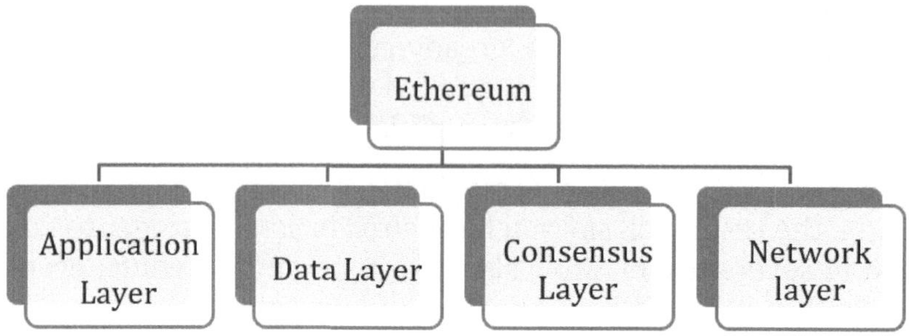

***Figure 2.14**: Layered Structure of Ethereum*

- **Application Layer:** The application layer of the Ethereum blockchain is where smart contracts are executed and decentralized applications (dApps) are built. We talked about smart contracts earlier, and here I would like to emphasize how users interact with the Ethereum blockchain. This can be done in the following ways.
    - **web3-enabled browser**: Many modern web browsers, such as MetaMask, Brave, and Opera, come with built-in support for the Ethereum blockchain. Users can install these browser extensions to interact with dApps and smart contracts directly from their browser.
    - **Ethereum wallet**: Users can download and install a dedicated Ethereum wallet, such as MyEtherWallet, Trust Wallet, or Coinbase Wallet. These wallets allow users to send and receive Ethereum, as well as interact with smart contracts and dApp.
    - **Command-line interface**: Advanced users can interact with the Ethereum blockchain using a command-line interface (CLI) such as Geth or Parity. These tools provide direct access to the Ethereum network and allow users to perform more complex operations, such as deploying their own smart contract.
    - **Geth(Go-Ethereum)**: Geth is an Ethereum execution client, which means that it runs smart contract deployment, execution, and transactions. It also has an embedded computer called the Ethereum Virtual Machine.
- **Consensus Layer:** Ethereum has switched on its proof-of-stake mechanism considering it is more secure, less energy-intensive, and better for implementing new scaling solutions compared to the previous proof-of-work architecture.

- Proof of Stake (PoS) is an alternative consensus mechanism to Proof of Work (PoW) used by some blockchain networks, including Ethereum. Unlike PoW, which relies on miners to solve cryptographic puzzles to validate transactions and create new blocks, PoS relies on validators to secure the network.

In a nutshell, the PoS consensus layer in Ethereum is designed to be more energy-efficient and secure than PoW, as it does not require miners to solve computationally expensive puzzles to validate transactions and create new blocks. Instead, validators are chosen based on the amount of Ether they have staked and are incentivized to act honestly and follow the rules of the network to avoid losing their stake.

- **Data Layer:** The data layer of Ethereum refers to how data is stored and managed on the Ethereum blockchain. The Ethereum blockchain is a decentralized, distributed ledger that stores transactions and data in a series of blocks. Each block contains a cryptographic hash of the previous block, creating an unbreakable chain of the block.

In Ethereum, the data layer consists of two main components: the state trie and the transaction trie. The state trie is a data structure that stores the current state of the Ethereum network, including account balances and contract codes. The transaction trie is a data structure that stores all the transactions that have been processed by the network.

- **Network Layer:** The network layer of Ethereum is responsible for managing the peer-to-peer network of nodes that make up the Ethereum network. It allows nodes to communicate and share information with each other and is crucial for ensuring that the blockchain is secure and operates smoothly.

  To break it down, it comprises the following:

  - **Peers**: The Ethereum network is made up of nodes, also known as "peers". These nodes run Ethereum software and are connected to each other via the internet.
  - **Communication**: Nodes on the network communicate with each other using the Ethereum Wire Protocol, which is a peer-to-peer networking protocol that allows nodes to send and receive messages.
  - **Discovery:** Nodes can discover other nodes on the network through a process known as "node discovery". This involves sending messages to other nodes to find out information about their peers, such as their IP address and port number.

- **Synchronization**: Nodes on the network synchronize with each other to ensure that they have the latest copy of the blockchain. This is done through a process known as "blockchain synchronization", which involves downloading and verifying each block.
- **Consensus**: Nodes on the network work together to reach a consensus on the current state of the blockchain. This is achieved through the consensus layer, which has been transitioned from Proof of Work (PoW) to Proof of Stake (PoS) to validate transactions and create new blocks.
- **Incentives**: Nodes on the network are incentivized to participate in the network by earning transaction fees and block rewards. This helps to ensure that the network is secure and that there are enough nodes participating to prevent centralization.

Ethereum security review

Now that you have understood the fundamentals, Ethereum architecture and different layers, now we are in a position to review the Security posture. Before we go any further, take a look at the following picture, it shows the attack history on the Ethereum blockchain, one thing which is evident by examining the following figure, most exploits are done on the application layer, which includes EVM and smart contracts, exploiting code vulnerabilities, the other attacks fall under blockchain design weakness, such as consensus mechanism, oracle feeds, clients interaction, and so on. whereas other layers like the network, data layer are generally solid.

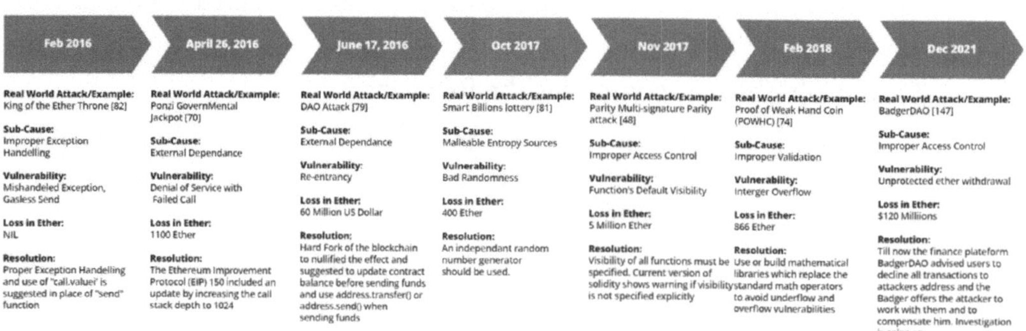

***Figure 2.15**: Ethereum Security breaches overview*

Smart contract review

There have been several high-profile smart contract vulnerabilities that have been exploited over the years. Some of the main ones include:

- **Re-entrancy attacks**: This is when a malicious contract repeatedly calls back into itself before the initial transaction is completed. This can allow an attacker to drain the contract of its funds.
- **Integer overflow/underflow**: If a contract uses integers to track balances or other values, an attacker may be able to manipulate these values by causing them to overflow or underflow. This can lead to unexpected behavior and potentially allow an attacker to steal funds.
- **Unchecked external calls**: If a contract makes external calls to other contracts without checking the return value, an attacker can create a malicious contract that reverts the transaction or steals funds.
- **Access control**: If a contract relies on a single address or account to control access, an attacker may be able to take control of the contract by compromising that account.
- **Time manipulation**: If a contract relies on timestamps to determine when certain actions can be taken, an attacker may be able to manipulate these timestamps to their advantage.
- **Lack of input validation**: If a contract does not validate input data, an attacker may be able to submit malicious data that can cause unexpected behavior or lead to the theft of funds.
- **Bad randomness**: If a contract relies on a source of randomness that is predictable or controllable by an attacker, the attacker can manipulate the results to their advantage.

The root cause of these vulnerabilities falls under either one of these sub-causes, the following figure can give an idea about what to look for when you audit smart contracts.

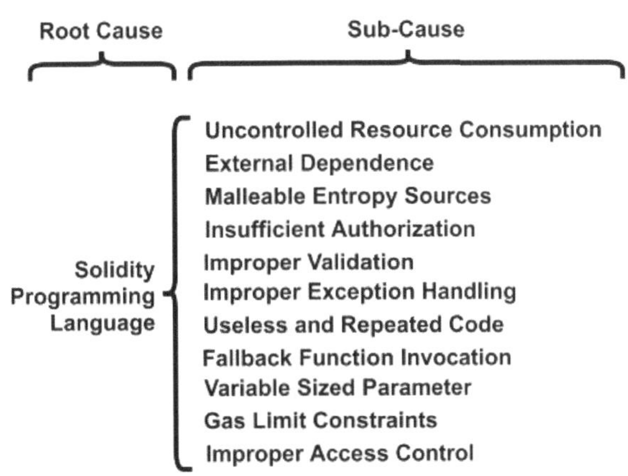

Figure 2.16: *Vulnerabilities Breakdown*

It is important for developers, architects, and security leads to perform threat modeling, see if any of these attack vectors make sense, assess their impact from a confidentiality, data integrity, and traceability standpoint, perform a thorough test on their contracts, and follow the best practices to minimize the risk of exploitation. Also, there are security audit tools available, such as Mythril, Slither, and Remix, but it is important to note that no tool can guarantee the absence of vulnerabilities, and manual code review and testing should also be conducted.

We will go into more details on the vulnerabilities analysis and remediation later in this book, but here to just give an idea about what to expect.

EVM security review

The Ethereum Virtual Machine (EVM) is a crucial component of the Ethereum network, as it is responsible for executing the smart contracts that power decentralized applications (dApps) on the blockchain. However, like any other software, the EVM is not immune to vulnerabilities and exploits; the vulnerabilities fall under the following categories:

- **Denial-of-service attacks:** The EVM can also be vulnerable to denial-of-service (DoS) attacks, where an attacker floods the network with transactions that consume excessive gas, leading to slower transaction processing and higher fees.
- **Immutable bugs or mistakes:** It is related to the immutability of the Ethereum blockchain. Because once a contract is deployed on the blockchain, it cannot be altered due to the immutability feature of the blockchain. It is against the legal law that allows being modified and terminated. However, it may lead to problems if the deployed smart contract contains bugs because after deployment it is impossible to alter.
- **Missing orphan block:** Ether can be lost in the transfer. Ethers can be transferred to a contract to its unique address, but the contract must not be orphan, because in that case the transferred ether will be lost forever. There is a mechanism to revert the ether transfer. Developers need to physically guarantee the rightness of the recipient addresses. The address of the recipient contract must be verified manually to avoid the loss of ether in the transfer.

Ethereum security design review

Ethereum design principles are set by the architecture, which shows how the transaction is mined, the call flow of the architecture, and the network components parameters, the vulnerable areas fall into the following sub-categories:

- **Transactional privacy:** Transaction balance details of the users are publicly available. But, users want that their financial details and transactions should not be visible to others. It may limit the users of smart contracts since attackers can monitor the transaction-related details of users. Attackers can use this information for various kinds of unethical uses.

  It is suggested the encryption of the smart contracts before deploying them on the blockchain, also never share the financial transaction information on smart contracts.

- **Malleable user:** This vulnerability is related to the execution order of two dependent transactions that are invoking the same smart contract. A malevolent user can utilize this vulnerability to attack if the transactions are not executed in the proper order. The order of transaction execution is decided by the miners, but if the adversary is the miner itself, then this will be a very disastrous situation. Suggested to enforce such that the contract code either returns the expected output or fails. Order of transaction should be enforced, otherwise should be an error generated.

- **Untrustworthy data feeds:** Some smart contracts need data feeds from outside the blockchain, but there is no guarantee that the external data source is trustworthy. So, in the case when an attacker is intentionally sending wrong information to fail the smart contract operation then it will be a hazardous situation. Any request coming from outside needs to be properly authenticated and authorized, such as using HTTPS with a valid Certificate, which should land on an API Gateway.

- **Consensus mechanism:** After Ethereum has moved to Proof of Stake, it has adopted the following security measures to overcome malicious users exploiting the network.

- **Slashing:** Ethereum has implemented a mechanism called **slashing** to deter and mitigate attacks on the network. Slashing is a penalty imposed on validators who act maliciously or fail to follow the rules of the network. If a validator is found to have acted maliciously or in violation of the network rules, their staked funds are partially or entirely confiscated, depending on the severity of the offense. The Ethereum community has the power to burn the coins for dis-honest validators.

- **Checkpointing:** Ethereum also has a mechanism called **checkpointing** to help recover from the attack. Checkpointing involves creating a reference point or "checkpoint" at regular intervals in the blockchain. If an attack occurs, the network can roll back to the most recent checkpoint, effectively undoing the malicious activity and restoring the network to a previous state.

In a PoS system, the network is resilient for 51% of attacks, and validators are required to stake their own cryptocurrency as collateral in order to participate in the consensus process. This means that a validator who tries to cheat the system by creating invalid blocks or approving fraudulent transactions will have their stake confiscated. This serves as a strong deterrent against malicious behavior, as validators have a financial incentive to act honestly and protect the network.

There is a range of defense strategies that the Ethereum network can leverage upon any attack, A minimal response could be to forcibly exit the attackers' validators from the network without any additional penalty, the community could also decide to penalize the attacker more harshly, by revoking past rewards or burning some portion (up to 100%) of their staked capital.

Ethereum security considerations

Although the Ethereum foundation has done its due diligence in identifying and taking care of all the vulnerabilities in the smart contract layer, through bounty programs and then there are different audit tools that can be adapted to identify and mitigate bugs in protocols, clients, and solidity. But still, there are some areas which can be looked upon.

Do you know?

You can earn up to $250,000 and a place on the leaderboard by finding protocols, clients, and solidity bugs affecting the Ethereum network – Ethereum.org

Centralization of the consensus layer

One potential vulnerable area is in the consensus layer, with the majority of the validators coming under the umbrella of big exchanges such as Coinbase, Kraken, and Binance. This may lead to a centralization issue, with an attack surface at the core. For example, for some reason, if the regulator sanctions or bans some of the big names, then the whole Ethereum validation ecosystem would be at risk, it is like having the risk of being *too big to fail.*

Another vulnerable domain is the wallets, like meta masks and software where you interact with Ethereum, like the use of geth (go Ethereum client).

MetaMask

When you use MetaMask, ensure that the latest version is installed on your browser and you have saved the passphrase securely. You receive the 12-word Secret Recovery Phrase when you first create your wallet.

MetaMask does not use the cloud. Assuming your gadget breaks, is lost, taken, or has information defilement, it is impossible for the MetaMask Backing group to recuperate this for you. The only way to recover your MetaMask accounts is to use this Secret Recovery Phrase. Secondly, Keep your private keys and secret recovery phrases confidential. If you have a large value of tokens in your account(s), consider getting a hardware wallet.

Vulnerability management

When you interact with the Ethereum Geth client or EVM, cross-verify the CVE under the **https://www.cvedetails.com/vulnerability-list/vendor_id-17524/product_id-51210/Ethereum-Go-Ethereum.html and then go through vulnerability disclosure** - **https://geth.ethereum.org/docs/developers/geth-developer/disclosures**

If you look at the following CVE, you can have a good idea of what to expect. Ensure that there are no open CVEs in your software and you are running the latest patch.

Protect yourself from typical smart contract weaknesses such as Reentrancy, Integer underflows and overflows, and Oracle manipulation. Ensure that all related bugs are fixed, tested, and validated.

Ethereum : Security Vulnerabilities (CVSS score >= 6)

CVSS Scores Greater Than: 0 1 2 3 4 5 6 7 8 9

Sort Results By : CVE Number Descending CVE Number Ascending CVSS Score Descending Number Of Exploits Descending

Copy Results Download Results

<table>
<tr><th>#</th><th>CVE ID</th><th>CWE ID</th><th># of Exploits</th><th>Vulnerability Type(s)</th><th>Publish Date</th><th>Update Date</th><th>Score</th><th>Gained Access Level</th><th>Access</th><th>Complexity</th><th>Authentication</th><th>Conf.</th><th>Integ.</th><th>Avail.</th></tr>
<tr><td>1</td><td>CVE-2018-18920</td><td>119</td><td></td><td>Exec Code Overflow</td><td>2018-11-12</td><td>2019-02-04</td><td>6.8</td><td>None</td><td>Remote</td><td>Medium</td><td>Not required</td><td>Partial</td><td>Partial</td><td>Partial</td></tr>
<tr><td colspan="15">Py-EVM v0.2.0-alpha.33 allows attackers to make a vm.execute_bytecode call that triggers computation._stack.values with '"stack": [100, 100, 0]' where b'\x' was expected, resulting in an execution failure because of an invalid opcode. This is reportedly related to "smart contracts can be executed indefinitely without gas being paid."</td></tr>
<tr><td>2</td><td>CVE-2018-15890</td><td>502</td><td></td><td></td><td>2019-06-20</td><td>2019-06-20</td><td>10.0</td><td>None</td><td>Remote</td><td>Low</td><td>Not required</td><td>Complete</td><td>Complete</td><td>Complete</td></tr>
<tr><td colspan="15">An issue was discovered in EthereumJ 1.8.2. There is Unsafe Deserialization in ois.readObject in mine/Ethash.java and decoder.readObject in crypto/ECKey.java. When a node syncs and mines a new block, arbitrary OS commands can be run on the server.</td></tr>
<tr><td>3</td><td>CVE-2017-14457</td><td>125</td><td></td><td>DoS +Info</td><td>2018-01-19</td><td>2023-01-30</td><td>6.4</td><td>None</td><td>Remote</td><td>Low</td><td>Not required</td><td>Partial</td><td>None</td><td>Partial</td></tr>
<tr><td colspan="15">An exploitable information leak/denial of service vulnerability exists in the libevm (Ethereum Virtual Machine) `create2` opcode handler of CPP-Ethereum. A specially crafted smart contract code can cause an out-of-bounds read leading to memory disclosure or denial of service. An attacker can create/send malicious a smart contract to trigger this vulnerability.</td></tr>
<tr><td>4</td><td>CVE-2017-14451</td><td>125</td><td></td><td>Exec Code</td><td>2020-12-02</td><td>2020-12-09</td><td>7.5</td><td>None</td><td>Remote</td><td>Low</td><td>Not required</td><td>Partial</td><td>Partial</td><td>Partial</td></tr>
</table>

Figure 2.17: *Ethereum Common Vulnerability Exposures (CVE)*

Note

it is always better to do your due diligence on any open software you are using on your blockchain product, for example, running the patches up to date, routinely performing threat modeling, auditing, classifying risk by performing simulation, AKA *red vs blue teaming exercises, etc.* CVE *gets posted once the exploit has been made, you can take the* CVE *matrix as a reference only.*

More to come later in the book, where we will go through blockchain vulnerabilities and remediation in much detail.

Hardening access control

Any externally owned account (EOA) or contract account can call functions marked public or external in smart contracts. Indicating public perceivability for capabilities is important assuming that you believe others should connect with your agreement. However, functions within the smart contract—not external accounts—can only call private functions. Problems can arise if every network participant has access to contract functions, particularly if this means that anyone can carry out sensitive operations (like minting new tokens).

Secure access controls are required to prevent unauthorized use of smart contract functions. A smart contract's access control mechanisms limit who can use certain functions, like accounts that are in charge of managing the contract. Two patterns that can be used to implement access control in smart contracts are the Ownable pattern, role-based control, and by using multi-signature.

- **Ownable pattern**: Using the Ownable pattern, an address is chosen as the **owner** of a contract during the process of making it. The Only Owner modifier is added to methods that are private. This makes sure that the contract checks the name of the calling address before running the code. So that people who aren't the contract owner can't get in without permission, calls to protected services from addresses other than the contract owner always go back.

- **Role-based access control**: A single point of failure occurs when a single address is registered as the Owner of a smart contract, increasing the risk of centralization and a vulnerability to be used as an attack vector.

  Under role-based access management, a group of known people are given access to different private functions. For example, one account might be in charge of making tokens, while another might be in charge of upgrading contracts or stopping them. By making access control less centralized in this way, customers' expectations of trust are lowered, and single points of failure are taken away.

- **Multi-signature**: With multi-sig, accounts are owned by multiple entities and require signatures from a minimum number of accounts to execute a transaction. Since multiple parties must agree before taking any action on the target contract, using a multisig for access control adds an additional layer of security. Since it makes it more challenging for an attacker or rogue insider to manipulate sensitive contract functions for malicious purposes, this is especially helpful if the Ownable pattern is required.

Testing and auditing

Smart contracts necessitate a more rigorous degree of quality evaluation throughout the development process due to the immutability of code executing in the Ethereum Virtual Machine. Long-term security will be greatly enhanced and your users will be protected if you thoroughly test your contract and keep an eye out for any unexpected outcomes.

It is advisable to ask others to review the source code for potential security flaws once you have tested your contract. While testing won't find every bug in a smart contract, getting an outside opinion increases the likelihood of finding security flaws.

Just unit and regression testing on the code is not enough. A more effective strategy is to combine property-based testing with unit testing, which is carried out via static and dynamic analysis. To examine attainable program states and execution routes, the static analysis uses low-level representations like control flow graphs and abstract syntax trees. Dynamic analysis methods, like fuzzing, execute contract code with random input values in order to find actions that go against security principles.

- **Bug bounty**

  Another useful approach is to set up a bug bounty program is another approach for implementing external code reviews. A bug bounty is a financial reward given to individuals (usually white hat hackers) that discover vulnerabilities in an application.

  When implemented effectively, bug bounties provide the hacker community with an incentive to review your code for serious issues. The **infinite money bug** on Optimism, a Layer 2 protocol running on Ethereum, is a real-world illustration of this. It allowed an attacker to generate a limitless supply of Ether. Fortunately, a whitehat hacker found the vulnerability and alerted the team, earning an enormous prize in the process.

  Setting a bug bounty program's reward proportionate to the amount of money at risk is a smart move. This strategy, known as the **scaling bug**

bounty offers cash incentives for people to properly report vulnerabilities as opposed to abusing them. I will cover this topic in much more detail in *Chapter 5, Blockchain Application Audit.*

Immunefi is a good Bug bounty platform for smart contracts and DeFi projects, where security researchers review code, disclose vulnerabilities, get paid, and make crypto safer.

- **Smart Contract Weakness (SWC) registry**

  The weakness classification system described in EIP-1470 is implemented in the Smart Contract Weakness Classification registry (SWC registry).

Note

There are multiple opcodes in the Ethereum bytecode, which is written in assembly language. On the Ethereum blockchain, each opcode carries out a particular function. Ethereum Virtual Machines compile smart contract functionalities into low-level language as bytecodes to carry out actions, while developers construct them using high-level languages like Solidity.

It can be seen from the following figure, that smart contract weakness decreased over time. It shows three stages of smart contract security with respect to mean and variance. It was high in the initial stages, but right after April 2017, the smart contract got solid.

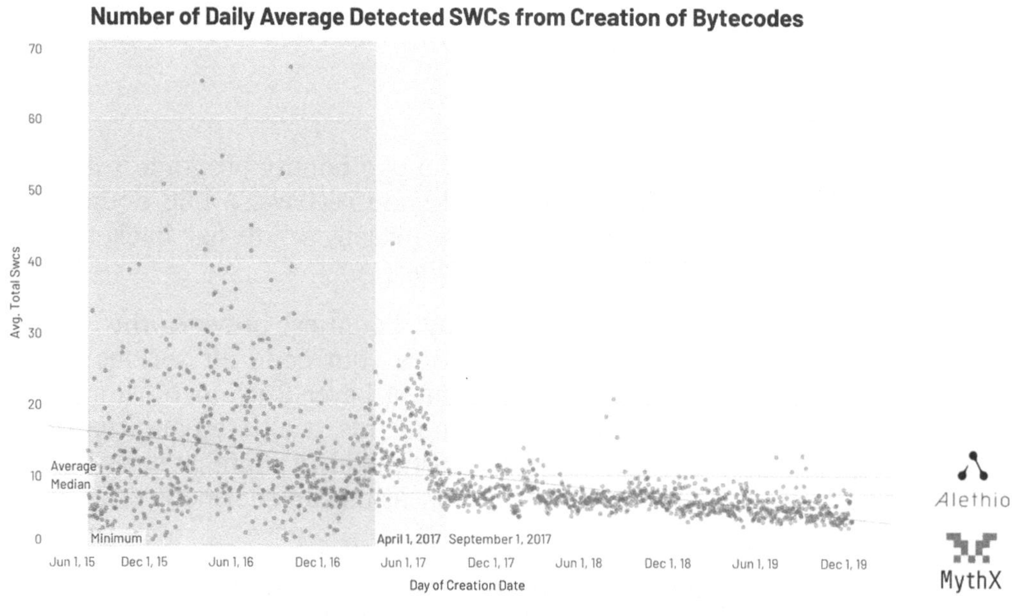

Figure 2.18: *Analysis of SWCs over time*

It is recommended to scan your smart contract through all SWCs and use the following test cases to ensure that the contract is hardened. The following table extracted from **https://swcregistry.io/** is a good starting point in your Ethereum security journey.

ID	Title	Relationships	Test cases
SWC-136	Unencrypted Private Data On-Chain	CWE-767: Access to Critical Private Variable via Public Method	• odd_even.sol • odd_even_fixed.sol
SWC-135	Code With No Effects	CWE-1164: Irrelevant Code	• deposit_box.sol • deposit_box_fixed.sol • wallet.sol • wallet_fixed.sol
SWC-134	Message call with hardcoded gas amount	CWE-655: Improper Initialization	• hardcoded_gas_limits.sol

Figure 2.19: *SWC Registry*

Some useful resources related to Ethereum security testing and auditing are as follows.

https://ethereum.org/en/developers/docs/smart-contracts/testing/#testing-tools-and-libraries.

Hyperledger fabric

Hyperledger Fabric is a permissioned, open-source, enterprise-grade distributed ledger technology (DLT) platform designed for use in business settings that offers a few key capabilities that set it apart from other popular DLT platforms.

Fabric's architecture is highly modular and configurable, allowing for innovation, adaptability, and optimization for a wide range of industry use cases, such as supply chain, healthcare, human resources, and even digital music delivery.

Fabric is the first distributed ledger platform to support smart contracts written in general-purpose programming languages like Java, Go, and Node.js as opposed to domain-specific languages (DSL), which are constrained. This indicates that no additional training to learn a new language or DSL is required for the majority of businesses to develop smart contracts.

In addition, the Fabric platform is permissioned, which means that, in contrast to a public permissionless network, participants are known to one another rather than completely untrusted. This means that a network can operate under a governance model based on the trust that exists between participants, such as a legal agreement or framework for handling disputes, even though the participants may not fully trust one another (for instance, they may be competitors in the same industry).

The platform's support for pluggable consensus protocols, which makes it easier to tailor the platform to specific use cases and trust models, is one of its most significant points of differentiation. For instance, a fully byzantine fault-tolerant consensus may be deemed unnecessary and detrimental to performance and throughput when implemented within a single company or under the direction of a reputable authority. A crash fault-tolerant (CFT) consensus protocol may be sufficient in such circumstances, whereas a more conventional byzantine fault-tolerant (BFT) consensus protocol may be required in a multi-party, decentralized use case.

Fabric can use consensus protocols that do not need a native cryptocurrency to encourage expensive mining or drive the execution of smart contracts. The absence of cryptographic mining operations means that the platform can be deployed at roughly the same cost of operation as any other distributed system. Avoiding cryptocurrencies also reduces some significant risks and attack vectors.

Fabric is one of the best-performing platforms currently available in terms of transaction processing and confirmation latency thanks to the combination of these distinguishing design features. Additionally, Fabric makes it possible to maintain the privacy and confidentiality of transactions as well as the smart contracts (which Fabric refers to as "chain code") that carry them out.

The following are the architecture components of fabric:

- **Peer nodes:** Peer nodes are the foundation of the Fabric architecture. The distributed ledger is hosted by these nodes, which also carries out chain codes or smart contracts. In Fabric, there are two types of peer nodes: committing and recommending peers.
- **Endorsing peers:** These nodes carry out the chain code and provide the client application with a proposal response. Peers who endorse, validate transactions, and support the outcomes.
- **Committing peers:** These nodes commit the transaction to the distributed ledger and verify the endorsement policy.
- **Ordering service:** The broadcasting of the block to the committing peers for validation and commitment to the ledger is the job of this service, which is in charge of receiving endorsed transactions from the committing peers, and organizing them into a block.
- **Membership service providers:** The management of the permissions and identities of network participants is the responsibility of this component.

- **Client software:** To carry out transactions and obtain data from the ledger, the client application communicates with the peer nodes.
- **Chain code:** The smart contract, known as chain code, specifies the rules and logic that govern the ledger's transactions.
- **Channels:** Within the Fabric network, channels enable the creation of private subnetworks that guarantee the privacy and confidentiality of transactions between specific participants.

Hyperledger Fabric's modular and adaptable architecture makes it a popular choice for building enterprise-grade blockchain applications because it can be customized and integrated with other enterprise systems.

Now that you have understood the basics of Fabric, let us review it from a security standpoint.

Hyperledger Fabric security review

The purpose of Hyperledger Fabric is to make it possible for multiple organizations with limited trust to work together securely. Despite Hyperledger Fabric's security enhancements, deployments still require careful configuration and monitoring to ensure their safe operation. In this section, we'll look at various threats that HyperLedger Fabric administrators should be aware of and discuss ways to mitigate them.

Hyperledger Fabric's network threats differ from those of popular permissionless chains because it is a permissioned blockchain. On permissioned networks, for instance, users are known, their activities can be monitored, and access is managed by access control lists, so 51% of attacks and network partitioning attacks are less of a threat. Denial of Service (DoS) attacks and consensus manipulation are two examples of these types of attacks that affect all distributed systems. The Membership Service Provider (MSP) is a target of other attacks in a Hyperledger Fabric network.

- **DOS attack:** DoS attacks pose a threat to any distributed system and disrupt the availability of the network. Denial of service attacks can come from a wide variety of sources, making proactive prevention difficult. By collecting performance metrics like transaction throughput and latency, compromised availability can be detected early on, reducing this risk.

  DOS can impact the availability of any of the components of the Hyperledger fabric network, so there have to be proper measures of identification, remediation like network isolation and monitoring principles to be applied.

- **Consensus mechanism:** Assaults on the organization agreement incorporate DoS and exchange reordering assaults. Crash Fault Tolerant (CFT) consensus algorithms are the only ones Hyperledger Fabric currently uses, so they cannot tolerate any malicious actors. Byzantine Fault Tolerant (BFT) algorithms are currently being developed, which will be able to tolerate up to one-third of the network being malicious. This threat can be mitigated by early detection of malicious behavior, regardless of the consensus algorithm used. For the purpose of detection, it is essential to log threat indicators like elections in leadership and transaction delays.
- **MSP downtime:** Fabric-specific threats can be significant when an MSP is compromised. The MSP has the ability to alter network access control and, if malicious, could deny service and launch sybil attacks. Private key theft or a rogue insider can compromise the MSP, which may only be discovered after it has been exploited. It is essential to adhere to best practices with key management to reduce this risk. In the event of a breach, logging MSP actions like certificate creation and revocation can assist in identifying malicious behavior. Early detection and remediation are the results of alerting based on that logging.
- **Chain code exploits:** In contrast to cryptocurrencies, where the cost of smart contract attacks is easier to quantify, attacks on Hyperledger Fabric can compromise business logic and network performance. Notwithstanding standard programming rationale bugs, normal mistakes can likewise come from improperly taking care of simultaneousness or non-determinism. Using a secure software development life cycle framework, smart contracts should be designed with security in mind from the start to reduce this risk. Utilizing smart contract analysis tools like the Hyperledger Lab Chain code Analyzer, smart contract security should be evaluated before deployment to identify potential threats. Consider a formal verification or external security audit for more sensitive applications. Finally, after the smart contract has been deployed, it should be monitored to identify unusual behavior.

Use Case - Central Bank Digital Currency

Over 105 nations, representing more than 95% of the worldwide Gross Domestic Product (GDP), are exploring a central bank that utilizes just digital currency. A record-breaking fifty nations are well on their way towards implementing a blockchain-based economy. This has been made conceivable by private blockchains, which are the basic foundation for these enormous tasks.

Several Central Bank Digital Currency projects have used hyper ledger fabric as the blockchain platform. One good example that can be seen is the ABER project between Saudi Arabia and the UAE. It is important to use the best security practices outlined as follows while using a private blockchain. We will explore more on the Central Bank Digital Currency security design later in the book.

Private blockchain security consideration

Network sharing at the corporate level frequently requires a higher level of privacy due to concerns about data confidentiality. A private blockchain is your best option if this is one of your requirements. Since only a small number of users have access to specific transactions, private blockchains are unquestionably a more stable alternative to the network. However, that doesn't mean they can't be penetrated.

Network availability

While having complete control over who has access to the network increases security, it also creates a single point of failure for the server(s) that act as validation computers. This means that anyone can enter the network without proper verification if the certified authority is attacked or fails.

You can add back-ups and modify the architecture of your network to make it more resilient against failures of this kind.

On-premise deployment

You can store data using an on-premise model with a private blockchain. Traditional security measures like data confidentiality, integrity, availability, and non-repudiation are able to be taken in this scenario. The data can only be accessed by participants who have agreed to be kept private. Respectability implies that information should be communicated without alteration. Similar to redundancy, availability requires a backup for each computer processing messages. Lastly, network access log monitoring is made possible by the non-repudiation principle, which states that if someone catches you doing something wrong, you cannot deny it.

Cloud deployments

On the other hand, you can decide to run your private blockchain network on cloud administration. However, keep in mind that you are still responsible for anything that happens to your cloud-based data; consequently, you must ensure that service level agreements and security controls are in place.

Governance

Governance may influence the choice of architecture in a DLT-based implementation, a fixed architecture may limit the available governance models. To put it succinctly, governance is concerned with authorities, decision rights, and rewarding good behavior. Who is a part of the system, for example, is decided by governance models. It is likely that a private blockchain would be having a permissioned environment and necessitate a hierarchy for defining participant roles. A design challenge is how security can be effectively managed through the governance structure, one that is likely to be managed by the enterprise with public stakeholder involvement, because this complexity has the potential to introduce additional vulnerabilities.

Roles and authority are defined by governance models, but the consensus is used to make decisions in DLTs, particularly when determining the finality of a transaction. The governance model determines which nodes participate in the consensus process, and as the number of nodes grows, so does the system's complexity of communication. Additionally, the utilization of nodes that are not directly controlled by the organization, for instance, third-party vendors—increases the system's attack surface and the amount of time required to reach finality, which has an impact on throughput.

The system architecture should clearly define boundaries in a private blockchain for security governance, as should clear roles, authorities, and permissions. It is necessary to apply security frameworks in such a way that governance models adequately address authorities and responsibilities. Governance is also essential in operational stages, where the system must quickly distribute code updates, vulnerability patches, and other system changes. Additionally, tasks like incident reporting and system maintenance may require coordination among system participants to guarantee security. If the structure were decentralized, participating bodies would be required to clearly communicate their expectations regarding the observance of security requirements.

Key management

Current iterations of DLTs rely heavily on the use of public key cryptography for verifying and signing transactions and in some cases for securing blocks. This use of public key cryptography poses a problem for usability in scenarios where users may be more familiar with biometric or password-enabled security functionality. To address usability challenges, key management custodians have emerged in the cryptocurrency landscape. As third parties outside of the blockchain system itself, custodians constitute an attractive attack target and have been demonstrated to be a key point of vulnerability for many cryptocurrencies, their evaluation should be done thoroughly.

- The use of a bare metal hardware security module, to serve as a vault, with strict access control and key rotation is enforced with envelope encryption. Meaning that keys inside the vault are encrypted with a secondary key.

- Keys are generated with a key ceremony process, which has data security standards in transit and the rest has been implemented.
- Testing for Key Backups and System Resiliency is ensured of the vaults.

Conclusion

Congratulations! You have made it to the end of this chapter. We have covered lots of important information. It may seem draining considering the amount of content we covered, but trust me you will be connecting all the dots once you apply this knowledge in your organization.

We started this chapter with a discussion of blockchain types, by showing you the differences, so you know exactly which one to choose over another. Then we started the Ethereum blockchain, where we explained the fundamentals and the architecture in detail so that when we review the vulnerabilities, you can relate to it. Since Ethereum is the heart of blockchain applications, it was important to cover it in depth. Later in this chapter, we shifted our focus to private blockchains, where we covered Hyperledger Fabric, showcased the components and what vulnerabilities exist, and covered security considerations while explaining both public and private blockchains. Now with this knowledge, you will feel confident about how security varies across different blockchain types, and how to architect the solution securely, no matter what use case you land up with.

Points to remember

- Every blockchain platform is not the same. The variation mainly depends upon who can write, validate and read the data in the blockchain.
- The selection of a blockchain platform depends upon the use case if it supports the transaction speed, data privacy concerns and validation concerns over the consensus layer, compatibility with existing systems, and cost.
- Ethereum blockchain is a preferable platform to build Dapps, due to its massive ecosystem due to its surging popularity of its dApps in areas such as finance (decentralized finance, or DeFi apps), arts and collectibles (non-fungible tokens, or NFTs), gaming, and technology.
- Ethereum's vulnerable areas include the consensus layer, smart contract bugs, transaction privacy, contract calls, common vulnerabilities, and client endpoints like metamasks and wallets.

- Hyperledger Fabric is the most popular enterprise blockchain solution, with 38% of the top 100 global companies implementing it, including Microsoft, Amazon, Alphabet, and Visa, also being the preferred platform for CBDC projects.
- HL Fabric vulnerability domain includes Membership service providers, validation nodes, code bugs, key management systems, prevention against DOS attacks, centralization, and availability attacks that need to be considered.

References

- **https://ethereum.org/**
- **https://swcregistry.io/**
- **https://www.cvedetails.com/vulnerability-list/vendor_id-17524/Ethereum.html**
- **https://www.hyperledger.org/**

Multiple choice questions

1. **What does SWC stand for?**
    a. Smart Contract Weakness Classification
    b. Smart contract weakness class
    c. Smart channel Weakness Classification
    d. All of the above

2. **What does EVM consist of?**
    a. Gas
    b. Bytecode
    c. Memory
    d. Program Counter
    e. All of the above

3. **Which of the following is an example of externally owned accounts in Ethereum?**
   a. They are controlled by private keys and have no code associated with them
   b. They are controlled by Public keys and have code associated with them
   c. They are controlled by Public keys and have no code associated with them
   d. All of the above

4. **What is the prevention against Re-entrancy Attack?**
   a. Use the checks-effects-interactions design while coding smart contracts
   b. Sign the transactions and block the external calls
   c. Ensure all state changes happen before calling external contracts
   d. None of the above

5. **How do you prevent overflow in Solidity?**
   a. Use at least a 0.8 version of the Solidity compiler
   b. Clamp any values that exceed either this minimum or maximum
   c. Use at least a 0.7 version of the Solidity compiler
   d. Store the transactions in an externally owned contract

Answers

1. **a**
2. **e**
3. **a**
4. **a, c**
5. **a, b**

CHAPTER 3
Attack Vectors Management on Blockchain

Introduction

Crypto investors lost nearly $4 billion to hackers in 2022, with DeFi protocols being hit the hardest by cryptocurrency hacks. To better understand what has happened in recent years, the following analysis chart can provide you with the seriousness of the matter. What could have been the main reason for these exploitations? If you are thinking about code, AKA Smart contract vulnerabilities, you are right. However, that is just the tip of the Iceberg.

The truth is, all of these losses could have been significantly reduced if platform vulnerabilities had been identified early in the design. It could have been much less if the risk management had been performed, based on the impact and probability of occurrence, and followed up with mitigating controls and remediation procedures.

It is a well-known known fact that if hackers can see your application on the internet, they will do whatever they can to exploit the weakness, as evidenced by news reports and the numbers on social media. It is also true that the hacks can be mitigated; there are methods for handling these risks and safeguarding your system.

To accomplish this, it is crucial to detect any potential vulnerabilities in your system at an early stage, classify and filter whether these risks can be exploited, and do the math to determine if it makes sense to safeguard them. As an example of effective risk management, there are cases when vulnerable network elements, which you are trying to secure, are present in a private subnet, not exposed to the outside world nor part of critical assets. The risk score for such elements can be low, you wouldn't want to spend 100$ worth of a lock to protect 10$ worth of an isolated asset.

In this chapter, I will walk you through the cycle of blockchain risk management. We will then learn the tools like threat modeling and the classification matrix to scope and prioritize the risk domains. While doing all this, we will explore and analyze some use cases and examples of sample attacks to see how all of this applies.

Structure

We will be covering the following topics in this chapter:

- Blockchain risk management
- Top security risk in blockchain
- Threat model overview and architecture
- Applying Threat Modeling to Blockchain
- Mitigation against STRIDE Attack Vectors

Blockchain risk management

New technologies may have drawbacks that need to be discovered and dealt with. This is especially true when the technology is a fundamental component of the organization's underlying IT infrastructure, rather than just an overlaying application, as is frequently the case with the blockchain.

If I ask you a simple question: how much security is enough in your blockchain application? Or rather how much are you willing to spend on security controls? The answer to this depends on your risk management exercise. However, before we go any further, let's start with the basics, by defining risk, attack vector, and mitigation.

- **Risk** is a potential problem and its effects if the problem occurs.
- **Threat or Attack vector** is a path that can be exploited in the risk occurrence. A common example includes infected email attachments and malicious web page pop-ups.
- **Mitigation** is a countermeasure against a threat, something you can do to prevent the threat or, at a bare minimum, reduce the likelihood of its success.

To better understand all this, consider a good example where there is a risk that someone could steal your car keys from your house and drive off in your car. The attack vector is the different way the attacker can accomplish this, such as breaking a window to reach in or breaking the door lock, all this can happen if the breakpoints are not hardened. Mitigation is something when you keep the car key out of sight or store it in a vault protected with strong cryptographic passwords. Other ways could be to protect against all possible attack vectors, such as window and door locks should be protected with alarms and watched by a security guard.

Businesses should be proactive when they look for new risks linked to blockchain. You shouldn't wait until the last minute to do risk management. This should be a part of every step of the planning and marketing process for a blockchain project from the very beginning.

The blockchain risk management cycle starts with defining the security objective, performing a threat and vulnerability assessment, classifying and quantifying risk, and then take the remediation actions.

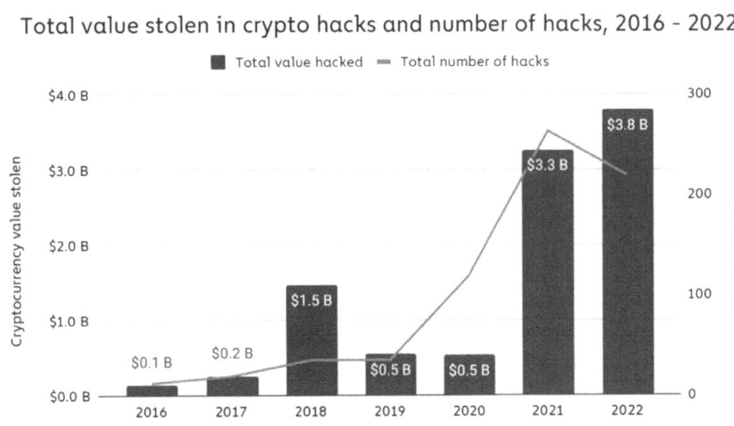

Figure 3.1: *Risk Management lifecycle*

Security objective

This forms the basis for the risk assessment as a whole and provides guidance for all subsequent steps. Considering the plan of action that will be upheld by blockchain, what are the key security targets to develop? Should availability be more important than confidentiality? Should complete anonymity be ensured? What parts of the framework should safeguard data integrity other than a blockchain stage?

The security objective should align with the business goal and be clearly verified. For example, providing secure and reliable data storage to authorized third parties with the assurance that the platform is appropriate to process sensitive information. Here, we are targeting availability and confidentiality. It varies for different blockchain platforms; private blockchains support availability and confidentiality, whereas data integrity can be difficult to achieve. This is because you rely on access control for who can write but cannot control the intent of validators, due to no incentive program. On the other hand, with public blockchains, data integrity and availability can be achieved, but the goal of data confidentiality is difficult to achieve.

Risk Identification

This exercise will identify the top security threats in your blockchain architecture. There are numerous techniques for achieving this, like threat modeling, vulnerability scanning, end point detection agents, security audits, and penetration testing are the most common tools an organization uses. The goal is to identify what and where are the weak links are in our solution before the attacker catches it. This evaluation exercise also tells how strong the security posture is, in terms of the types of security controls implemented. what would be the outcome of a potential attack, and what key data assets do we need to guard against.

Note

You will end up with more than 1000 weaknesses if you do this practice all the way through. It's a good idea to start with a high-level design, then do some threat modeling to see how the system reacts to an attack, such as what security controls are built in by default. This will help you narrow down what's important to you, like if the Man in the Middle (MIM) attack is done by an intruder using a sniffer to look for incoming traffic and if you already have strong access control with TLS enabled.

Next, put your blockchain app's images, smart contracts, OS, and files through a vulnerability check to look for common vulnerabilities (CVEs). This will let you know if there are any out-of-date patches and how exposed the apps are to major attacks. Finally, use all the knowledge you got in the previous steps to do a penetration testing exercise with both red and blue teams. This will make it easy for you to choose the right risk to deal with. This is the point: get the risk from various tools and assess them until you have a good idea of how bad it is.

Note

A review of vulnerabilities helps the project team understand what parts of the blockchain solution will be open to attackers and what weak places could cause problems in the future. Finding holes is hard, so all companies that use blockchain solutions should regularly do security testing on every part of those solutions. Tests for smart contracts need to be given extra care. To limit the risks, it's important to set up a way to protect smart contract code early on.

We will cover the threat assessment using threat modeling in the next topic in much more detail, whereas the other topics like vulnerability scanning, penetration testing will be covered in the following chapters.

As the next step, let us understand the concept for classifying the risk.

Risk classification

Vulnerabilities and threats combine to form risks, as defined in the previous steps. Prioritizes risks by figuring out how likely it is that a particular vulnerability will cross paths with threats and, if that does happen, how important the impact will be. A risk with a significant impact but very unlikely to occur will be managed differently than a risk with a moderate impact that is likely to occur frequently.

You can use the following grid to rank the risks that come with different blockchain application options.

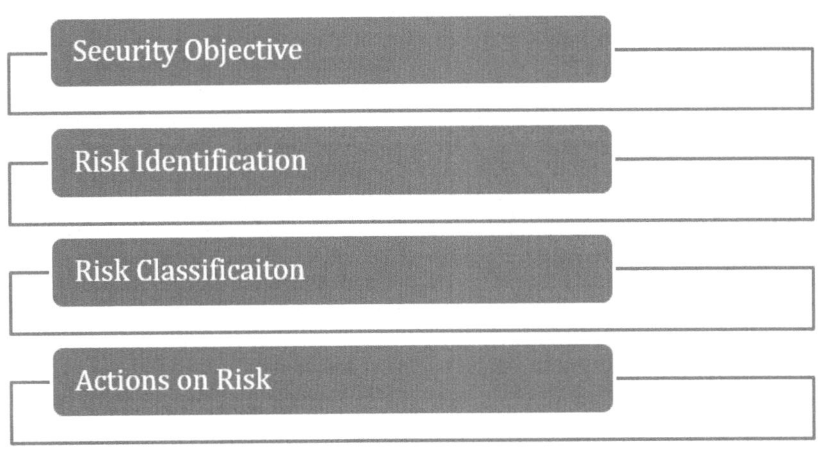

***Figure 3.2**: Criticality estimates by likelihood and impact*

Bring all your teams together for a tabletop exercise. The people who own the assets should figure out how important the data they hold is, and the people who design the networks should be able to say whether the endpoints' IP addresses, ports, and services are open or not. The company that sold the goods should also be involved to explain any controls that are in place to make up for any mistakes or false results.

When classifying risks, the best thing to do is to group them down to a very fine level. For instance, for any CVE or risk that has already been discovered, if the underlying application has a routable IP address and holds PI or SNPI data or any cryptographic keys, this means that anyone in the network can reach that IP address. During the risk assessment process, direct and compensating controls should also be checked to make sure they prevent CVEs for getting exploited. A high score would be given to the risk that has high-value data, an IP address that can be routed, and no security controls.

Next, you need to put a dollar amount on the risk. Let's say that the protected keys are lost or stolen. It will be harder to get the data back. You can only handle clear text input, so this would make things take longer. The program that has that data won't be able to be used for a few hours while the backups are being restored. In terms of money, this might be around $10,000.

Note

The numbers don't have to be exact; a calculate estimate will do.

Mitigation strategy

Deciding what to do with each risk in an important task. There are mainly the following ways of addressing the risk.

- **Mitigate or reduce the risk**: Do something about the risk and/or the defect right away to lessen its effects. It might be harder to limit the effects of blockchain than with other technologies. More attention should be paid to making systems less vulnerable and preventing risks. This approach controls risk the best, but it usually costs a lot. It's best for very high and very important risks.

  Example: Code hardening of smart contracts, patching the endpoints, and API Firewall filtering for any incoming traffic towards blockchain oracles.

- **Accept the risk**. Risk acceptance is when you choose to live with or accept a potential risk instead of taking steps to reduce or avoid it. This approach is best advised for low to medium risks.

  Example: No security measures on securing the consensus layer, assuming that the trust is achieved through the computation process, the risk is low since the likelihood of pulling off a 51% attack is low in a public blockchain as compared to the private blockchain, assuming the public blockchain network is highly distributed.

Note

But it's much more likely that a 51% attack will work when there are hard forks that leave behind a smaller blockchain with fewer nodes. A very small network can become even smaller during times of the day when most miners turn off their nodes. This makes 51% strikes very easy.

In other case, the small to medium-sized business that made the blockchain wallet might decide to take the chance of a breach by not spending money on a hardware security tool for key management.

- **Avoid the risk**. Change the way the system works to get rid of the unique security problem. Usually, this means making trade-offs and letting go of some features to build a system efficiently.

  Example: No PI or SNPI information is taken from the users in the blockchain onboarding process to avoid privacy breaches in case of a cyber-attack.

- **Transfer the risk**. Involve a third party, such as an insurance company or an external service provider, to address the risk.

  Example: Using a custodial wallet service using an HSM on a cloud provider, where the cloud provider will be responsible to manage security around the key lifecycle management.

  But for the HSM product, the wallet service provider needs to work out a service level agreement with a cloud provider. If they do this, there is a risk of going against the other party or terms not been followed. When you buy insurance, on the other hand, you can give the risk to the insurance company in exchange for a price. It all depends on the use case

---

Note

Transferring risk never frees the owner from some risk. Not all risk can be transferred, but it can be shared.

The following table is a good summary to understand the strategies.

In the matrix below, avoid would also include the consideration of how costly the mitigation is. If the cost of remediation is reasonable, then mitigation is the recommended path. But if remediation is either cost prohibitive or there is no known solution, coupled with the high-risk ranking (vulnerability * threat), then risk avoidance would be recommended.

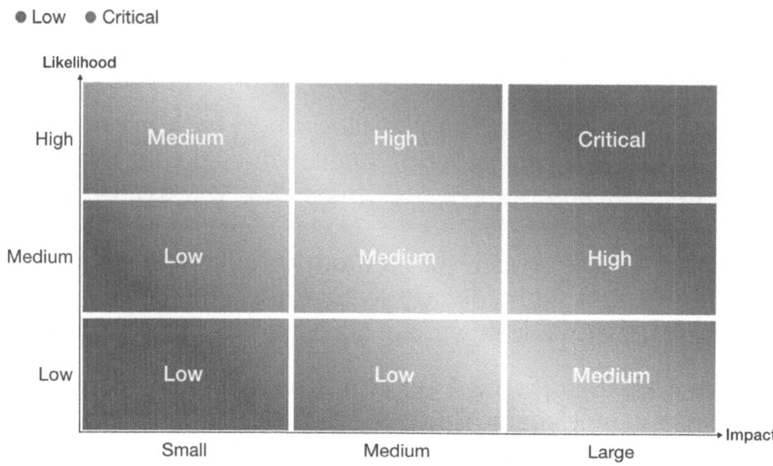

***Figure* 3.3**: *Strategies to counter the risk*

Risk management template

There can be different attack scenarios and risk events that can happen on the blockchain application, such as:

- A scenario where an attacker rewrites the ledger by compromising enough nodes. This will put the community (in this case, a consortium) at serious risk.
- The administrator's secret key becomes accessible to other parties, who can then impersonate the administrator and even change the smart contracts.
- Node administrators can access confidential data stored in the node.

To arrive at the best course of action, the following worksheet will give you a good cheat sheet. While doing the risk assessment for your blockchain application, ensure that you have knowledge of all these areas and then adopt the controls appropriately.

Objective	Info Type	Vulnerability	Threat Actor	Likelihood	Impact	Risk Response	Compensative Control	Security Control
Confidentiality	User Funds and Transaction Data	Encryption Key stolen from a wallet	External (incentive)	High	High	Mitigate	Envelope Encryption at Rest	Access request Validation check

Table 3.1: *Risk Management Template*

Note

Compensating controls are a good way to check how much the solution is secure if the direct security controls are missing. It also ensures the defense's in-depth coverage. If the attack launches a sophisticated attack, it prevents the attacker to penetrate further, moving laterally within the network.

Top security risk in blockchain

Blockchain security risk can be broadly categorized into four main categories, as shown in *Figure* 3.4. Each of these categories can be further divided. However, to start assessing your blockchain solution, you need to see how you are handling these risks.

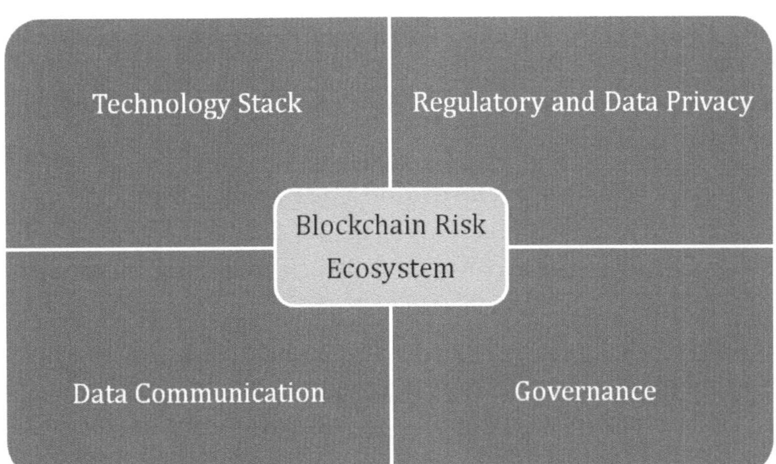

Figure 3.4: *Blockchain Risk Ecosystem*

Technology stack

Blockchain protocol has some underlying features such as cryptographic keys, consensus mechanisms, confidentiality concerns, availability drawbacks, process logic of smart contract layer, and validation nodes.

Risk management of the protocol stack is equally as important as any other domain. Let me explain further by breaking down each element.

- Cryptographic keys created to store digital assets are an integral part. Considerations include how the keys are created, shared, stored, and managed throughout the lifecycle. Is there enough awareness given to the user to handle their sensitive keys? How are funds restored if a user loses their keys?
- Validation nodes pose a potential security risk. How are the nodes patched and configured? Is there any endpoint detection and response tool configured to detect malicious events and take responsive actions?
- Has secure development practice been adopted to develop the App throughout different layers, from UI to Smart contact, extending all the way to the infrastructure?
- How is the availability risk addressed? What happens if the blockchain networking nodes are compromised? Is a Disaster recovery plan prepared to recover services through backups? What is the Recovery time objective (RTO) and Recovery point objective (RPO) metrics and have they been tested?
- Are the performance checks been performed on the application and underlying blockchain platform in terms of measuring transaction throughput, settlement time, CPU, I/O, and memory utilization.
- Are there standards that can be used to connect blockchain apps to enterprise systems?

The recommendation is to perform due care and due diligence and apply a defense-in-depth strategy to each layer of the technology stack, which means securing data confidentiality, integrity, and availability while designing the architecture.

Controls should be designed for hardening and the store of the public/private keys, addressing application, infrastructure and smart contract vulnerabilities, and strong consideration for consensus committee delegations.

Regulatory and Data privacy

The privacy risk deals with how the sensitive data call flow is handled within the blockchain architecture and which regulatory framework applies to your solution in your jurisdiction. The checks include the following:

- Could non-compliance with data-related regulations or confidentiality agreements result from design flaws in a blockchain-based system? For example, does the application include by and by recognizable data personally identifiable information (PII)? Do the requirements require data to be stored off-chain, or can it be stored on-chain?
- Does the application have the right controls in place throughout the data lifecycle, such as when data is collected or created, stored, used, and shared between blockchain nodes?
- Is there a gamble of openness of delicate information because of insufficient strategies, methods, principles, and rules for information encryption and confusion?
- Is there a possibility of incorrect data entering the system? If so, how can errors be identified and corrected?
- Is it necessary for the blockchain system to adhere to regulations regarding the *right to be forgotten*? If so, does it conflict with the possibility that data stored on a blockchain cannot be changed?
- Is there a legal requirement indicating that data must be seen by certain participants, with strong access and security control enforced on Personal Identifiable information, known as PII? If so, then implementing such a policy across thousands of computers in a network requires a massive amount of infrastructure and resources.
- How are the smart contracts perceived legally in your jurisdiction?
- Are the Anti-money laundering (AML) and know your customer (KYC) checks are passed?
- Are there ways to make sure that money does not go to or come from people or countries that are subject to international penalties or the position of *politically exposed person*?

  The general rule of thumb is to always set up the data privacy framework of your blockchain solution by understanding the compliance requirements around data management in your jurisdiction. The second is to collect the minimum amount of data to avoid spending too much on maintenance and compliance. Last, but not least, consult with a lawyer and make sure your blockchain solution is properly audited from the legal standpoint.

Governance

Governance risks emanate primarily from the decentralized nature of blockchain solutions and require strong controls on decision criteria, governing policies, and handling of security incidents.

Here are some checklists you can go through while setting up a governance model:

- How will incident, fault, and change management be handled for any operational issue?
- Do we have any policy and guidelines, or RACI matrix defined for different teams across various domains in the blockchain solution?
- Consistency on the accountability and auditing criteria for different design and operational phases.
- How the Security baseline golden configuration will be maintained?
- Security policy regarding bringing in new vendors, integration with APIs, blockchain exchanges, and protocols.
- What Security standards are to be followed for interoperability?
- How will communication be conducted with internal and external stakeholders upon any incident?
- How is the liquidity risk taken care of? how the disputes are handled? in the traditional business model intermediary take on the counterparty risk and resolve disputes.
- How the Permanence or the data immutability will be handled incase if the transaction or the smart contract needs to be revised? When people carry out a deal through a smart contract, they usually can't go back on it. When two people use a third party's smart contract system, they can't back out of the deal or change its rules.

Note

To make changes to the smart contract, you must stop the old one and start a new one with the new terms, however the parties holding the private key of the contract can only modify the contract if the code allows it.

The best way to tackle data governance issues in your blockchain solution, is to design a data governance program by firstly defining objectives and policies around all above points, Next is to set desired outcomes and identify key stake holders. The policy objectives should meet the organizational goals and stakeholders should take the ownership. Lastly, ensure if the policies defined are getting executed and measured.

Data communication

Data communications risks relate to the security posture of the data in transit, during processing, and at rest. It means how vulnerable the communication is in the architecture. If an attacker gets between two network elements while they are talking, can he read the data? This is known as a "man-in-the-middle" attack. Are there any security tools that can find and stop this kind of attack? In addition, the network elements accept and process the data from a trusted source. If data is stored across the network, who can access the data under what circumstances? Where is it hosted and how the access is granted?

Security controls involved in these domains includes identity and access management, Public Key Infrastructure, infrastructure security hardenings, and service level agreements with cloud service providers if the network is hosted on the public cloud. Some important checklists to follow are as follows:

- Is data encrypted between two network elements in your blockchain architecture?
- Is data encryption applied to sensitive information such as secrets, tokens, and information containing PII data?
- Is there any policy governing data access, and how is authorization granted to subjects?
- How do you ensure that the network nodes in the network are trusted?
- How are security controls defined by the cloud providers in case of any security incident, and how soon the network is restored to its full service?
- How much downtime is expected after the incident?
- How is the data request coming inside your blockchain network, is the request getting authentication and authorized.
- Are the subjects only given access to specific allowed resources or they can access multiple data sets.
- Are there any audit logs maintained of the activity?
- Is there any network management system in place to monitor the activity happening inside your blockchain network.

Now you have the tools to identify and classify the risks in your blockchain solution based on the various checklist you have learned. Use them early in your solution design to keep you aligned with a security posture. This topic has given you a good overview of the risk management tactics for your blockchain application. The next step is to focus on how to identify the attack patterns in your application, which we will learn in the threat modeling topic.

Threat model overview

Understanding blockchain can be challenging. Keeping its decentralized and distributed nature in mind, knowing how many assets and participants a blockchain network has, and tracking the flow of data across different components can make your head spin. The dizzying data can prevent you from identifying potential risks and assessing their impact, making risk mitigation control an afterthought - a corrective measure when it should be a proactive move.

The best way to cover all this is through a tool known as threat modeling. Threat modeling is an exercise designed to help an organization identify potential threats and cybersecurity risks within their organization and systems. This is an essential first step toward designing defenses and solutions to help eliminate or reduce these risks. I'll give you the framework for threat modeling to uncover hidden vulnerabilities in your blockchain application and get one step closer to securing the solution by design.

First things first, what is threat modeling?

Threat modeling is a process by which potential vulnerabilities, or the absence of appropriate safeguards, are identified so that countermeasures can be prioritized.

The process can be divided into four sections: digging down on the architecture, drawing a data flow diagram to show zones of trust, discovering threats with STRIDE, and following up with architecting mitigation and security controls mapping with OWASP. We will explain all the components in detail. Let us get straight to this.

Threat model architecture

In the first stage, you need to build the data flow diagram (DFD), outlining the detailed architecture of your application, the interaction between different assets, how requests come into the network from different subjects, how it is been processed, and where the data is stored.

The main reason to use a Data Flow Diagram in threat modeling is to have a simple and common understanding of the main components and communication flows within threat modeling among all team members. It has five main components as follows:

- **Data Flow**: Consists of an arrow symbol that shows how the data is flowing from source to destination.
- **Data Store**: Consists of two lines or a database symbol (you can choose from both options). It depicts the storage location.
- **Process:** Consists of a circle or a rounded rectangle, it shows the process that modifies the data.
- **Interactors**: Consist of a rectangle. It depicts an endpoint (person or system) that interacts with or uses the process. An Interactor is external to the system in scope and can be an individual person or system, or can also be an entity such as a *Customer*, or *Third Party*.
- **Trust boundary**: Consists of a dotted line, multiple dotted lines. It depicts a boundary between trust zones (that is, the boundary between trusted and non-trusted zone).

Figure 3.5 is a good representation of the topics we have just discussed.

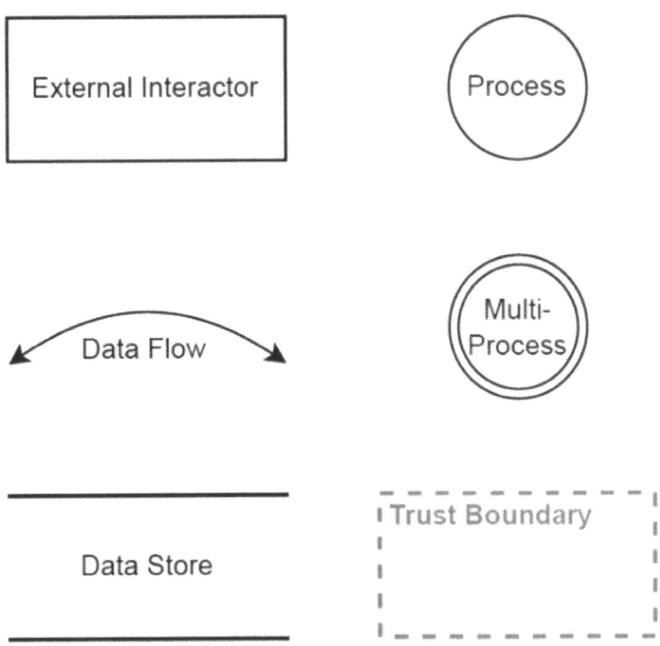

Figure 3.5: *Data flow diagram symbols*

It is recommended that you use only these symbols in your architecture diagram to make it look neat.

Next, the Blockchain Threat model consists of three main architecture components as follows:

- **Assets:** What, where, and how is the data stored?
- **Security Controls:** What Security measures/controls do we have?
- **Threat Actors:** Who can penetrate the network, and what kind of acts (internal, external)?

Figure 3.6 provides a sample of how it will look once you complete all phases of the cycle. Doesn't that look good? Believe me, you will feel a sense of accomplishment that you have carried out due diligence. In addition, you will uncover some hidden attack patterns in your network, which you might have missed with your current security posture.

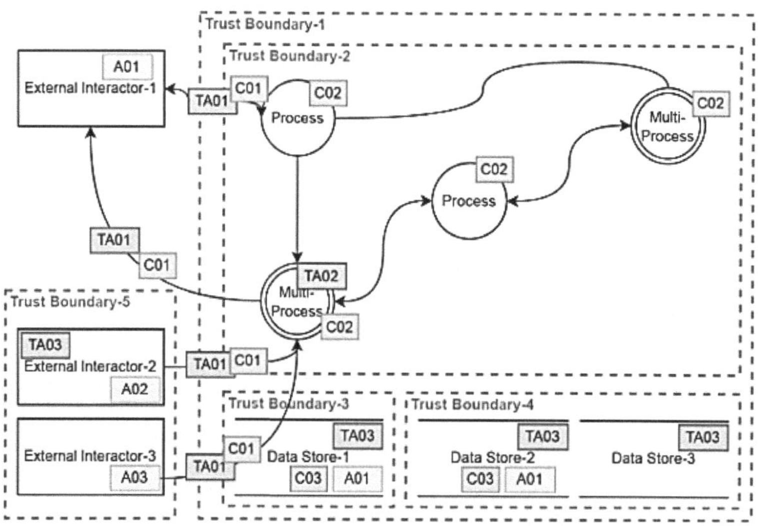

Assets	
ID	Description
A01	Asset-1
A02	Asset-2
A03	Asset-3

Threat Actors	
ID	Description
TA01	Threat-1
TA02	Threat-2
TA03	Threat-3

Security Controls	
ID	Description
C01	Control-1
C02	Control-1
C03	Control-1

Figure 3.6: *Sample Threat Modeling Diagram*

Applying Threat Modeling to Blockchain

Now that you have looked at the sample architecture, let us try building a new one from scratch. We will consider a common use case: A *Crypto wallet Application for* IOS.

First, what do we need to draw the architecture diagram for this use case? We first need the tool which we can use to draw; it should have all the components built in.

The following is the URL of the free tool, which can you leverage in your project:

https://online.visual-paradigm.com/app/diagrams/#diagram:proj=0&-type=ThreatModelDiagram&width=11&height=8.5&unit=inch

In the first section, we need to identify the architecture components, which are assets, interaction with various actors, and the trust boundaries across these components.

The actors and their interactions can be as follows:

- Users - User onboarding
- Cloud provider - API server, database, HSM
- Third-party services - Crypto exchange
- Security administrator - Penetration testing and compliance

Assets can be classified as follows:

- Private key
- User email address
- User passcode
- Public blockchain data
- Device data
- Transaction history
- Tokens and keys

Trust boundaries are created depending on the asset type and actors' interaction. As a general rule, sensitive information such as private keys, tokens, and key access, should be restricted to a private boundary. Anything exposed to the public should be in a separate zone, while interaction with external API or cloud providers sits in a different zone.

Each zone will have its own security posture. There will be a separation between each zone, and inter-zone movement will be restricted through confidentiality, integrity, and authentication checks.

Based on the information we have of the use case, this is what the architecture looks like, as shown in *Figure 3.7*.

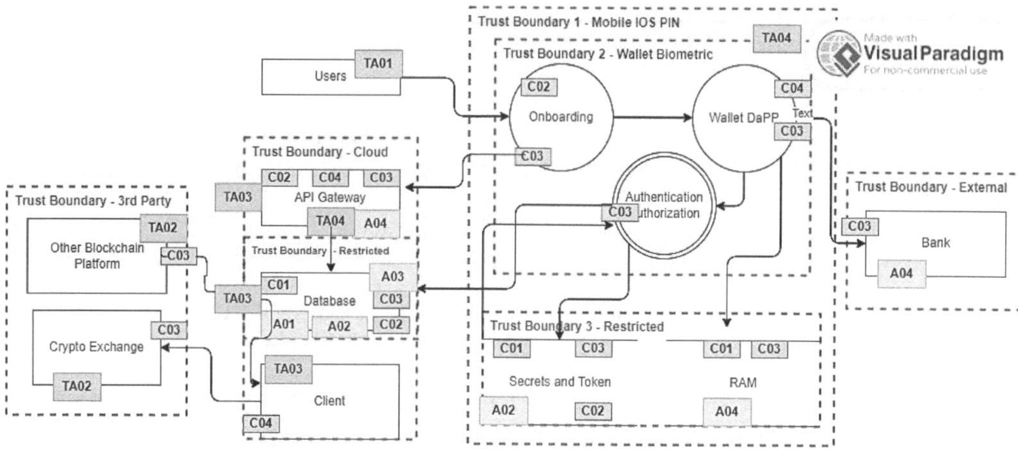

Threat Actors	
TA01	Malicious App User
TA02	Network Attackers
TA03	Malicious Employees
TA04	Malicious Cloud Provder

Assets	
A01	User Data
A02	Secrets and Tokens
A03	Private Key
A04	Public Blockchain Data

Security Controls	
C01	Encryption at Rest
C02	Integrity Check
C03	TLS Cert Verification
C04	Security Logging

***Figure 3.7**: Crypto Wallet threat modeling diagram*

The third step is to discover threats using STRIDE, which can potentially be attacked, keeping in view the security architecture that we build earlier.

But what is STRIDE, and how does it apply to the threat modeling data flow? Let me explain.

STRIDE is an acronym for Spoofing, Tampering, Repudiation, Information disclosure, Denial of service, and Escalation of privilege.

Let me expand on what STRIDE means by explaining the meaning of each letter:

- **Spoofing** is the act of disguising a communication or identity so that it appears to be associated with a trusted and authorized source.
- **Tampering** is when someone hacks the software parameters in the e-wallet to produce different behavior.
- **Repudiation** is when someone denies another from performing their action.
- **Information Disclosure** is sharing some of the system's private information with others.

- **Denial of service** occurs when users are unable to access information, systems, or resources.
- **Elevation of Privileges** gives authorization permissions beyond those initially granted.

Note

Not all of the STRIDE elements apply to each use case. Quickly evaluate if it applies. For example, if you're using a public cloud like AWS to host your infrastructure, then Denial of service on hardware isn't your responsibility because it's taken care of by the cloud provider under a service-level agreement.

In *Figure* 3.8, we have mapped the STRIDE framework into the data flow diagram where it applies. For example, Spoofing applies to users who are onboarded into the application. This can also be targeted for the banks where users will go to withdraw the cryptocurrency into cash.

On the other hand, tampering attempts can be done on crypto exchanges, and information disclosure can be carried out in the database and memory where sensitive data like user information, token, and secrets are stored.

Lastly, a Denial of service (DOS) attack can be carried out on the DaPP and API gateway, since they are mostly exposed to the internet. So, they can be the low-hanging fruit for attackers.

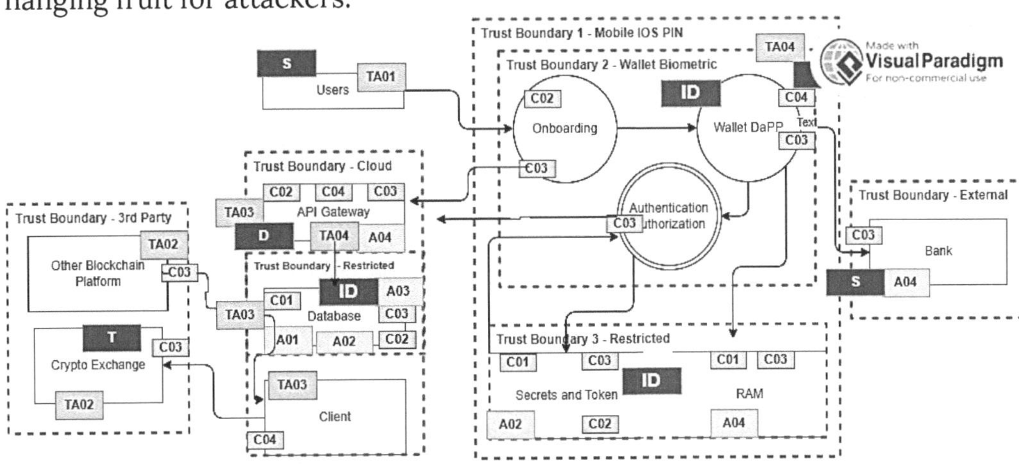

Threat Actors	
TA01	Malicious App User
TA02	Network Attackers
TA03	Malicious Employees
TA04	Malicious Cloud Provder

Assets	
A01	User Data
A02	Secrets and Tokens
A03	Private Key
A04	Public Blockchain Data

Security Controls	
C01	Encryption at Rest
C02	Integrity Check
C03	TLS Cert Verification
C04	Security Logging

STRIDE	
Spoofing	User, Banks
Tampering	Crypto Exchange
Info Disclosure	Database, User data, Tokens
Denial of Service	API Gateway, DaPP

Figure 3.8: *Threat Modeling Implementation on Blockchain with STRIDE*

Mitigations against STRIDE Attack Vectors

The final step of the threat modeling exercise is to tighten your architecture with mitigating controls against the STRIDE attack vectors. There are several ways to accomplish this, and my recommendation is to understand and classify each of these attacks in terms of probability and impact, and then apply the control.

Let us take a detailed look at each STRIDE vulnerability and mitigation control:

- **Spoofing**: Spoofing attacks include cookie replay attacks, session hijacking, and cross-site request forgery (CSRF) attacks.

  Since spoofing is an attack on user authentication, the best form of prevention is to implement secure user authentication methods, including both secure password requirements and multi-factor authentication (MFA).

- **Tampering**: Tampering attacks such as Cross-Site Scripting (XSS) and SQL injection damage the integrity of the application. In order to protect against tampering, the application should be designed to validate user inputs and encode outputs. Static code analysis should be used to identify vulnerabilities to tampering in the application, both during the development stage and once the application is in production.

- **Repudiation**: A repudiation attack is an attack on the validity and integrity of actions on the application. Repudiation attacks take advantage of a lack of controls that properly track and log user actions, using this to manipulate or forge the identification of new, unauthorized actions, delete logs, log wrong data to log files, and deny actions or receipt of service (for example, committing fraud).

  This can be prevented by incorporating digital signatures in the application, which provide proof of actions, or by ensuring that there are full, tamper-proof logs in place.

- **Information Disclosure:** This information can then be used by attackers to force access to the application, gathering information about customers, which can be used in a further crime, or gaining privileges that will give access to more sensitive areas of the application.

  Prevention methods include ensuring that error messages, response headers, and background information should be as generic as possible to avoid revealing clues about the application's behavior.

  Proper access controls and authorizations should be in place to prevent unauthorized access to information.

- **Denial of service:** Denial of service (DoS) attacks flood the target with traffic, triggering a crash and shutting it down to legitimate traffic. DoS attacks typically cost time and money but do not cause other damage to their victims. The most common form of DoS attack is a buffer overflow attack, which simply sends excessive traffic to the application. Other attacks exploit vulnerabilities to cause systems to crash.

  Applications can be protected against DoS attacks by configuring firewalls to block traffic from certain sources, such as reserved, loopback, or private IP addresses, unassigned DCHPDHCP clients, or introducing rate limiting to manage traffic.

- **Escalation of privilege**: Privilege escalation attacks exploit vulnerabilities and misconfigurations in the application to gain illicit access to elevated or privileged rights. Privilege escalation attacks may exploit credential and authentication processes, compromise vulnerabilities in code and design, take advantage of misconfigurations, or use malware or social engineering to gain access.

  Mitigation includes hardening systems and applications through configuration changes, removing unnecessary rights and access, closing ports, and more.

  The following table provides a good, summarized view for your reference.

Threat	Property	Definition	Controls
Spoofing	Authentication	Impersonating someone or something	Authentication Stores, Strong Authentication mechanisms
Tampering	Integrity / Access Controls	Modifying data or code	Crypto Hash, Digital watermark/ isolation and access checks
Repudiation	Non-repudiation	Claiming to have not performed a specific action	Logging infrastructure, full-packet-capture
Information Disclosure	Confidentiality	Exposing information or data to unauthorized individuals or roles	Encryption or Isolation
Denial of Service	Availability	Deny or degrade service	Redundancy, failover, QoS, Bandwidth throttle
Elevation of Privilege	Authorization / Least Privilege	Gain capabilities without proper authorization	RBAC, DACL, MAC; Sudo, UAC, Privileged account protections

***Figure 3.9**: Summary of STRIDE with Controls*

Conclusion

Great job on completing the third chapter! With this knowledge, you can easily do risk management for your blockchain application. You can identify risks, quantify them in terms of probability and impact, and most importantly, apply mitigation controls. You have also learned the tool of threat modeling, equipping you to build a security architecture for your blockchain application. Any direct security controls can be applied to the architecture as you build the data flow diagram, and any security gaps can be filled up through STRIDE evaluation. This chapter has given you a lot of hands-on work and will prove vital as you progress through this book.

In the next chapter, we will look at the ways to exploit blockchain applications, which means taking a deep dive into attack vectors, penetration testing tools, infrastructure, and smart contracts with real-world examples.

Points to remember

- Blockchain risk management is like risk management you would do in any other project. It includes identification, classification, and mitigation stages.
- Remember the top security risk in Blockchain, and how to classify and apply the mitigation controls.
- Threat modeling starts with the data flow diagram, there are fundamental architecture components and symbols that you can leverage.
- STRIDE framework in threat modeling only applies to the components that are more critical and lack available compensating controls.
- Mitigation controls on your security architecture can be applied through OWASP mapping or by understanding the impact and occurrence.

References

- **https://www.chainalysis.com/ (Figure 3.1)**
- **https://ennowallet.com/security/threat-model/**
- **https://widgets.weforum.org/blockchain-toolkit/cybersecurity/index.html**

Exercise

I would recommend you take a look at the threat modeling of ENNO Wallet. You can relate this to everything we have studied in this chapter. You are now in a position to do all of this yourself.

Case Study: Enno Wallet Threat Model for Mobile Apps

https://blog.ennowallet.com/introducing-enno-wallet-threat-model-for-mobile-apps-22a519df46bc

CHAPTER 4
Blockchain Application Exploitation

Introduction

With the developing prominence of digital currencies, the number of individuals entering the market is expanding emphatically. Tragically, a portion of these individuals aren't keen on putting resources into digital currencies as their only object is to hack and take resources that have a place with others. To make their task even more easier, there isn't enough attention given in this area.

Take a look at various blockchain applications, one common thing you will notice is the neglecting attitude towards securing the blockchain applications. Either they are too naïve to think that the blockchain is built-in secure, or the only security they need is just the testing and auditing of smart contracts. All of this results in widening the attack surface, leaving backdoors and vulnerabilities for hackers to exploit.

Now the question arises: How do we know where are the weaknesses and how much security is enough? We tried to partially cover this topic through threat modeling analysis in the previous chapter, but there is more to that. No matter how closely we analyze, there is only a handful that we can do, considering the width of the blockchain paradigm we are dealing with. Another argument that arises as we progress in securing blockchain is: Why should I put my efforts and resources in the security aspect of blockchain? How do we know these weaknesses are exploitable? In other words, I need a business reason to implement security - Security isn't cheap.

To answer this tricky question, we have to use tools and strategies such as penetration testing, validate the strength of crypto wallets, examine smart contracts code, and lastly, understand the scenarios where hackers were successful in their attempts. By doing so, you can take these considerations into account when you architect security solutions in your application.

Structure

We will be covering the following topics in this chapter:

- Blockchain Penetration Testing
- Hacking Smart Contract with Lab
- Integer Overflow and Underflow Threat Mitigations
- Top attack vector analysis on Smart contracts.
- Useful tools and resources

Blockchain Penetration Testing

Imagine a team competition to hack a secure blockchain application, with winners earning huge cash prizes for a weekend's worth of work exploiting weaknesses. These Hackathons actually happen frequently in real life. Cybersecurity companies put them on to identify weaknesses in their systems. It's a practice known as ethical hacking because you intentionally invite someone to hack your computer so you know how to fortify your defenses. It gives you the following benefits:

- Protects against hacks and attacks by identifying vulnerabilities that attackers can exploit.
- Ensures trust and compliance, which can build trust and credibility with investors and customers.
- Improves user experience by helping to identify issues and bugs, such as broken links or slow loading time.
- Saves time and money by findings issues upfront; it is cheaper to fix vulnerabilities in the development stage rather than after rollout.

In this lesson, I'll explain how penetration testing works and how it helps blockchain solutions strengthen their security defences by identifying a probable adversarial path to compromise and move laterally within a blockchain network. As always, let's start with the basics.

What is penetration testing or Ethical hacking?

Ethical hacking, also known as penetration testing or pen testing for short, refers to the security process of evaluating your computer system's applications for vulnerabilities and susceptibility to threats like hackers and cyberattacks.

Let me break down the roadmap for blockchain penetration testing. It has mainly six phases, as shown in *Figure* 4.1.

Figure 4.1: *Roadmap for blockchain penetration testing*

Planning

This is the information-gathering stage. It includes the following checks:

- Determining the objectives and scope of a test, as well as the systems that will be tested and their methods.
- Acquiring intelligence, such as the names of a target's network and domain, its mail server, and other details, to comprehend a target's workings and potential weaknesses.

In this stage, information is collected about the blockchain platform. Here, you analyze the architecture, determine threat entry points, and collect data for potential threats. The popular tools you can leverage are Nessus, Nmap, and Spyse to check open ports, public-facing Ips, and common vulnerabilities.

https://pentestlab.blog/2020/06/15/spyse-a-cyber-security-search-engine/

For example, using Spyse:

To make asset discovery easier, subdomains of a given domain can be easily found. During Open Source Intelligence Assessments or when examining the client's external attack surface, penetration testers and red teamers should be able to use it. The results also include A records, DNS CNAME, and the version of TLS/SSL. Since there are a number of vulnerabilities in TLS and SSL, they could be used first before any other tools. *Figure 4.2* is the snapshot for the same.

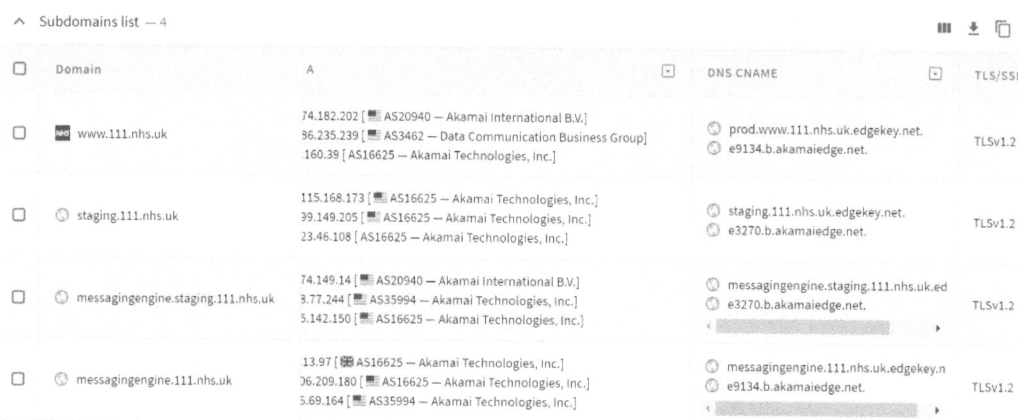

***Figure 4.2**: Discovery of sub-domains list*

In order to retrieve information such as links, robots.txt files, and HTTP headers, you can also perform web spidering (following links on the web page to find useful information) on the target domain. This can help towards fingerprinting the current advancements used by the site in scope, recognizing proof of sensitive URLs, and planning the application.

Figure 4.3 depicts a snapshot of the information under the links tab.

robots.txt HTTP headers links (8)

anchor	href
1 1 1 online	https://111.nhs.uk/
Get information and advice	/PWCorona/5cc6af1f-f496-44de-98c3-36445674f0f8/COVID-19/about
health problems	https://www.nhs.uk/conditions/
NHS.UK	https://www.nhs.uk
emergency prescription	/emergency-prescription
terms	/Help/Terms
we use cookies.	/Help/Cookies
Privacy statement	/Help/Privacy

***Figure 4.3**: Application Mapping on links tab*

In addition, *Figure* 4.4 displays the information under the HTTP headers tab. Here, you can see the payload information and cookies being used.

robots.txt HTTP headers links (8)

```
Content-Length: 6640
Content-Type: text/html; charset=utf-8
Set-Cookie: .ASPXANONYMOUS=d1UE0KNFgw9_ltvTgb4wyz-B8GJIOvQ5JJxGI_TsLzDVzdA7AN_6LgWBgTNveBmsxQzawa9qm-UBkwyt6
Set-Cookie: nhs111-session-id=5cc6af1f-f496-44de-98c3-36445674f0f8; expires=Tue, 03-Mar-2020 17:13:54 GMT; path=/; secure
Cache-Control: private
Strict-Transport-Security: max-age=15552000;
Date: Tue, 03 Mar 2020 13:13:54 GMT
Connection: close
```

***Figure 4.4**: HTTP Headers*

Next is the information that you can see under the robots.txt. The asterisk (*)is listed as a wildcard, meaning any user agent can access it. However, this can also be a signal for an attacker.

robots.txt HTTP headers links (8)

```
User-agent: *
Disallow: /Location/
Disallow: /PWCorona/
```

***Figure 4.5**: Robots.txt content*

Vulnerability Scanning

It's the scanning against open ports, public IP address scanning, and detection of potential exploits through business logic errors and common vulnerabilities against software libraries that are used.

The Nessus vulnerability is the preferred option. It has good coverage and provides a template that you can customize as per your blockchain application design. Nessus works by testing every port on a blockchain network, figuring out which services are running, and testing each service for vulnerabilities.

Figure 4.6 depicts the snapshot taken from the Nessus scanning result. Here, you can see vulnerabilities with ratings and a summarized result. This can give you an idea of the security posture of your application.

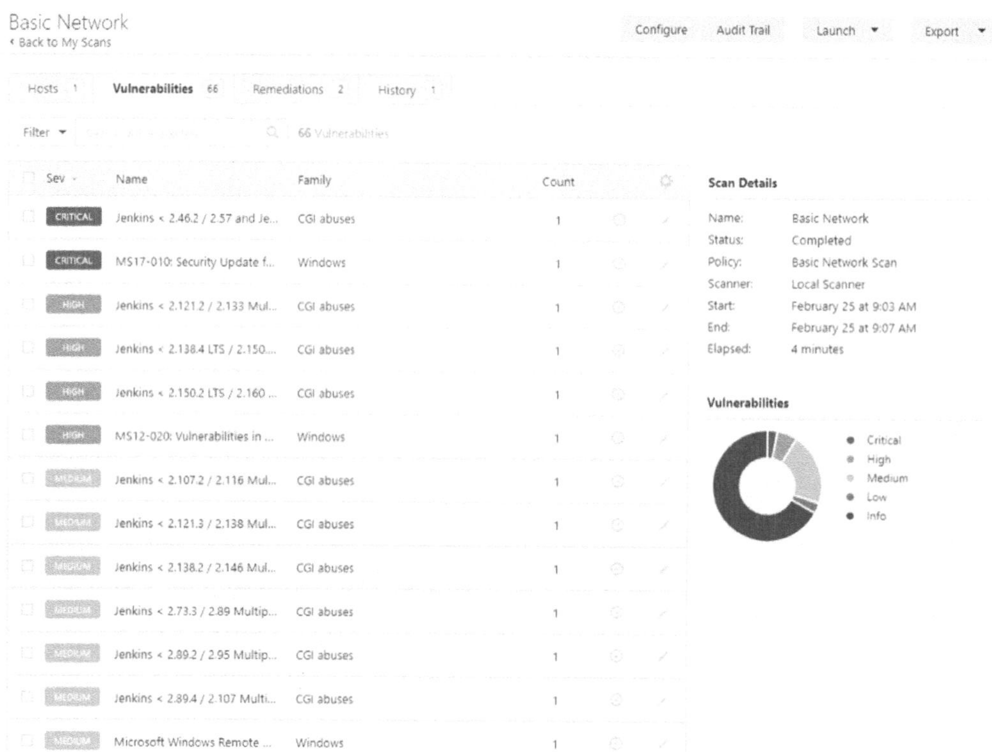

Figure 4.6: *Nessus Vulnerability Scan result*

Additionally, Nessus offers excellent extensibility. You can utilize the Nessus pre-arranging language to compose tests quite certain to your framework. Additionally, plug-ins written in the Nessus Attack Scripting Language (NASL) are available through Nessus. The modules incorporate weakness information, brief data on suggested remediation, and a calculation to take into consideration further testing of the security issue. Here are some plug-in examples: ***https://www.tenable.com/plugins***.

Did you know?

Nessus is frequently contrasted with OpenVAS. OpenVAS is an open-source weakness scanner made as a fork of the open-source code initially used for Nessus. The Nessus fork of the code, GNessUs, was later renamed OpenVAS once Tenable Networks began selling Nessus. Nessus occupies an enviable position due to the breadth and depth of its vulnerability coverage. Over 47,000 common vulnerabilities and exposures (CVEs) may be known to Nessus, providing excellent coverage.

In addition to Nessus, you can also leverage smart bugs framework for analyzing Ethereum smart contract. Smart bugs framework is available at GitHub, that can be expanded and has a standard way to connect to tools that check blockchain programs for bugs and other issues. The best part is, it supports several tools with multi-mode of operations on solidity, deployment bytecode and the runtime code.

Figure 4.7 is the snippet taken from the GitHub, on the number of tools the smart bug framework supports.

Note

The list just show some of the tool, not the entire list.

	version	Solidity	bytecode	runtime code
ConFuzzius	#4315fb7 v0.0.1	✔		
Conkas	#4e0f256	✔		✔
Ethainter				✔
eThor	2021 (CCS 2020)			✔
HoneyBadger	#ff30c9a	✔		✔
MadMax	#6e9a6e9			✔
Maian	#4bab09a	✔	✔	✔
Manticore	0.3.7	✔		
Mythril	0.23.15	✔	✔	✔
Osiris	#d1ecc37	✔		✔
Oyente	#480e725	✔		✔
Pakala	#c84ef38 v1.1.10			✔
Securify		✔		✔
sFuzz	#48934c0 (2019-03-01)	✔		
Slither		✔		
Smartcheck		✔		

***Figure 4.7**: Tools supported by Smart Bug Framework*

More details on the installation, usage, requirements of Smart bugs, can be seen on the GitHub URL - **https://github.com/smartbugs/smartbugs**

Exploitation

Web application attacks, such as cross-site scripting, SQL injection, and backdoors, are used in this stage to find a target's weaknesses. Ethical hackers then attempt and take advantage of these weaknesses, commonly by escalating privileges, taking information, catching traffic, and so forth, to comprehend the harm they can cause.

An example of this is an SQL Injection attack, which is one of the most happening web hacks pervasive today in the web3 industry, wherein an attacker utilizes site page contributions to embed a noxious code in SQL proclamations. This usually occurs when a website asks for user input, such as a username or user ID. The attacker takes advantage of this to insert an SQL statement into your database, which then runs without your knowledge. *Figure* 4.8 depicts the attack process flow.

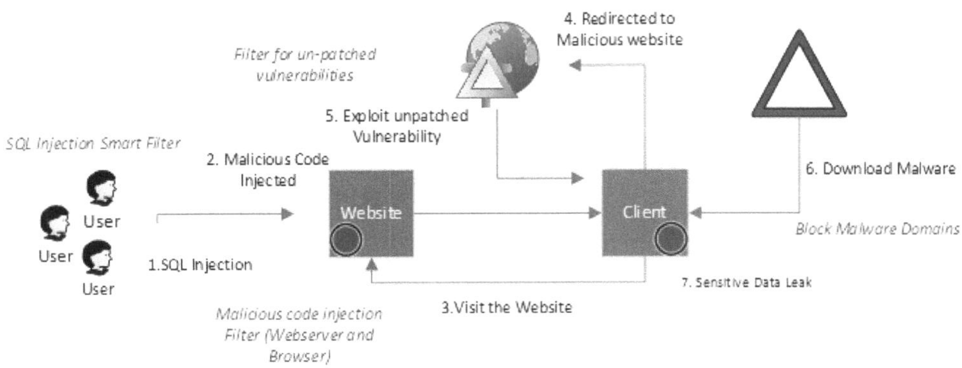

Figure 4.8: *SQL Injection attack*

Note

Injection attacks on Ethereum and Hyperledger platforms have cost millions of dollars. From XSS -cross-site scripting impact on Ether Delta to the delegate call injection vulnerability, which resulted in stealing over $31M from a wallet.

Following are a few more examples of similar injection attacks on the blockchain with their related CVE. I am showing you all this to give you an idea of the magnitude of these issues.

- TransferFrom overflow - CVE-2018-11411
- Integer Overflow - CVE-2018-11687
- Easy Trading Token (ETT) Integer Overflow - CVE-2018-13113
- TransferFlaw - CVE-2018-10468
- Batch overflow - CVE-2018-10299

An SQL injection is considered a highly serious weakness. The attacker's skill and imagination determine how much damage can be done and whether or not there are countermeasures.

When an SQL injection occurs, the following kinds of attacks are typically possible:

- Without providing any of the necessary credentials, the attacker can gain access to the application, possibly with administrative privileges, by evading authentication.

- The attackers can compromise the availability of data by deleting log or audit information in a database. The attackers can jeopardize the operations of the host operating system through command execution through a database.
- The attackers can compromise the integrity of the data by altering the contents of the database, defacing a web page, or inserting malicious content into other harmless websites.

Maintaining Access

This stage aims to determine if the vulnerability can be exploited to establish a long-term presence in the exploited system long enough for a malicious party to gain full access. The goal is to mimic advanced persistent threats, which frequently stay in a framework for quite a long time to take an association's most delicate information.

Here, I would like to introduce you to APT (Advanced persistent threats). APT is a broad term for an attack campaign in which an intruder or a group of intruders establish an illegal, long-term presence on a network to mine highly sensitive data.

Just looking at how APT attacks are different from traditional web application threats, I have listed a few checkpoints as follows:

- They are notably more complicated.
- They are not just hit-and-run attacks, meaning once the network is penetrated, the perpetrator remains in there to discover more.
- They are not automated against a specific target but are executed against a large pool of targets.
- They often target to penetrate an entire network, instead of a specific one. This is similar to the preceding point.

  Examples of such are remote file inclusion (RFI), SQL injection, and cross-site scripting (XSS), which are frequently utilized by criminals to gain access to a targeted network. Then, Trojans and backdoor shells are frequently used to extend that traction and make a steady presence inside the targeted area.

  Figure 4.9 provides details on APT progression and some of the security measures.

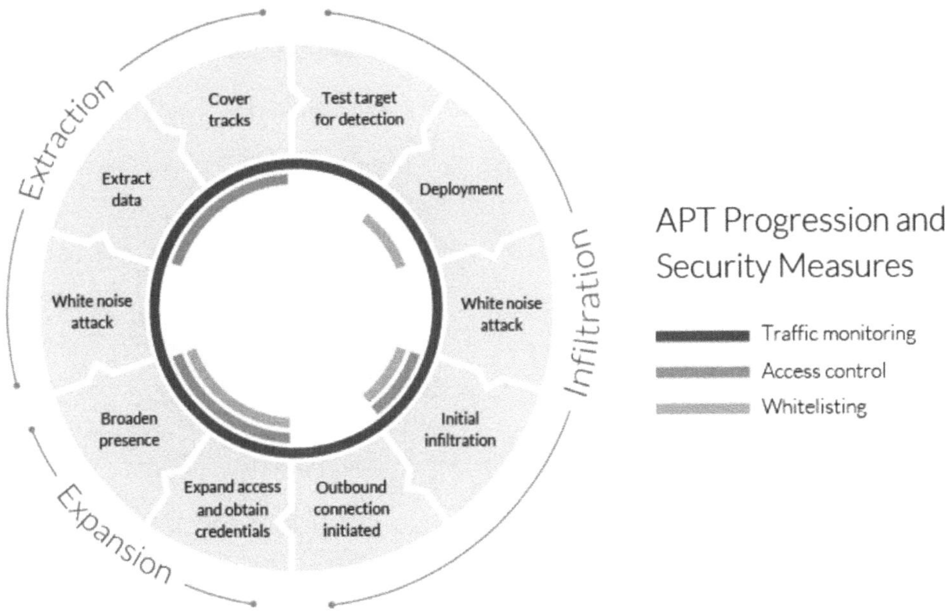

Figure 4.9: *APT Progression Matrix*

Analysis and Reporting

The pen tester must complete everything during this phase, keeping an eye on everything they do, particularly during the process of discovery and exploitation. In order to provide a report that highlights the methods used to successfully penetrate the dApp, as well as any security flaws and other relevant information discovered, they are analyzing every detail and step, delving into each problem in great detail and devising strategies to reduce vulnerabilities.

To sum up, this stage includes reviewing and documenting the findings to make a report. The sample report should cover the following:

Firstly, there should be an executive summary – which should contain the scope of testing, for example, the application involved, Smart contract, Infrastructure details, and the list of vulnerabilities with severities, and also should contain the remediation measures with status, as shown in *Figure* 4.10.

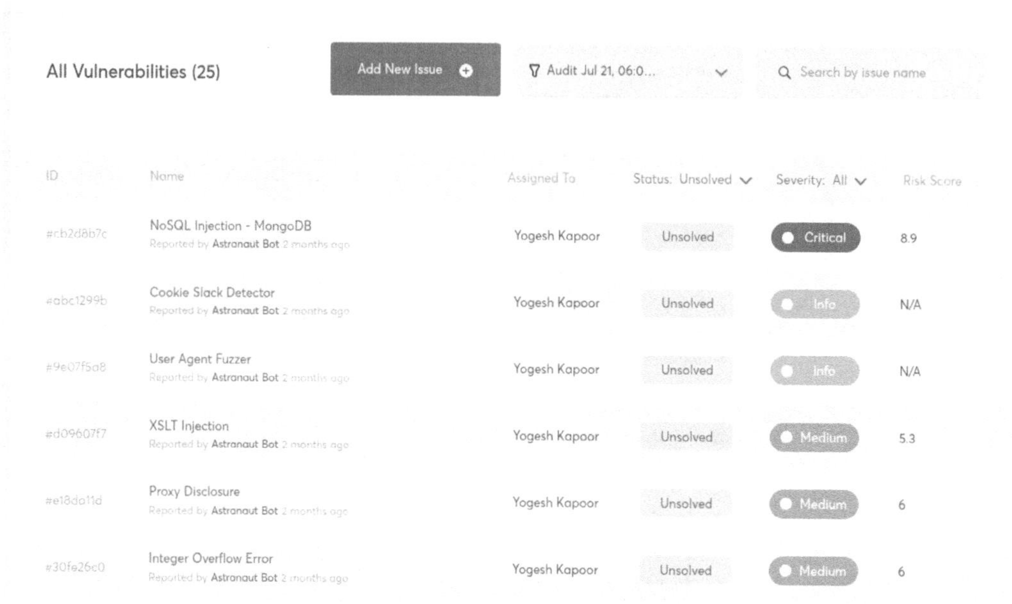

Figure 4.10: *Vulnerabilities Summary*

Secondly, the other section of the report should tell us about the discovered vulnerabilities. *Figure* 4.11 shows a sample snapshot of how the discovered vulnerabilities should be reported.

The details of the vulnerabilities must include the impact, the CVSS Score, and suggested fixes. It is also recommended to show if the vulnerability impact can affect key performance indicators, such as customer experience, increase the CPU, Memory utilization, and so on.

On the other hand, the suggested fix should include a mixture of direct and compensating controls. In some cases, compensating controls can be useful if direct security controls are costly and the organization is willing to accept the risk.

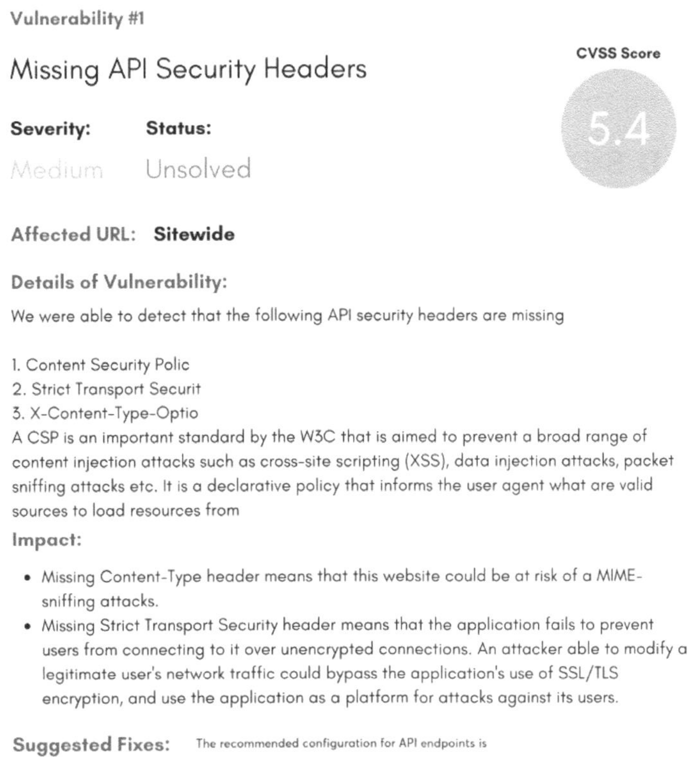
Vulnerability #1

Missing API Security Headers

CVSS Score

5.4

Severity: Medium

Status: Unsolved

Affected URL: **Sitewide**

Details of Vulnerability:

We were able to detect that the following API security headers are missing

1. Content Security Polic
2. Strict Transport Securit
3. X-Content-Type-Optio

A CSP is an important standard by the W3C that is aimed to prevent a broad range of content injection attacks such as cross-site scripting (XSS), data injection attacks, packet sniffing attacks etc. It is a declarative policy that informs the user agent what are valid sources to load resources from

Impact:

- Missing Content-Type header means that this website could be at risk of a MIME-sniffing attacks.
- Missing Strict Transport Security header means that the application fails to prevent users from connecting to it over unencrypted connections. An attacker able to modify a legitimate user's network traffic could bypass the application's use of SSL/TLS encryption, and use the application as a platform for attacks against its users.

Suggested Fixes: The recommended configuration for API endpoints is

***Figure 4.11**: Vulnerability details of missing API Security header*

A detailed sample report can be found here - ***https://www.getastra.com/blog/wp-content/uploads/2021/06/Astra-Security-Sample-VAPT-Report.pdf***

Remediation

In the final stage, this is where you take action on the remediation actions that come out from the report. The best practice is to use a change management window to apply the changes. The changes have to be applied through the Method of procedure (MOP). This should contain Pre-checks, Activity details, Rollback procedures, and a combination of functional, unit, and regression testing to ensure that the fix is applied without any issues happening to the system.

Hacking Smart contracts

In this section, we will try to explain how smart contracts can be exploited using PWNX Labs. We will look at overflow and underflow vulnerabilities with remediation measures.

PWNX provides CTF labs on computer systems and applications for training purposes.

The Lab setup

Using VPN, try to connect to the PWNX's internal network, where a server exposes a local blockchain via Ganache.

Note that Ganache is a personal blockchain for rapidly developing Ethereum and other blockchains. You can use Ganache throughout the blockchain development lifecycle to develop, deploy, and test your decentralized applications (dApps) in a secure and sandboxed environment.

Figure 4.12 just shows the setup that you need to do. You can install OVPN on your laptop and download the VPN configuration file by accessing the settings of PWNX's website.

To install Ganache, please visit **https://trufflesuite.com/docs/ganache/**.

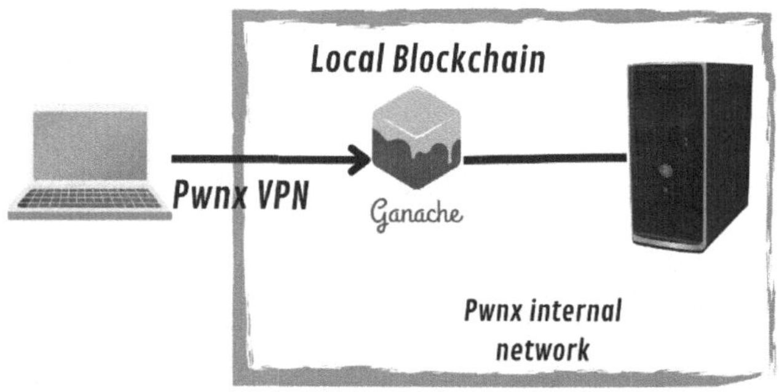

***Figure 4.12**: Connectivity diagram between Local terminal to PWNX internal network*

Examining the source code

There will be some data and code when you enter the lab and connect to the internal network. On the left, you will see the Solidity-written smart contract code that explains the contract's logic. A code for the ABI can be found on the right side, as shown in *Figure* 4.13.

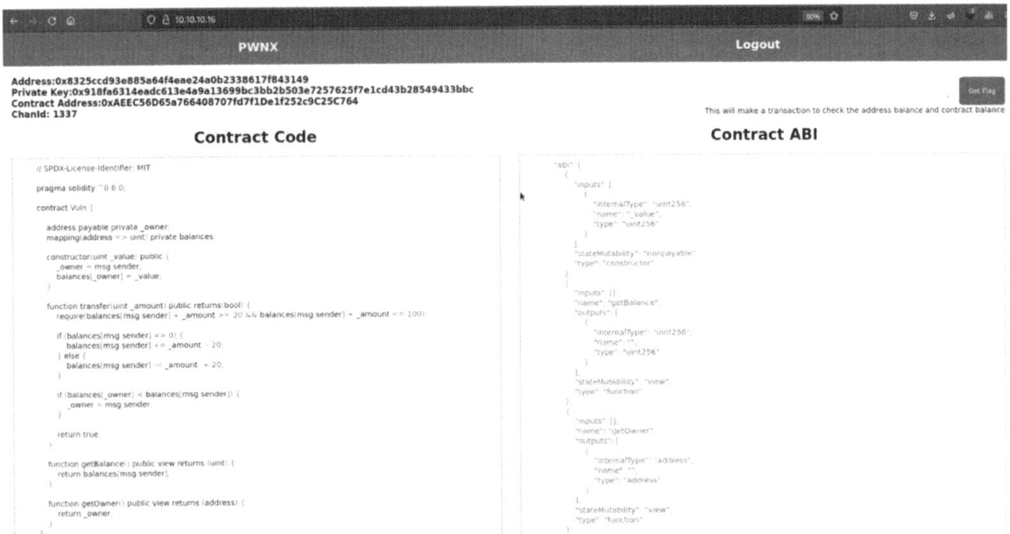

Figure 4.13: *Comparison of contracts code with ABI*

The most common way to interact with contracts in the Ethereum ecosystem, both outside of the blockchain and between contracts, is through the Application Binary Interface (ABI).

Keep in mind that the goal is to claim ownership of the following smart contract.

You ought to have a wallet address, a confidential key to sign, and the location of the shrewd Agreement.

As an initial step, begin by breaking down the Smart contract code locally. We can compile and test the contract on our local system with the help of REMIX IDE.

Remix Online IDE is a powerful toolset for developing, deploying, debugging, and testing Ethereum and EVM-compatible smart contracts. It requires no setup and has a flexible, intuitive user interface

---

The solidity code PWNX.SOL can be copied to Remix IDE. This is a vulnerable contract, which consists of different functions, as shown in *Figure* 4.14. The details of the following contract will be explained before we get into the exploitation stage.

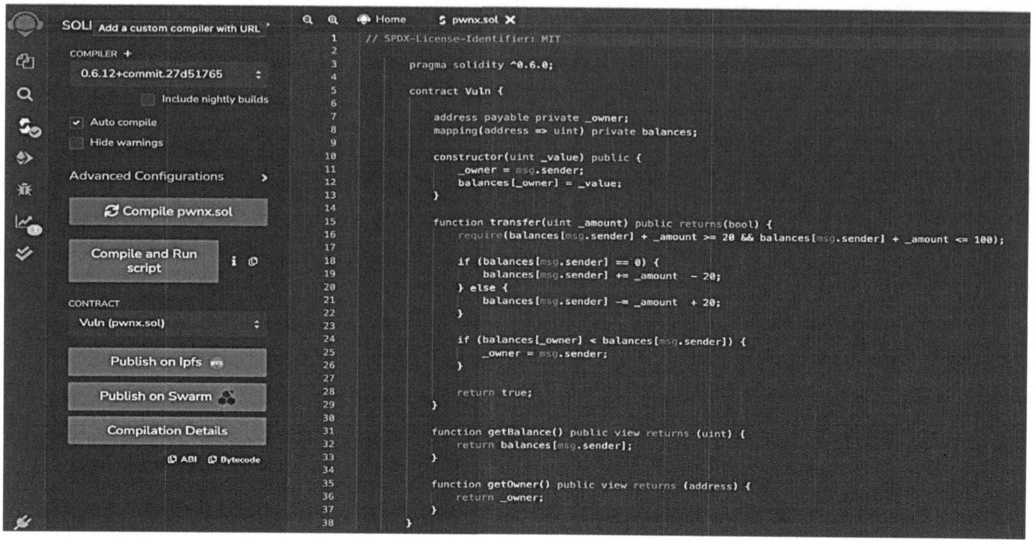

***Figure 4.14**: Vulnerable smart contract*

Note that once smart contracts are placed on the blockchain, the constructor function is called, and the address that was assigned to the contract becomes the contract's owner (ownership action).

Here are the details:

- When the constructor is called, a private variable of the type address, known as the owner, is set.
- On the agreement, there is a planning called balances. The mapping in Solidity is a dictionary or HaspMap (similar to Java).
- In our scenario, this mapping is a **database** of addresses that records the amount of ether or tokens each address possesses.
- Two smaller functions, **`getOwner`** and **`getBalance`**, are visible to the public. They do not affect the blockchain's state; **`getBalance`** returns the amount of ether or tokens the user has in the mapping data structure, returning data only. We can use the **`msg.sender`** in Solidity to accomplish this.
- The transaction's global variable, msg, can be found in your Solidity code. The source worth of the msg object is the actual sender of the exchange that conveyed the smart contract.

- As the _owner parameters were declared in the constructor, the **getOwner** function returns the smart contract's owner address.

Now, let us understand the vulnerability in the following section.

The vulnerability explanation

We can see a function named **transfer** in the following code snippet that enables an address to transfer money into the smart contract:

- A `uint` (unsigned integer value), a public function that returns a boolean value, is needed for the function transfer.
- Line 16 contains the necessary statement. Two boolean values, either true or false, are returned by the command required. If the indicated condition yields a true response, the code can proceed and operate as intended. The code ends there if the returned value is false and an error is triggered.
- The address must be greater than or equal to 20, but less than or equal to 100, for the condition to be satisfied.
- Line 24 has a second if statement that determines whether the account balance of the owner's address is lower than the account balance of the transaction's performer, **msg.sender**, to enable ownership of the smart contract.

The if statement (line 18) checks if the balance of the **msg.sender** inside the mapping data structure, which means that if the balance inside the mapping data structure of the address that makes the transaction is equal to 0, it will add the amount that has to be transferred and subtract 20. Otherwise, it will deduct the amount inserted into the transfer function and add 20 to it.

Note that this is a classic example of an Overflow/Underflow Vulnerability on smart contracts, as shown in *Figure* 4.15.

```
15  function transfer(uint _amount) public returns(bool) {
16      require(balances[msg.sender] + _amount >= 20 && balances[msg.sender] + _amount <= 100);
17
18      if (balances[msg.sender] == 0) {
19          balances[msg.sender] += _amount  - 20;
20      } else {
21          balances[msg.sender] -= _amount  + 20;
22      }
23
24      if (balances[_owner] < balances[msg.sender]) {
25          _owner = msg.sender;
26      }
27
28      return true;
29  }
```

Figure 4.15: *Vulnerability snapshot for Overflow and underflow*

The `uint` underflow/overflow is one of the most common security flaws in smart contracts. The underflow/overflow issue could easily make the crypto hacker rich and result in a significant loss for the crypto holder's account.

The `uint` overflow/underflow, otherwise called `uint` wrapping around, is a math activity that creates an outcome that is bigger than the maximum above for an N-bit integer or produces a result that is smaller than the minimum below for an N-bit integer.

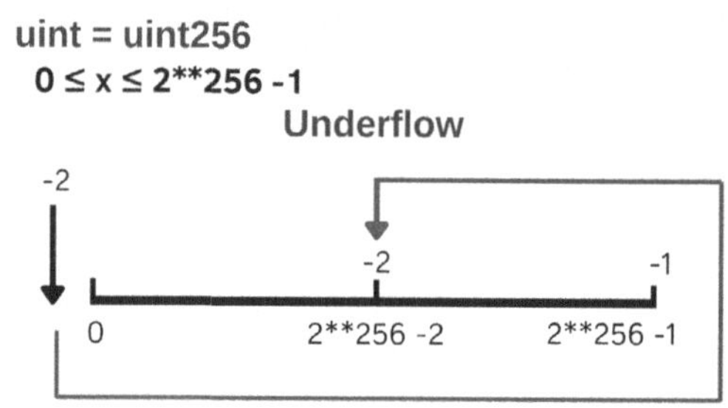

Figure 4.16: *Underflow Logic arithmetic view*

Figure 4.15 displays a good example of Underflow. If you subtract 2 from a `uint` that is 0, it will change the value to 2**256 -2.

On the other hand, overflow shows the opposite. Adding +3 to a `uint` that is 2**256 -1 would result in an overflow situation. The `uint` overflow occurs when there is a number greater than the `uint` max, which results in the number looping back to 0.

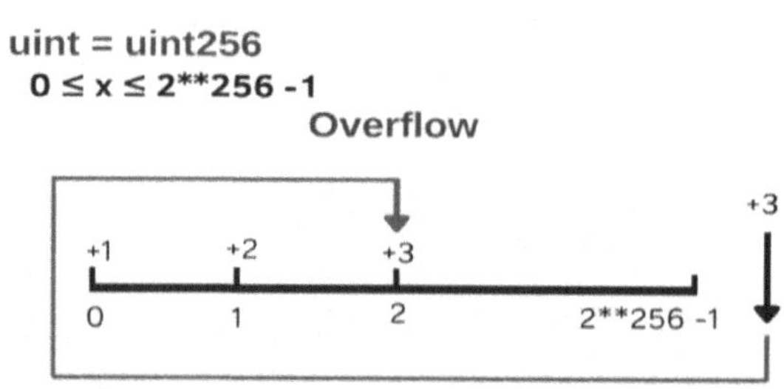

Figure 4.17: *Overflow Logic arithmetic view*

Now that we have understood the vulnerability, let us exploit the smart contract in the next step.

Local Exploitation

We will start by initially compiling and deploying the smart contract. To send the smart contract, we will need an address that will become the owner (you can utilize the REMIX ones), and we want to enter a value that will go into its balance mapping.

Once it is deployed, the contract will show all of the functions that are available at the bottom. We can see that the capabilities that don't change state are displayed in blue, while the transfer function is in orange, as shown in *Figure 4.18*.

We can check the owner's balance by calling the getBalance function as the first call.

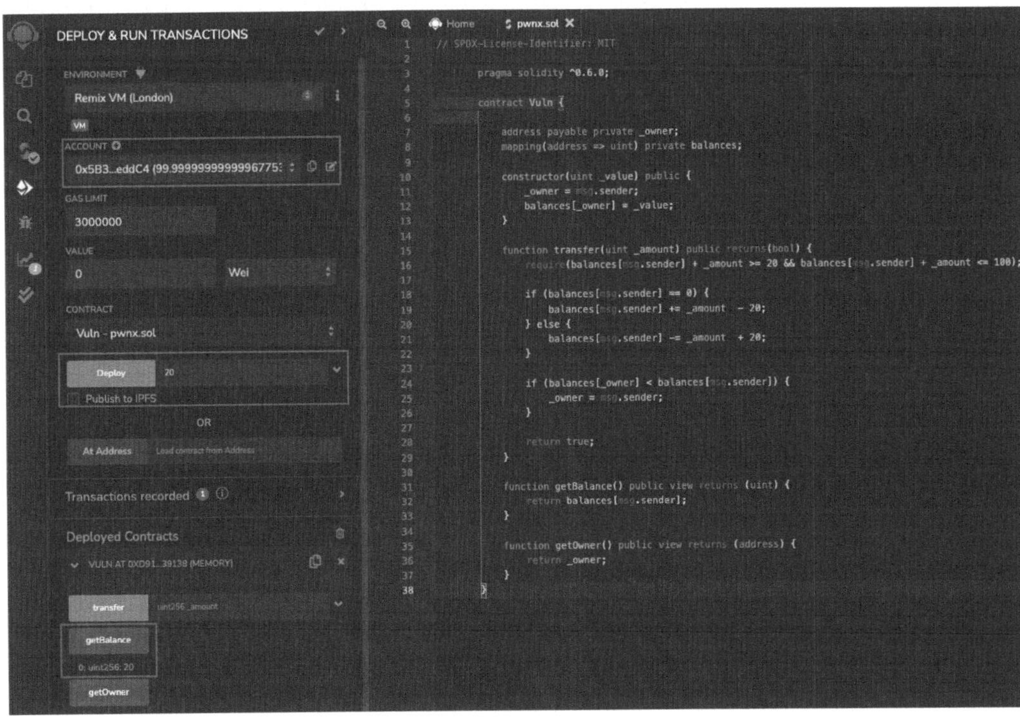

Figure 4.18: *Snapshot of the function to get balance*

Now that the account has been changed, we go to the transfer function to send21 as the amount to the smart contract using a different address (also from Remix). We can see that the transaction was successful in the console, anwhen we call the **`getbalance`** function, we get 1.

This is because line 18 of the first statement is where the contract is. We get 1 because the address's current balance is zero the first time it transfers money.

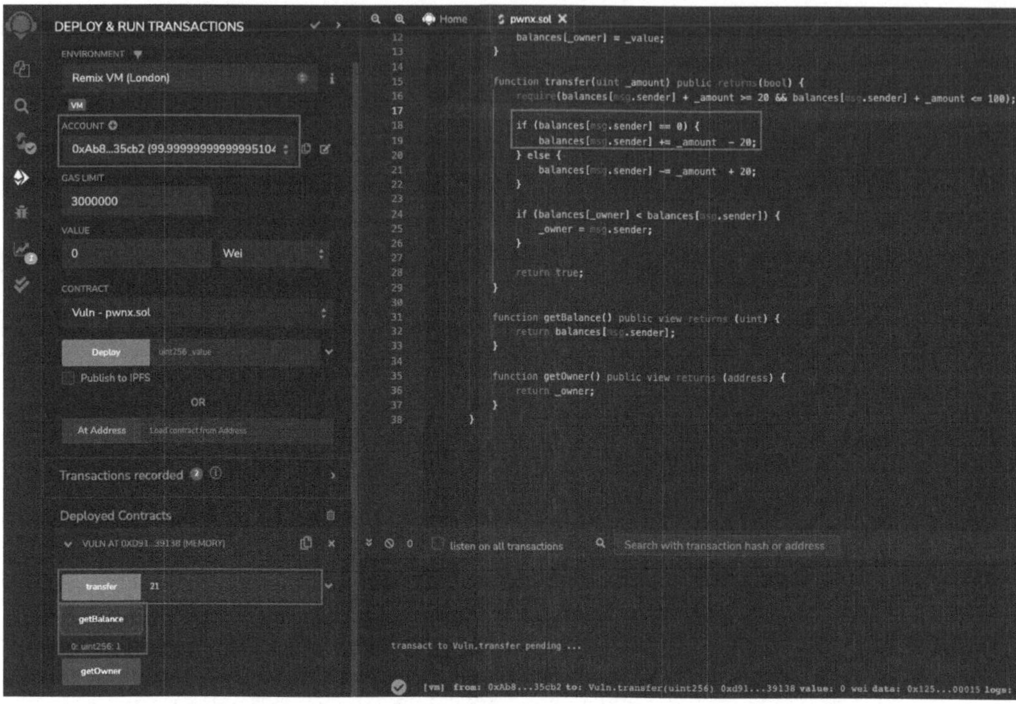

Figure 4.19: *Snapshot for the explanation of the vulnerability*

Now, the next step is to repeat the procedure. By calling the transfer function once more, our balance within the mapping will not be zero. The code in the second if statement will be executed by the contract, resulting in the mathematical underflow. This time, the address balance of **`msg.sender`** will be greater than the owner's balance in the second if statement, allowing us to take advantage of the smart contract's flaw and claim ownership.

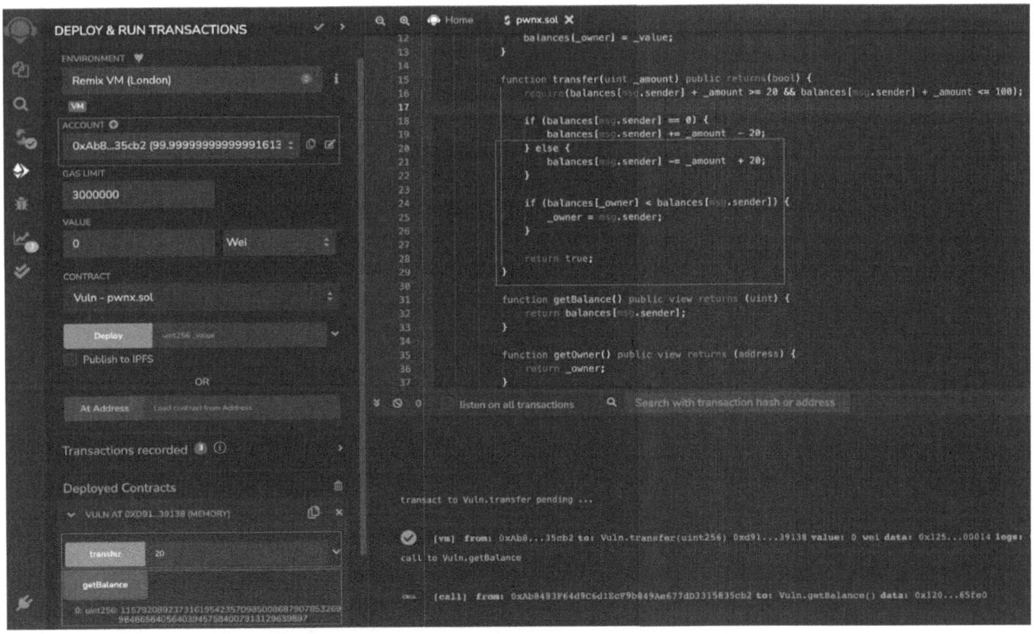

Figure 4.20: *Snapshot for the explanation of the vulnerability*

Now that we understand the vulnerability, we can return to the PWNX challenge and complete the lab.

Since we need to communicate with an external blockchain, we must create a script capable of doing what we just tested on our local system.

Remote Exploitation

A Python library for interacting with Ethereum is called Web3.py. It is frequently used in decentralized apps (dapps) to facilitate transaction sending, smart contract interaction, block data reading, and other applications.

By calling the relevant functions, we can use the ABI to communicate with smart contracts.

Let's understand the code underneath in the depiction:

- We have a URL for HTTP; this is the ganache provider that makes it possible for us to use RPC calls to communicate with the smart contract.
- We import our ABI from this point to call necessary functions.
- We connect to the we3.eth.contract command and establish the smart contract's address.

- From here, we can call functions like **getOwner**. Note that the calls that do not change the state are called calls because they go to read values without changing the state of the blockchain.

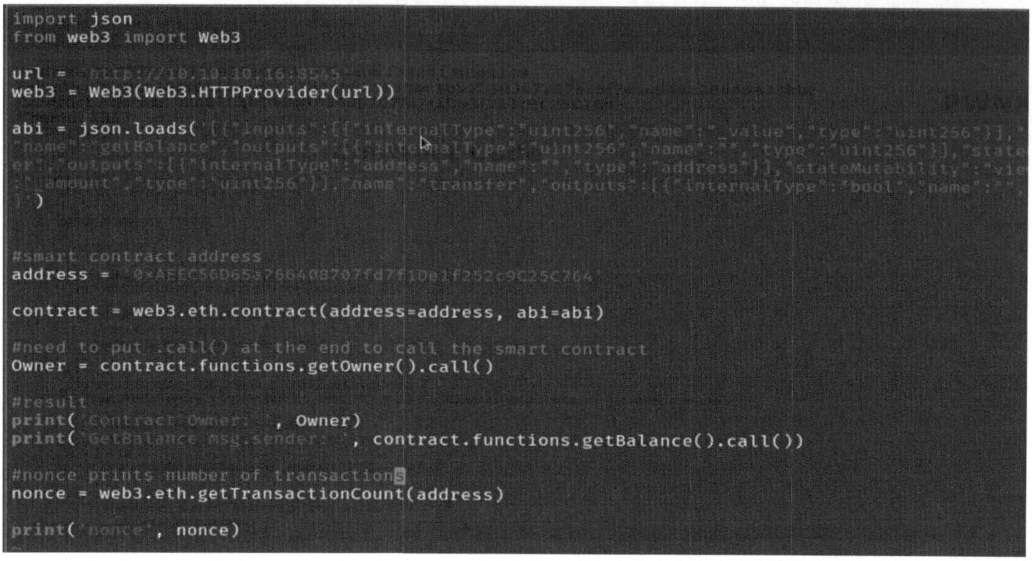

***Figure 4.21**: Communication with smart contracts through the ABI*

After running the script, we can see the owner of the contract, the balance, and the nonce in the console. See the following snapshot:

***Figure 4.22**: Output from the script*

The nonce is only a counter that records notifications of transactions made. In this example, there was only one transaction because the contract was deployed only once.

The transaction that invokes the transfer function and causes underflow will now be created once we tweak our exploit.

As you can see, once the transaction is created, we sign it using the challenge's private key before executing it using the **rawTransaction** function. This time, we use the **buildTransaction** method to generate the transaction that will alter the blockchain's state.

```
address = '0xA6EC56D65a766408707fd7f1De1f252c9C25C764'

contract = web3.eth.contract(address=address, abi=abi)
nonce = web3.eth.getTransactionCount(address)

print('GetBalance msg.sender: ', contract.functions.getBalance().call())
#need to put .call() at the end to call the smart contract
totalOwner = contract.functions.getOwner().call()

# Transaction need to be send 2 times to cause underflow
transaction = contract.functions.transfer(21).buildTransaction(
        {
                "gasPrice": web3.eth.gas_price,
                "chainId": 1337,
                "from": account_from,
                "nonce": 0
                })
#result
signed_trans = web3.eth.account.sign_transaction(transaction, private_key = private_key)
transaction_hash = web3.eth.send_raw_transaction(signed_trans.rawTransaction)
transaction_receipt = web3.eth.wait_for_transaction_receipt(transaction_hash)


transaction = contract.functions.transfer(20).buildTransaction(
        {
                "gasPrice": web3.eth.gas_price,
                "chainId": 1337,
                "from": account_from,
                "nonce": 1
                })
#result
signed_trans = web3.eth.account.sign_transaction(transaction, private_key = private_key)
transaction_hash = web3.eth.send_raw_transaction(signed_trans.rawTransaction)
transaction_receipt = web3.eth.wait_for_transaction_receipt(transaction_hash)

print('Contract Owner: ', totalOwner)
print('Signed Transaction', signed_trans)
print('Receipt', transaction_receipt)
```

Figure 4.23: *Result of sending the transactions*

After running the script, we can see that the transaction is successful by returning the transaction hash and other data. Once we've changed the state of the blockchain and exploited the vulnerability, let us verify.

```
┌──(rea㉿h4t4way)-[~]
└─$ python3 web1.py
Contract Owner:  0xf7332D30437F14d5aB31109Fe612f92D9B72a6e4
GetBalance msg.sender:  20000000000
nonce 1

┌──(rea㉿h4t4way)-[~]
└─$ python3 web1.py
Contract Owner:  0x8325CCD93E885a64F4eAe24A0B2338617f843149
GetBalance msg.sender:  20000000000
nonce 1
```

Figure 4.24: *Verification of the exploit*

Now, check whether the address owner is different. After exploiting the code, our contract address now becomes the owner of the contract. Hence, we have successfully exploited the vulnerability, as shown in *Figure 4.25*.

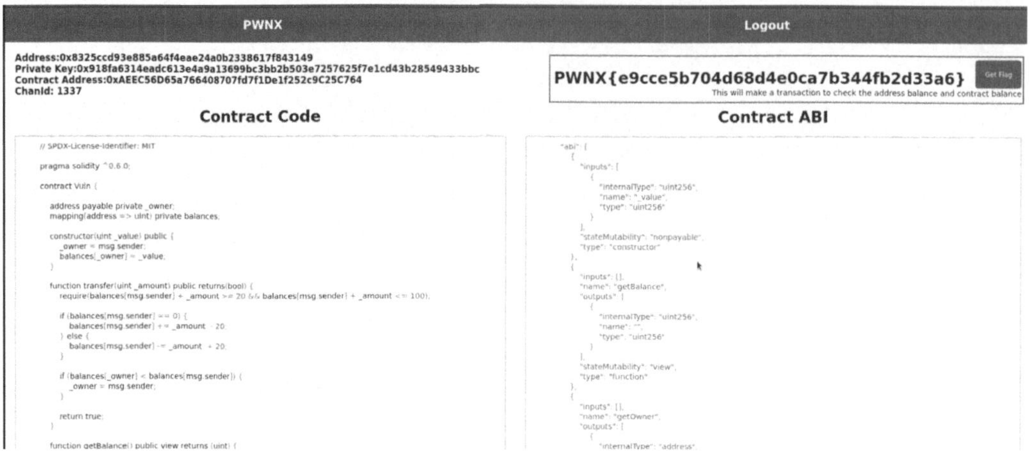

***Figure 4.25**: Comparison of contract address after exploiting the vulnerability*

Congratulations on making it this far! You have successfully hacked the smart contract. Now, repeat this exercise and try to take the challenge yourself. Follow the steps that we have just learned.

Before we go to the next topic, let us see the mitigation that you can use to prevent buffer overflow and underflow attacks.

Mitigations against Overflow and Underflow Attacks

Following are some of the ways to mitigate overflow and underflow attacks:

- **SafeMath library**: Developers should use safeMath libraries or appropriate types with overflow detection to avoid an integer overflow or underflow attack. This library not only gives fundamental math activities but can also really look at the preconditions and postconditions to decide if a flood has happened or not. In the event of an error, the library cancels the transaction and changes its status to *Reverted.*

- **Compiler Version**: The attack can be prevented by using robustness >= 0.8. Compile smart contracts with a newer variation of the compiler. The preventative code of external libraries like SafeMath is thus incorporated into the compiled code.

- **Use modifier 'onlyOwner'**: You can also use security-enhancing modifiers like "`onlyOwner`" or check their code to ensure that the values never exceed their expected range.
- **Regularly update code**: It is also important to keep the code updated.

  Data Execution Prevention: Attackers frequently inject malicious code into locations like stacks and heaps when utilizing buffer overflows to gain unauthorized application execution. As a result, data execution prevention, a new buffer overflow mitigation strategy, is presented. This is referred to as NX (No Execute) in Linux. Both hardware and software levels can enable DEP. When NX is enabled, the stack is no longer executable, and any malicious code added as part of an attack is also no longer considered to be executable.
- **Address Space layout randomization:** Address space layout randomization (ASLR) randomizes the base addresses of the libraries and other memory areas such as the stack. This makes it harder for an attacker to build ROP chains. As ROP chains rely on the addresses of instructions from these libraries, which are loaded into the program.

To check if ASLR is enabled on a Linux machine (specifically, Ubuntu), the following command can be used:

```
$ sudo cat /proc/sys/kernel/randomize_va_space

1
```

As you can see, the value of the file shown in the preceding excerpt is set to 1, which means ASLR is fully enabled is enabled.

For more deep understanding of this topic, it is recommended to go through the following article:

https://www.geeksforgeeks.org/overflow-and-underflow-attacks-on-smart-contracts/,

Now that you have understood the case study in detail and also looked at the mitigation steps for a few vulnerabilities, let us take a deeper dive into understanding more smart contract vulnerabilities.

Smart Contract Attack Vectors Analysis

Solidity's security flaw stems from smart contracts not operating in accordance with their intended behavior. The outcome of such can be as follows:

- Funds getting stolen

- Funds getting locked up or frozen inside a contract
- People receiving fewer rewards than anticipated (rewards are delayed or reduced)
- People receiving more rewards than anticipated (leading to inflation and devaluation)

I will try to cover most of the vulnerabilities here, although these lists do not cover every bug that Solidity has and have come across. However, it serves as a checklist of things to keep an eye out for and study. If a subject seems unfamiliar, it should be an indication that practicing identifying that category of vulnerability is worthwhile.

As a pre-requirement, I assume you have a reasonably good proficiency in Solidity. There is a good tutorial available at ***https://www.rareskills.io/learn-solidity.***

Re-entrancy

In a re-entrancy attack, an attacker calls a function that interacts with another contract and then immediately calls the same function again before the first function call completes. This can exploit a flaw in the contract's logic and allow the attacker to manipulate the contract's state, causing significant damage.

It happens whenever a smart contract calls the function of another smart contract, sends Ether to it, or transfers a token to it, then there is a possibility of re-entrancy.

- When Ether is transferred, the receiving contract's fallback or receive function is called. This hands the control over to the receiver.
- Some token protocols alert the receiving smart contract that they have received the token by calling a predetermined function. This hands the control flow over to that function.
- When an attacking contract receives control, it doesn't have to call the same function that handed over control. It could call a different function in the victim smart contract (cross-function re-entrancy) or even a different contract (cross-contract re-entrancy)
- Read-only re-entrancy happens when a view function is accessed while the contract is in an intermediate state.

Real-world Example: The DAO Hack: The attacker took advantage of Ethereum's fallback function to perform re-entrancy. Every Ethereum smart contract byte code contains the so-called default fallback function. More details can be found at ***https://quantstamp.com/blog/what-is-a-re-entrancy-attack***

More such attacks can be found at ***https://github.com/pcaversaccio/reentrancy-attacks***

Where to find re-entrancy attacks: As of April 2023, 46 re-entrancy attacks have been documented in that repository. More details can be found at ***https://www.rareskills.io/post/where-to-find-solidity-reentrancy-attacks***

This default fallback function contains an arbitrary code if the developer overrides the default implementation. If it is overridden as payable, the smart contract can accept ether. The function is executed whenever ether is transferred to the contract.

Figure 4.25 provides a good example of the process flow of a re-entrancy attack.

Figure 4.26*: Illustration of a DAO Attack*

- **Prevention**

  The following are the best practices to follow when writing your smart contract code to prevent re-entrancy attacks from occurring.

- **Simplicity and code reuse**

  A simple code reduces the likelihood that your code will encounter a bug and assists in preventing an unanticipated effect. Keep the code basic and spotless, following the DRY guideline. Glance through the brilliant agreement code and attempt to track down ways of simplifying it utilizing fewer lines of code. This will make it simple for you to find any part of your code that is vulnerable.

- **Checks effects interactions patterns (CEI)**

  This example is a powerful method for preventing re-entrancy attacks in a smart contract code. Checks and verifications in the contract flow are the first steps in using this pattern. Before interacting with another contract, changes to the current contract's state variables should be made.

- **Setting gas limit**

  Using both the send() and transfer() functions set the gas limits that can be used in a transaction to 2300 units. This helps prevent a re-entrancy attack from occurring because there wouldn't be enough gas to recursively call back into the vulnerable function to exploit funds.

- **Mutex/re-entrancy guard**

  Open Zeppelin has a re-entrancy guard library. The re-entrancy guard provides a modifier called `nonReentrant()` that blocks re-entrancy attacks in the function it is applied. Following is the code of how it applies.

```
3  contract Reentrancy {
4
5      mapping (address => uint) private userBalance;
6
7      bool private locked;
8      modifier nonReentrant() {
9      require(!locked, "No re-entrancy");
10     locked = true;
11     _;
12     locked = false;
13     }
14
15     function withdraw() public nonReentrant() {
16         uint withdrawAmount = userBalance[msg.sender];
17         (bool success, ) = msg.sender.call.value(withdrawAmount)("");
18     require(success);
19         userBalance[msg.sender] = 0;
20     }
21 }
```

Figure 4.27: *Re-entrancy Contract Code*

Check Line 7 and Line 8:

- Create a boolean locked and make it private.
- **`nonReentrant()`** modifier is created that locks the withdraw() function after a single transfer.

When we apply the **`nonReentrant()`** modifier to the `withdraw()` function that was stated earlier, it prevents reentrancy. This is because the first required statement will equate to false and revert the transaction. As a result of this, the attacker is no longer able to exploit the withdraw function with a recursive call. In addition, when the modifier is applied to the cross-function reentrancy attack, the function will be locked when that attacker tries to call it repeatedly.

Access Control

It may appear to be a straightforward error, but it is actually quite common to forget to restrict who can call a sensitive function, such as changing ownership or withdrawing ether.

Even when a modifier is in place, there have been instances in which the modifier was not used appropriately, as in the case where the require statement is missing in the following example:

```
// DO NOT USE!
modifier onlyMinter {
    minters[msg.sender] == true_;
}
```

Figure 4.28: *Access control vulnerability example#1*

This preceding code is a real example from this audit: https://code4rena.com/reports/2023-01-rabbithole/#h-01-bad-implementation-in-minter-access-control-for-rabbitholereceipt-and-rabbitholetickets-contracts
Here is another way access control can go wrong:

```
function claimAirdrop(bytes32 calldata proof[]) {

    bool verified = MerkleProof.verifyCalldata(proof, merkleRoot,
keccak256(abi.encode(msg.sender)));
    require(verified, "not verified");
    require(alreadyClaimed[msg.sender], "already claimed");

    _transfer(msg.sender, AIRDROP_AMOUNT);
}
```

Figure 4.29: *Access control vulnerability example#2*

In this case, **`alreadyClaimed`** is never set to true, so the claimant can issue call the function multiple times.

Real-life example: Trader bot exploited

A fairly recent example of insufficient access control was an unprotected function to receive flashloans by a trading bot (which went by the name 0xbad, as the address started with that sequence). It racked up over a million dollars in profit until one day an attacker noticed any address could call the flashloan receive function, not just the flashloan provider.

As is usually the case with trading bots, the smart contract code to execute the trades was not verified, but the attacker discovered the weakness anyway.

For more details, please visit **https://rekt.news/ripmevbot/**

Improper Input Validation

If access control is about controlling who calls a function, input validation is about controlling what they call the contract with.

This usually comes down to forgetting to put the proper required statements in place.

Here is an example:

```
contract UnsafeBank {
    mapping(address => uint256) public balances;

    // allow depositing on other's behalf
    function deposit(address for) public payable {
        balances += msg.value;
    }

    function withdraw(address from, uint256 amount) public {
        require(balances[from] <= amount, "insufficient balance");

        balances[from] -= amount;
        msg.sender.call{value: amout}("");
    }
}
```

Figure 4.30: *Improper Input Validation example*

This contract checks that you aren't withdrawing more than you have in your account, but it doesn't stop you from withdrawing from an arbitrary account.

Real-life example: Sushiswap

Sushiswap experienced a hack of this type due to one of the parameters of an external function not being sanitized.

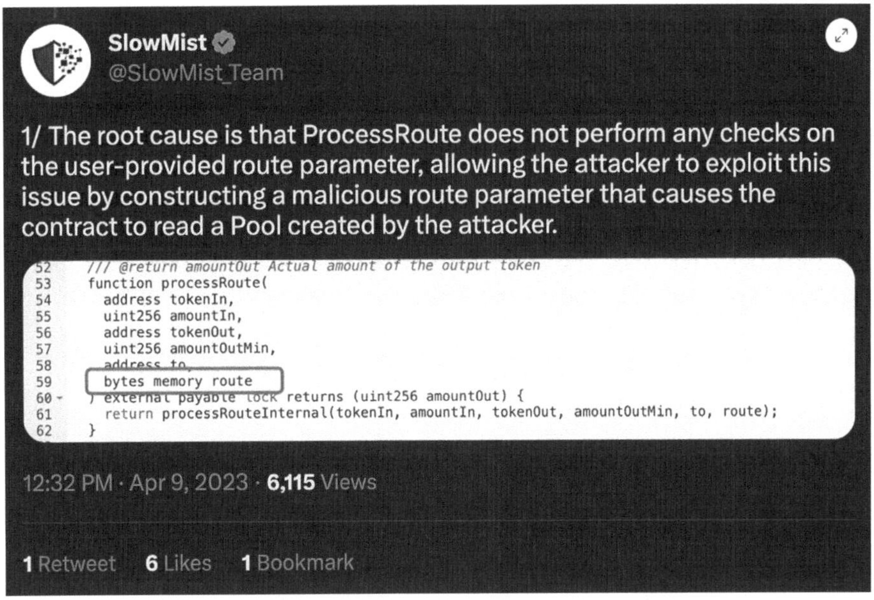

Figure 4.31: *Twitter feed of sushiswap exploit cause*

For more details, please visit **https://twitter.com/peckshield/status/1644907207530774530**

Denial of Service

A security issue that can result in code logic errors, compatibility issues, or excessive call depth (a feature of blockchain virtual machines), causing smart contracts to fail to function properly.

An example of this is when a smart contract can maliciously use up all the gas forwarded to it by going into an infinite loop. Consider the following example:

```
contract Mal {

    fallback() external payable {

        // infinite loop uses up all the gas
        while (true) {

        }
    }
}
```

Figure 4.32: *Malicious code of a loop for DOS exploit*

If another contract distributes ether to a list of addresses, as follows:

```
contract Distribute {
    funtion distribute(uint256 total) public nonReentrant {
        for (uint i; i < addresses.length; ) {

            (bool ok, ) addresses.call{value: total / addresses.length}
("");
            // ignore ok, if it reverts we move on
            // traditional gas saving trick for for loops
            unchecked {
                ++i;
            }
        }
    }
}
```

Figure 4.33: *Distribute contract for DOS*

Then the function will revert when it sends ether to Mal. The call in the preceding code forwards 63 / 64 of the gas available (read more about this rule in our article on EIP 150), so there likely won't be enough gas to complete the operation with only 1/64 of the gas left.

A smart contract can return a large memory array that consumes a lot of gas.

Consider the following example:

```
function largeReturn() public {

    // result might be extremely long!
    (book ok, bytes memory result) =
        otherContract.call(abi.encodeWithSignature("foo()"));

    require(ok, "call failed");
}
```

Figure 4.34: *Vulnerability example of a contract to consume gas*

Memory arrays use up quadratic amounts of gas after 724 bytes, so a carefully chosen return data size can grief the caller.

Even if the variable result is not used, it is still copied to memory. If you want to restrict the return size to a certain amount, you can use assembly.

```
function largeReturn() public {
    assembly {
        let ok := call(gas(), destinationAddress, value, dataOffset,
dataSize, 0x00, 0x00);
        // nothing is copied to memory until you
        // use returndatacopy()
    }
}
```

Figure 4.35: *Example of a Mitigation measure to avoid DOS vulnerability*

Note that deleting arrays that others can add to is also a denial of service vector. In addition, there are also cases where ERC777, ERC721, and ERC1155 contracts can also come under DOS. For example, if a smart contract transfers tokens that have transfer hooks, an attacker can set up a contract that does not accept the token (it either does not have an onReceive function or programs the function to revert).

Now that you have understood the major attack vectors with examples and case studies, let us take a look at some of the best practices to strengthen your smart contract. Finally, in the end, we will take a look at some tools and resources.

Best Security Practices and tools to secure Smart Contracts

A smart contract is an integral feature of blockchain technology since it enables the secure and automated management of digital assets. However, these smart contracts might be protected from malicious attacks with direct and compensating security measures. To preserve their security, organizations must ensure their smart contracts are correctly updated and security hardened.

The following are the best practices for smart contract security:

- Use secure programming languages
- Implement proper input validation and sanitization
- Conduct thorough testing and auditing
- Implement access control and permissions
- Avoid unnecessary complexity

- Use standard libraries and avoid custom code
- Implement circuit breakers and other fail-safe mechanisms

The following tools can help smart contract developers ensure the security of their code:

- Development frameworks: Truffle, Embark, Hardhat
- Security analysis tools: Mythril, Oyente, Slither
- Bug bounty programs
- Security auditing firms: QuillAudits for smart contract audit
- Testing frameworks: Brownie, Hardhat, Waffle
- Code review tools
- Security-focused programming languages: Solidity, Vyper, Rust
- Standard libraries: OpenZeppelin
- Documentation and resources: Ethereum Developer Documentation, Solidity documentation, EIPs (Ethereum Improvement Proposals)
- Community forums and channels: Ethereum Stack Exchange, Discord, and Telegram groups for specific projects or protocols.

Conclusion

Congratulations on completing this chapter; we have covered quite a lot of topics. I could have broken down the topics and covered them under different chapters, but understanding how important the penetration testing procedure is, it was critical to examine and analyze the different bugs and exploits the smart contracts have, since this is the core feature of the blockchain technology, including the decentralized finance. Always remember the steps of penetration testing and ensure that it is conducted at regular intervals. This chapter has also explained the importance of strengthening your smart contracts and the different areas of vulnerability that you can look for. Remember all of this as you move forward in this book.

In the next chapter, I will take you through the auditing techniques for your blockchain application, in which you will learn about the different programs such as bug bounty and tools for static and dynamic testing for the code and frameworks. In addition, we will also take a look at various case studies that would allow you to harden your blockchain code even more.

Points to remember

- Penetration testing, also known as ethical hacking, is a method through which you exploit weaknesses in a system and make a business case to include preventive measures in your solution.
- You can use a lab setup to audit your code using Ganache and Remix. Make sure that any vulnerabilities you identify should be classified and remediated.
- Lots of vulnerabilities and bugs have already been exploited in smart contracts and also have been patched. As you do the audits of smart contracts, ensure that top OWASP attack vectors are addressed, monitored, and remediated.

References

- **https://pentestlab.blog/2020/06/15/spyse-a-cyber-security-search-engine/**
- **https://www.tenable.com/blog/how-to-run-your-first-vulnerability-scan-with-nessus**
- **https://github.com/smartbugs/smartbugs**
- **https://www.imperva.com/learn/application-security/apt-advanced-persistent-threat/**
- **https://www.getastra.com/blog/**
- **https://www.cobalt.io/blog/hacking-solidity-smart-contracts**
- **https://www.openzeppelin.com/**
- **https://quantstamp.com/blog/what-is-a-re-entrancy-attack**
- **https://pwnx.io/**

CHAPTER 5
Blockchain Application Audit

Introduction

Due to the rise in cyber hacks on DeFi and blockchain platforms in general, the FBI has issued a public service announcement to perform security audits on various platforms. A Blockchain security audit is a systematic examination of the security of a blockchain-based application by measuring how well it conforms to an established set of standards and security checklists. An audit typically assesses the security of the system's physical configuration and environment, software, information handling processes, and system design and integrations.

Blockchain security audits are also used to define compliance with regulations and show customers and regulators that you focus on all aspects of security. It also protects your stack from vulnerabilities in design, smart contracts, and the data you are storing of your users. It optimizes your code and increases audience trust. This all looks important, so the question now is: do all blockchain projects needs to be audited? At what stages does the project need to be audited? What process does it have to follow? What are the solutions available in the market that one should adopt?

In this chapter, we will try to uncover all of this. We will start by taking a deep dive into smart contract testing, exploring different methods from unit to integration testing, testing frameworks, and formal verification of smart contracts. We will also take a look at independent audits, such as bug bounty programs. While discussing all of this, we will take a look at various use cases of how formal verification has been applied to smart contracts and other projects. This topic is so interesting that I can't wait to take a deep dive straight into it. Let's take a look at the contents of this chapter.

Structure

We will be covering the following topics in this chapter:

- Smart Contract Testing
- Formal verification overview
- Applying formal verification to smart contracts
- Case Study - Verifying Open Zeppelin's ERC-20 Implementation
- Bug Bounty Programs

Smart Contract Auditing

Because public blockchains like Ethereum cannot be changed, it is difficult to modify a smart contract's code after it has been deployed. There are contract upgrade patterns for *virtual upgrades*, but these are hard to put into practice and require social agreement. Furthermore, if an attacker discovers the vulnerability first, your smart contract is vulnerable to exploits because an upgrade cannot fix it.

If you want to explore more on how smart contracts can be upgraded, there is a good article available at **https://ethereum.org/pt/developers/docs/smart-contracts/upgrading/**

Due to this, it is important to test and audit the smart contracts before they get to the main net. Several methods can be adopted to test your code; there is no single best method. However, it is recommended to do the risk assessment, evaluate the threat vectors in terms of probability and impact, and then choose a suite test suite, which is a mixture of different tools. The objective should be to identify any possible minor or major issues your contract may have.

Methods for testing smart contract

Smart contract testing falls under two main categories of testing methods: automated and manual testing. Before we look at some examples, let us start from the basics.

Automated Testing

Automated testing includes tools to check if a smart contract executes and generates errors if something is not right. Scripts are involved in this process, allowing automation through the scheduling of test cases. These are useful for handling repetitive tasks or important tasks as you don't want human errors. The drawbacks that we see are false positives, which means the bugs that are coming out of the result are not correct.

To find more on false positives, please visit **https://www.contrastsecurity.com/glossary/false-positive**

The following are some of the examples and use cases for automated testing.

Unit testing

During unit testing, contract functions are evaluated separately, which ensures that each component functions properly. If a unit test fails, it should be clear what went wrong and should be easy to run.

Unit tests are useful for ensuring that contract storage is correctly updated following function execution and that functions return expected values. In addition, running unit tests after making changes to a contract's codebase makes sure that adding new logic doesn't cause problems. The following are some recommendations for running efficient unit tests:

- Understand your Smart contracts business logic and process flow

  First, check if your smart contract is delivering what it is designed for. You can try running the happy path test, which determines if functions in a contract return the correct output for valid user inputs. This is explained with a sample bidding contract as follows:

  ```
  **************************************
  constructor(
  uint biddingTime,
  address payable beneficiaryAddress
    ) {
  beneficiary = beneficiaryAddress;
  auctionEndTime = block.timestamp + biddingTime;
  }
  function bid() external payable {
  if (block.timestamp > auctionEndTime)
  revert AuctionAlreadyEnded();
  ```

```
if (msg.value <= highestBid)
revert BidNotHighEnough(highestBid);
if (highestBid != 0) {
pendingReturns[highestBidder] += highestBid;
}
highestBidder = msg.sender;
highestBid = msg.value;
emit HighestBidIncreased(msg.sender, msg.value);
}
function withdraw() external returns (bool) {
uint amount = pendingReturns[msg.sender];
if (amount > 0) {
pendingReturns[msg.sender] = 0;
if (!payable(msg.sender).send(amount)) {
pendingReturns[msg.sender] = amount;
return false;
}
return true;
function auctionEnd() external {
if (block.timestamp < auctionEndTime)
revert AuctionNotYetEnded();
if (ended)
revert AuctionEndAlreadyCalled();
ended = true;
emit AuctionEnded(highestBidder, highestBid);
beneficiary.transfer(highestBid);
}
**************************************
```

This is a simple auction contract designed to receive bids during the bidding period. If the highestBid increases, the previous highest bidder receives their money; once the bidding period is over, the beneficiary calls the contract to get their money.

The various functions that a user might call when interacting with this contract would be covered by unit tests for that contract. Examples of unit tests include checking whether a user can place a bid while the auction is ongoing (that is, calls to **`bid()`** succeed) or if a user can place a higher bid than the current **`highestBid`**.

Writing unit tests to determine whether execution satisfies requirements also benefits from understanding a contract's operational workflow. For instance, when auctionEndTime is lower than **`block.timestamp`**, the auction contract says that users cannot place bids. Consequently, a designer could run a unit test to check if calls to the **`bid()`** capability succeed or come up short when the closeout is finished (that is, when **`auctionEndTime`** > **`block.timestamp`**).

- **Evaluate all assumptions related to contract execution**

  It is critical to report any suppositions about an agreement's execution and compose unit tests to confirm the legitimacy of those suspicions. Testing assertions force you to think about operations that could break a smart contracts security model in addition to protecting unexpected execution. Going beyond *happy user tests* and writing negative tests to see if a function fails for the wrong inputs is a helpful trick.

  You can create assertions, which are straightforward statements stating what a contract can and cannot do, and run tests to see if those assertions hold up under execution with many unit testing frameworks. Before conducting negative tests, a developer working on the auction contract described earlier might assert the following about its behavior:

  - When the auction is over or hasn't started, users can't make bids.
  - If a bid is lower than the acceptable threshold, the auction contract is reversed.
  - The funds of users whose bids do not win are credited.

  Alternatively, to test assumptions, write test that triggers their function modifiers in a contract, such as "require, assert, and if...else statements". For more details, please visit ***https://docs.soliditylang.org/en/v0.8.16/contracts.html#function-modifiers***

- Evaluate code coverage

  The number of branches, lines, and statements executed by your code during tests is tracked by code coverage, a testing metric. If your tests fail to cover all the code, you might get *false negatives*, in which a contract passes all the tests but still has vulnerabilities in the code. High code coverage, on the other hand, ensures that all smart contract statements and functions have been adequately tested for accuracy.

For more details, please refer **https://en.m.wikipedia.org/wiki/Code_coverage**

- Use of testing frameworks

  When developing in web3 or security auditing the effectiveness of a code, smart contract frameworks are essential tools. They help engineers to test and deploy smart contracts rapidly and successfully.

  The tools you use to run unit tests on your smart contracts must be of high quality. A well-maintained testing framework is the ideal one and provides useful features, such as the ability to log and report, and must have been tested thoroughly by other developers.

  Smart contract unit testing frameworks for Solidity are available in a variety of languages, primarily JavaScript, Python, and Rust. For guidelines on running unit tests with various testing frameworks, the following are some of the well-known frameworks that you can use:Evaluate code coverage

  - Truffle
  - Brownie
  - Foundry
  - Waffle
  - Remix
  - Ape
  - Hardhat

Out of the aforementioned list, for a user-friendly experience, I would recommend Ethereum Remix and Truffle. Remix is more like a visual browser IDE that is easy to get started. It is also very flexible and allows you to choose the Solidity version, compile, and run Solidity tests. You Can connect your local disk to Remix to run code from your version-controlled repo. On the other hand, Truffle comes packed with Ganache and Drizzle and has built-in contract abstractions that make web3.js easy to use.

Other popular ones are Hardhat, Brownie, and Foundry, and using these allows you to expedite your Solidity testing. They provide built-in fuzz testing, which means injecting invalid, malformed, or unexpected inputs into a system to reveal software vulnerabilities. In addition, they have been adopted by most DeFI projects like Yearn Finance and Curve Finance.

For a good comparison between truffle and hardhat, please visit **https://www.slashauth.com/post/hardhat-vs-truffle**

Integration testing

Integration tests evaluate the entire smart contract, while unit testing debugs individual contract functions. Integration testing is capable of detecting cross-contract calls or interactions between functions in the same smart contract.

For example, integration tests can help check the inheritance and dependencies of a smart contract. To learn more about inheritance, please visit **https://docs.soliditylang.org/en/v0.8.12/contracts.html#inheritance**

Note

Multiple smart contracts can be inherited into a single one using Solidity. Using tools like Ganache or Hardhat, you can fork the blockchain at a predetermined height to conduct integration tests and practice how your contract and deployed contracts interact with one another.

The forked blockchain will have accounts with associated states and balances and behave similarly to the Mainnet. However, it only serves as a sandboxed local development environment, so you won't need real ETH for transactions or alter the Ethereum protocol in any way.

Property-based testing

The process of verifying whether a smart contract satisfies a specified property is known as property-based testing. **Arithmetic operations in the contract never overflow or underflow** is an example of a smart contract property. Properties assert facts about the behavior of a contract that are anticipated to remain true in various scenarios.

Static and dynamic analysis are two normal strategies for executing property-based testing, and both can check whether the code for a smart contract fulfills some predefined property.

Static analysis

A static analyzer uses a smart contract's source code as input to determine whether or not a contract satisfies a property. Static analysis, in contrast to dynamic analysis, does not require the execution of a contract to verify its correctness. Instead, the static analysis considers all smart contract's possible execution paths (by examining the structure of the source code to ascertain its implications for the contract's operation at runtime).

Linting and static testing are common methods for running static analysis on contracts. Both require analyzing low-level representations of the contract's execution, such as abstract syntax trees and control flow graphs output by the compiler.

For details on linting, please visit **https://www.perforce.com/blog/qac/what-lint-code-and-what-linting-and-why-linting-important**

In general, safety issues like unsafe constructs, syntax errors, or coding standards violations in a contract code can be found with static analysis. Static analyzers, on the other hand, are generally unreliable at detecting deeper vulnerabilities and may generate an excessive number of false positives.

Dynamic Analysis

Dynamic analysis generates symbolic or concrete inputs, like in fuzzing, to a smart contract's functions to see if any execution trace(s) violates specific properties. Fuzzing is a useful security test where you give malicious input to the contract. If the smart contract enters an error state (for example, one where an execution fails), the issue gets flagged and inputs that drive execution toward the vulnerable path are delivered in a report.

For details on symbolic inputs, please visit **https://en.m.wikipedia.org/wiki/Symbolic_execution**

This form of property-based testing differs from unit tests in that test cases cover multiple scenarios, and a program handles the generation of test cases.

- It is difficult to write test cases, the scenarios can be many and different.
- The test that you write may miss some important scenarios.
- Unit tests can only prove if the contract can execute correctly for the sample data provided, but whether the code executes correctly for inputs outside the sample data is not known.

The following are the guidelines for running property-based testing on the smart contract, which covers multiple scenarios.

First, running property-based testing regularly begins with characterizing a property (for example, the absence of integer overflows or the collection of properties you want to verify). While writing property tests, you may also be required to define a range of values within which the program can generate data for transaction inputs.

Also, once designed appropriately, the property tcsting apparatus will execute your smart contract capabilities with arbitrarily created inputs. Assuming there is any statement infringement, you ought to get a report with substantial information that disregards the property under assessment. To get started with property-based testing using different tools, check out the following guides.

To explain all this, let us take a look at how you can use foundry to perform fuzzing on a command-line tool, Forge, on the contracts.

Note

Forge tests, builds, and deploys your smart contracts.

Forge will look for the tests anywhere in your source directory. Any contract with a function that starts with test is considered to be a test. Usually, tests will be placed in test/ by convention and end with **.t.sol**.

Here is an example of running a forge test in a newly created project, which only has the default test:

****

```
$ forge test
No files changed, compilation skipped
Running 2 tests for test/Counter.t.sol:CounterTest
[PASS] testIncrement() (gas: 28312)
[PASS] testSetNumber(uint256) (runs: 256, μ: 27376, ~: 28387)
Test result: ok. 2 passed; 0 failed; finished in 24.43ms
****************************************************
```

Let's write a unit test using Forge, identify the general property we are testing for, and change it to a property-based test to see what that means.

```
pragma solidity 0.8.10;

import "forge-std/Test.sol";

contract Safe {
    receive() external payable {}

    function withdraw() external {
        payable(msg.sender).transfer(address(this).balance);
    }
}

contract SafeTest is Test {
    Safe safe;

    // Needed so the test contract itself can receive ether
    // when withdrawing
    receive() external payable {}

    function setUp() public {
        safe = new Safe();
    }

    function test_Withdraw() public {
        payable(address(safe)).transfer(1 ether);
        uint256 preBalance = address(this).balance;
        safe.withdraw();
        uint256 postBalance = address(this).balance;
        assertEq(preBalance + 1 ether, postBalance);
    }
```

Figure 5.1: *Figure sample contract*

Running the test, we see it passes:

****

```
$ forge test
Compiling 6 files with 0.8.10
Solc 0.8.10 finished in 3.78s
Compiler run successful
Running 1 test for test/Safe.t.sol:SafeTest
[PASS] testWithdraw() (gas: 19462)
Test result: ok. 1 passed; 0 failed; finished in 873.70µs
```

****

The ability to withdraw ether from our safe is tested in this unit test. However, how do we say whether it applies to all amounts or just one ether?

Here, the general property is as follows: If we have a safe balance, we should get whatever is in the safe when we withdraw.

As a property-based test, let us rewrite: Forge will execute any test that takes at least one parameter.

****

```
contract SafeTest is Test {
    // ...
    function testFuzz_Withdraw(uint256 amount) public {
        payable(address(safe)).transfer(amount);
        uint256 preBalance = address(this).balance;
        safe.withdraw();
        uint256 postBalance = address(this).balance;
        assertEq(preBalance + amount, postBalance);
    }
```

****

If we run the test now, we can see that Forge runs the property-based test, but it fails for high values of amount:

****

```
$ forge test
Compiling 1 files with 0.8.10
Solc 0.8.10 finished in 1.69s
```

```
Compiler run successful

Running 1 test for test/Safe.t.sol:SafeTest
[FAIL. Reason: EvmError: Revert Counterexample: calldata=0x215a
2f20000000000000000000000000000000000000001000000000000000000000000, ar
gs=[79228162514264337593543950336]] testWithdraw(uint256) (runs: 47, µ:
19554, ~: 19554)

Test result: FAILED. 0 passed; 1 failed; finished in 8.75ms
**********************************************************
```

The default amount of ether that the test contract is given is 2**96 wei (as in DappTools), so we have to restrict the type of amount to uint96 to make sure we don't try to send more than we have:

```
function testFuzz_Withdraw(uint96 amount) public {
```

Now, we see it passes:

```
******************************************************
$ forge test
Compiling 1 files with 0.8.10
Solc 0.8.10 finished in 1.67s
Compiler run successful

Running 1 test for test/Safe.t.sol:SafeTest
[PASS] testWithdraw(uint96) (runs: 256, µ: 19078, ~: 19654)
Test result: ok. 1 passed; 0 failed; finished in 19.56ms
*****************************************************
```

For configuring fuzz test execution, Fuzz tests execution is governed by parameters that can be controlled by users via Forge configuration primitives. Configs can be applied globally or on a per-test basis.

For details, please visit **https://book.getfoundry.sh/reference/config/testing, https://book.getfoundry.sh/reference/config/inline-test-config**

Manual testing

After running automated tests, manual testing of smart contracts typically occurs later in the development cycle. The smart contract is evaluated in this way as a single, fully integrated product to see if it meets the technical requirements.

Testing contracts on Local Blockchain

While automated testing performed in a local development environment can provide useful debugging information, you'll want to know how your smart contract behaves in a production environment. However, deploying to the main Ethereum chain incurs gas fees, not to mention that you or your users can lose real money if your smart contract contains bugs.

An alternative to testing on the Mainnet is to test your contract on a local blockchain, also known as a development network. A local blockchain is a local copy of the Ethereum blockchain that runs on your computer and mimics the behavior of the execution layer. As a result, transactions can be programmed to interact with a contract without causing a lot of overhead.

Manual integration testing can benefit from running contracts on a local blockchain. Although smart contracts are highly composable, you will still need to ensure that such intricate on-chain interactions result in the desired outcomes. However, smart contracts allow you to integrate with existing protocols.

Testing Contracts on Testnet

Similar to the Ethereum Mainnet, a test network or testnet uses Ether (ETH) with no real-world value. Anyone can interact with your contract on a testnet, such as through the dapp's frontend, without risking funds.

This kind of manual testing is helpful when looking at your application's flow from beginning to end from a user's perspective. Additionally, beta testers can conduct trial runs and report any issues with the contract's overall functionality and business logic.

After testing on a local blockchain, deploying on a testnet is preferable because of its close resemblance to the Ethereum Virtual Machine operations. As a result, it is common practice for many Ethereum-native projects to deploy dapps on testnets to test the operation of smart contracts in the real world.

When evaluating the correctness of a smart contract, manual testing, or human-assisted testing entails running each test case in your test suite sequentially. This is different from automated testing, where you can run multiple isolated tests on a contract at the same time and get a report showing all the tests that failed and passed.

A single person can perform manual testing by following a written test plan that covers various test scenarios. As part of manual testing, you can also have multiple individuals or groups interact with a smart contract over a predetermined time. The contract's actual and expected behavior will be compared by the testers, and any difference will be reported as a bug.

After running automated tests, manual testing of smart contracts typically occurs later in the development cycle. The smart contract is evaluated in this way as a single, fully integrated product to see if it meets the technical requirements.

Comparing this with automated testing, manual testing requires considerable resources (skill, time, money, and effort) and is possible—due to human error—to miss certain errors while executing tests. However, manual testing can also be beneficial—for example, a human tester (for example, an auditor) may use intuition to detect edge cases that an automated testing tool would miss.

For more details on Ethereum testnets, please visit: **https://ethereum.org/pt/developers/docs/development-networks/#public-beacon-testchains**

Formal Verification of a Smart Contract

While testing contributes to the confirmation that a contract returns the anticipated results for some data inputs, it is unable to definitively demonstrate the same for inputs that are not utilized during tests. As a result, *functional correctness*, or the ability to demonstrate that a program behaves as required for all sets of input values, cannot be guaranteed when testing a smart contract.

Hence, we need a process like formal verification to determine whether the software is correct by comparing the program's formal model to its formal specification. While a formal specification specifies a program's properties (that is, logical assertions regarding the program's execution), a formal model represents an abstract mathematical representation of a program.

Formal verification, in contrast to testing, can be used to check that an execution of a smart contract satisfies a formal specification for all executions (that is, it does not contain bugs) without having to execute it with sample data. This not only saves time when running dozens of unit tests but also finds previously undetected vulnerabilities more effectively. A traditional security audit is not the same as formal verification. With a formal check, the contract code is confirmed at the bytecode level utilizing tools developed in light of a numerical model of the EVM.

How Formal Verification of Smart Contracts Works

Let's take a look at the process of verifying a smart contract using formal verification. A smart contract is written in Solidity and then converted into bytecodes. Once reduced to bytecodes, a smart contract can be deployed on the blockchain as a contract account at some address.

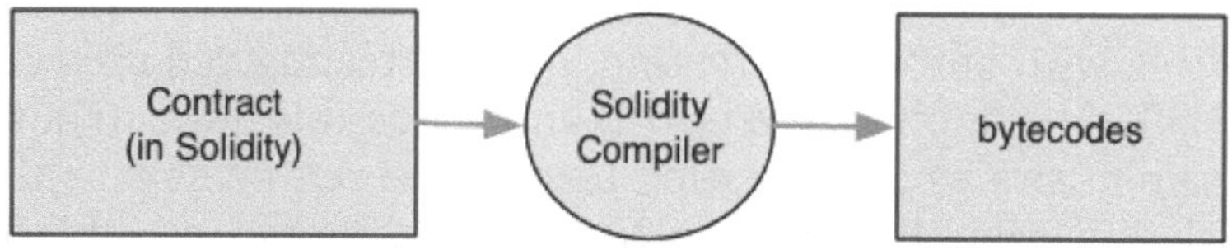

***Figure 5.2**: Solidity Contract with compilation*

In the following example, the contract has been deployed at 0x4ab05. A contract account contains funds, a compiled contract, and other data. The picture also contained an externally owned account (at 0x6eae7). Such an account contains only funds (100 ether in this case).

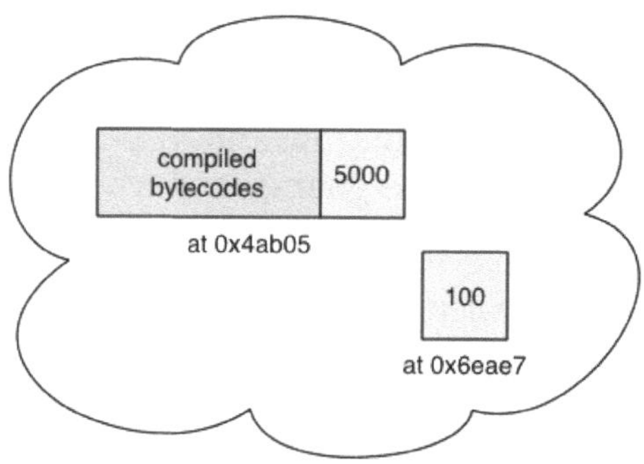

***Figure 5.3**: Address of a deployed contract*

A contract begins working after a transaction addressed to it is submitted to the network. Here's a transaction that transfers ether from the submitter's account to another account:

transfer(4000 ether, address(0x6eae7)).

Thousands of computers (miners) running identical copies of the same virtual machine (VM) will carry out this transaction. In this instance, the VM will be instructed to add 4000 ether to 0x6eae7 and subtract 4000 ether from 0x4ab05 by interpreting the bytecodes of the transfer function, as shown in *Figure* 5.4.

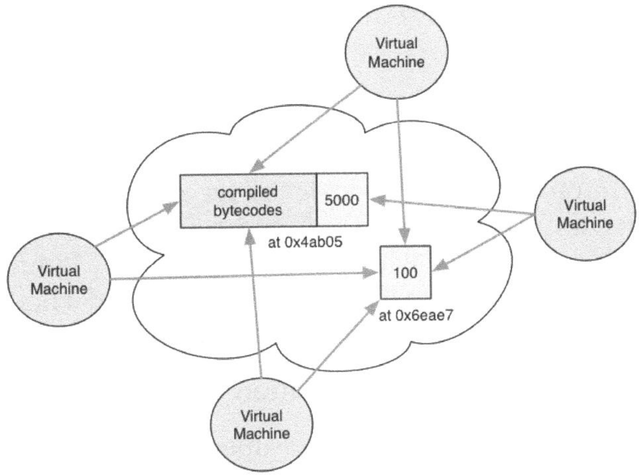

Figure 5.4: *Contract verification by nodes in virtual machines*

As all the VMs are processing the same data with the same bytecodes, they'll all produce the same answer.

Once again, our goal is to have great confidence that the contract will behave correctly, regardless of the value being transferred, the balances of the two accounts, and which account is to receive the value.

Following are the various ways that could prevent us from getting the desired result:

- The programmer could misunderstand the intent. For example, suppose no one said what to do if there was not enough money to transfer, should the transfer function fail? Or should the contract make a *best effort* and transfer only what was available?
- The programmer might assume one - the wrong one - is the *obvious* choice and implement it.
- Despite knowing what was needed, the programmer might make a mistake when implementing the intent. For example, the Hackergold exploit was due to mistyping += as =+.

During testing, the following conditions are usually checked:

1. Transfer zero ether
2. Transfer all the ether
3. Transfer slightly more than all the ether

4. Transfer the largest possible amount of ether (hoping to discover overflow bugs)
5. Transfer an account's value to itself

The tester would turn that into tests by picking specific values for each of the preceding points. (You cannot just *transfer all the ether*. Instead, you have to pick a specific number for both the contract and receiver's starting balances, and you need to provide a transfer with a specific address.) Running a test means predicting the final balances, making the transfer, and checking if what the contract did is the same as what it should have done.

So, what do we really do in formal verification that traditional testing cannot?

If we are to prove that a program always does what it should, we have to be precise about what *should* means. This is known as the contract's specification. This should apply in various hops, such as Solidity code, virtual machine, and bytecode specifications, and this all can be verified using K verification frameworks. The result of which can be either the contract is wrong or the proof is created where the contract is right.

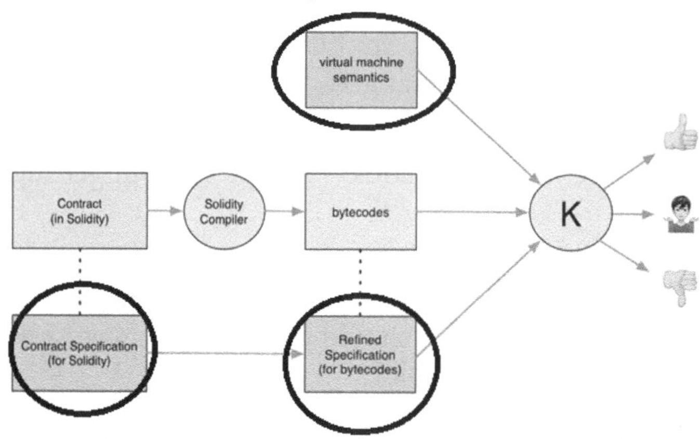

Figure 5.5: *Formal verification of a smart contract using the K framework*

Note

K is a rewrite-based executable semantic framework in which programming languages, type systems, and formal analysis tools can be defined using configurations and rules. Out of the several projects aiming to create formally specified execution environment, K frameworks are mostly used. It provides a user-friendly, modular, and mathematically rigorous meta-language for defining programming languages, type systems, and analysis tools. K includes formal specifications for C, Java, JavaScript, PHP, Python, and Rust.

The detailed analysis of this topic is beyond the scope of this book. We suggest you take a look at the following URLs and engage with concerned teams if you wish to pursue this.

Remember, the higher the stakes, the fancier the attack surface becomes.

For more details on the formal verification, please refer to the Wikipedia page: **https://en.wikipedia.org/wiki/Formal_specification**

Following are some useful links to see the formal verification done on smart contracts:

- **https://github.com/runtimeverification/verified-smart-contracts/blob/master/deposit/deposit-formal-verification.pdf**
- **https://runtimeverification.com/blog/end-to-end-formal-verification-of-ethereum-2-0-deposit-smart-contract**

KEVM as a specific application of the K Framework

The K semantics of the Ethereum Virtual Machine (KEVM) is an application of the K Framework on Ethereum. It specifies the full semantics of the Ethereum Virtual Machine (EVM), adding all the benefits of the formal specification to Ethereum smart contracts. The KEVM provides the first machine-executable, mathematically formal, human-readable, and complete semantics for the EVM.

The specification includes the following three main components:

- The syntax of the language.
- A description of the state/configuration.
- The transition rules that drive the execution of programs.

The KEVM implements both the stack-based execution environment, with all the EVM's opcodes, as well as the network's state, gas simulation, and even high-level aspects such as ABI call data.

This allows for the simplified creation of formal specifications for smart contracts. It provides auditors with all the tools necessary to verify a smart contract. And the KEVM isn't limited to any specific programming language.

Applying formal verification to a smart contract

A straightforward smart contract is used for a DEFI application. We define its specifications and verify it to test formal verification on the blockchain. When investigating formal verification, it is best to make use of an established framework. The most common tools for this job are the Ethereum virtual machine's K Framework and KEVM implementation. In every one of our examples, we'll use KEVM.

The following is the smart contract for an ICO, a part of an ERC-20 token. It has two callable functions as follows:

- **Buy**: receives Ether and distributes tokens.
- **BalanceOf**: returns the balance of any given account.

```
************************************************************
pragma solidity 0.4.25;
contract ICO {
    mapping (address => uint256) private _balances;
    uint256 private _totalSupply;
    uint256 private _decimals = 18;
    uint256 private _hardCap = 200 * (10 ** _decimals);
    uint256 private _rate = 2;

    function balanceOf(address owner) public view returns
(uint256) {
        return _balances[owner];
    }

    function buy() public payable {
        require(msg.value != 0);
        require(_hardCap <= _totalSupply + msg.value * _rate);
        _balances[msg.sender] += msg.value * _rate;
        _totalSupply += msg.value * _rate;
    }
}

************************************************************
```

The next step is to feed the requirements of a smart contract into specifications. This is a basic ICO example and the requirements are as follows:

- The ICO will collect 100 Ether at most and distribute 200 tokens.
- There's no time limit for the ICO.
- The emission rate is 2 tokens per Ether (for example, for 0.1 Ether, you will receive 0.2 tokens).

Figure 5.6 displays the high-level specification for this contract.

```
Solidity

module ICO
    syntax Value   ::= Int  // this can be changed
    syntax Address ::= Int  // this can be changed
    // defining the "syntax" of the contract
    syntax AExp ::= Value | Address
                  | "buy" "(" ")"
                  | "balanceOf" "(" AExp ")"                    [strict]
                  | "throw"
    // configuring cells for the contract's storage
    configuration <ico>
                    <caller> 0 </caller>
                    <value> 0 </value>
                    <k> $PGM:K </k>
                    <accounts>
                      <account multiplicity="*">
                        <id> 0 </id>
                        <balance> 0 </balance>
                      </account>
                    </accounts>
                    <supply> 0 </supply>
                    <hardcap> Int 200 * (Int 10 ^Int 18) </hardcap>
                  </ico>
    // balanceOf returns the balance of a given account
    rule <k> balanceOf(Id) => Value ...</k>
       <id> Id </id>
       <balance> Value </balance>
    // The buy function receives ether and distributes tokens appropriately.
    // Requirements:
    // - the buy function has to receive ether, so the value cannot be zero
    // - once the hard cap has been reached, no more tokens can be sold
    rule <k> buy() => .</k>
       <caller> From </caller>
       <value> MsgValue </value>
       <hardcap> HardCap </hardcap>
       <supply> Total => Total +Int MsgValue *Int 2</supply>
       <account>
         <id> From </id>
         <balance> BalanceFrom => BalanceFrom +Int MsgValue *Int 2 </balance>
       </account>
     requires MsgValue >=Int 0
       andBool Total +Int MsgValue *Int 2 <=Int HardCap
endmodule
```

Figure 5.6: *Specification of a smart contract*

You can see definitions for both functions as well as rules of what these functions should do in each case. Then, we have to define EVM specifications.

Defining the EVM specification

You must prepare an initialization file where the requirement for each function is defined, along with the details of all parameters in the EVM

```
// Defining EVM-level specification for the balanceOf function
[balanceOf]
k: #execute => #halt                                            //execution must stop eventually
statusCode: _ => EVMC_SUCCESS                                   //execution status must be success
output: _ => #asByteStackInWidth(BAL, 32)                       //the function returns the "balance" value
callData: #abiCallData("balanceOf", #address(OWNER))            //define ABI call data for the function (i.e. the signature balanceOf(address))
gas: {GASCAP} => _                                              //specify GAS usage (in this case we don't really care about GAS, since the function is so simp
refund: _                                                       //refunded GAS
storage:                                                        //specify changes to storage
    #hashedLocation({COMPILER}, {_BALANCES}, OWNER) |-> BAL     //loads balance of owner balances[owner] into BAL
requires:                                                       //specify requirements in this case - simple sanity checks for parameters
    andBool 0 <=Int OWNER    andBool OWNER    <Int (2 ^Int 160) //owner address is a 160 bit unsigned integer
    andBool 0 <=Int BAL      andBool BAL      <Int (2 ^Int 256) //balance is a 256 bit unsigned integer

// Defining EVM-level specification for the buy function
[buy]
k: #execute => #halt                                            //execution must stop eventually
statusCode: _ => EVMC_SUCCESS                                   //execution status must be success
output: _ => _                                                  //no return value
callData: #abiCallData("buy", .TypedArgs)                       //define ABI call data for the function (i.e. the signature buy())
gas: {GASCAP} => _                                              //specify GAS usage (in this case we don't really care about GAS, since the function is so simp
log: _                                                          //no logs
refund: _                                                       //refunded GAS unspecified
storage:                                                        //changes to storage
  #hashedLocation({COMPILER}, {_BALANCES}, CALLER_ID) |-> (BAL_FROM => BAL_FROM +Int MSGVALUE *Int 2)  //balance of caller is increased by MSGVALUE
  #hashedLocation({COMPILER}, {_SUPPLY}, _SUPPLY)     |-> (_SUPPLY => _SUPPLY +Int MSGVALUE *Int 2)    //total supply is also increased
requires:                                                       //specify requirements
    andBool MSGVALUE >=Int 0                                    //value is not zero (user actually has to pay Ether to buy tokens)
    andBool _SUPPLY +Int MSGVALUE *Int 2 <=Int _HARDCAP         //hardcap is not reached
// Program definition. Specifies the bytecode that will be tested. "code" is the compiled smart contract.
[pgm]
```

***Figure 5.7**: EVM specification details*

In order to produce a specification from it, we can simply call the gen-spec script from the KEVM repository as follows:

Shell Script >

```
python3 gen-spec.py spec-tmpl.k ico-spec.ini ico-spec ico-spec > ico-spec.k
```

Now, let's verify the smart contract:

```
kevm prove ./ico-spec.k
```

Once the proof executes as per the specification, the framework should display:

> True

Which means that the document has been verified successfully.

Now, let's try to see if we add a bug in a contract in the buy function, what the result will look like.

****

```
function buy() public payable {
    require(msg.value != 0);
    require(_hardCap >= _totalSupply + msg.value * _rate);
```

```
    if (msg.value == 42)
    {
        return;
    }
    _balances[msg.sender] += msg.value * _rate;
    _totalSupply += msg.value * _rate;
}
***********************************
```

We will receive a generic indication of an error if we carry out the verification right now. Although the bug is obvious, it would be very challenging to discover it by utilizing traditional unit tests or penetration testing methods without access to the source code

Case study - Formal verification of Open Zeppelin's contract

Web3 extensively uses the ERC-20 reference implementation from Open Zeppelin. Its numerous contracts would suffer greatly if it had a flaw. However, how do we know for sure that it is true? Also, how would we know that the data received from it is accurate and don't present bugs?

First, you need to have templates that specify the expected behavior of the ERC20 contracts. The main functions include **`functions transfer`**, **`transferFrom`**, **`approve`**, **`allowance`**, **`balanceOf`**, and **`totalSupply`**. Then, you need to add features related to each function, as explained here:

- **erc20-transfer-revert-zero**

  Function transfer Prevents Transfers to the Zero Address. Any call of the form transfer(recipient, amount) must fail if the recipient address is the zero address. Specification:

  ```
  [](started(contract.transfer(to, value), to == address(0)) ==>
    <>(reverted(contract.transfer) || finished(contract.transfer(to,
  value), return
      == false)))
  ```

- **erc20-transfer-succeed-normal**

  Function transfer Succeeds on Admissible Non-self Transfers. All invocations of the form transfer(recipient, amount) must succeed and return true if:

- The recipient address is not the zero address.

- Amount does not exceed the balance of the address **`msg.sender`**.
- Transferring the amount to the recipient's address does not lead to an overflow of the recipient's balance.
- The supplied gas suffices to complete the call.

Specification:

```
[](started(contract.transfer(to, value), to != address(0) && to != msg.
sender &&
    value >= 0 && value <= _balances[msg.sender] && _balances[to] + value <
    0x10000000000000000000000000000000000000000000000000000000000000000 &&
    _balances[to] >= 0 && _balances[msg.sender] <
    0x10000000000000000000000000000000000000000000000000000000000000000) ==>
  <>(finished(contract.transfer(to, value), return == true)))
```

With all these templates and features, you have to develop the formulas/ algorithms. For example:

```
function _transfer(address from
                  , address to
                  , uint256 amount) internal returns (bool) {
    require(from != address(0), "ERC-20 recipient address must not be zero");
    require(to != address(0), "ERC-20 recipient address must not be zero");
    _balances[msg.sender] -= amount;
    _balances[to] += amount;
    emit Transfer(msg.sender, to, amount);
    return true;
}
```

***Figure 5.8**: Transferfrom function in a contract*

The **`transferFrom()`** capability in ERC-20 agreements requires exceptional consideration. As the need might arise to recognize the initiator of the exchange (the location is **`msg.sender`**), the records that spend and get tokens, and because it needs to notice the cutoff points forced by the passages in **`_balances`** and **`_allowances`**.

```
function transfer(address to, uint256 amount) public returns (bool) {
    return _transfer(msg.sender, to, amount);
}

function transferFrom(address from
                     , address to
                     , uint256 amount) public returns (bool) {
    return _transfer(from, to, amount);
}
```

***Figure 5.9**: Transferfrom function balances allowance in a contract*

Specifying Correct Allowance Updates

At the point when transferFrom() succeeds, it should deduct how much tokens that have been moved from the remittance that the shipper has over the high-roller's record. Be that as it may, numerous ERC-20 symbolic agreements additionally permit the symbolic proprietor to give boundless remittance to another record. This is reflected by setting the record's recompense to the most extreme worth, for example, to ((2^256)- 1). Considering the exemption, a right recompense update can be determined by the accompanying LTL equation φ:

$$\begin{aligned}\varphi = \Box(&\mathit{started}(\mathsf{transferFrom}) \Rightarrow \Diamond \mathit{finished}(\mathsf{transferFrom}(\mathit{from}, \mathit{to}, \mathit{amt}), \mathit{return} = \mathsf{true}\\ &\Rightarrow \mathit{allowance}[\mathit{from}][\mathit{msg.sender}] = \mathsf{old}(\mathit{allowance}[\mathit{from}][\mathit{msg.sender}]) - \mathit{amt}\\ &\vee(\mathit{allowance}[\mathit{from}][\mathit{msg.sender}] = \mathsf{old}(\mathit{allowance}[\mathit{from}][\mathit{msg.sender}]\\ &\wedge(\mathit{msg.sender} = \mathit{from} \vee \mathit{allowance}[\mathit{from}][\mathit{msg.sender}] = 2^{256} - 1)))))\end{aligned}$$

***Figure 5.10**: Formula for allowance update*

The formula explains that when **`transferFrom()`** is invoked and terminates (without reverting) with a return value of true, it is expected that the sender's allowance is either reduced by the amount of tokens in amt (the red subformula) or that the sender either is the owner of the transferred tokens or has unlimited allowance over the spender's tokens. In such cases, the allowance must not be changed (the blue subformula).

Specifying Dismissal of Transfers that Exceed the Allowance

Attempts to use **`transferFrom()`** to transfer an amount of tokens that exceeds one's allowance should fail. This is formalized by ψ:

If the invocation of **`transferFrom()`** requests to transfer tokens from somebody other than their owner and if that transfer exceeds the sender's allowance, we expect the transaction to either revert or fail and signal its failure by returning false.

Here are just two examples that were shown to explain the mapping of templates into developing formulas to audit the behavior of a contract.

For more technical details for the specification, please visit:

https://www.certik.com/resources/blog/iLhagzcWkOVzOxoy0AWG3-erc-20-properties-for-formal-verification

In summary, following are the takeaways:

Formal verification can reliably identify bugs that testing and auditing frequently overlook, such as self-transfers or tricky arithmetic overflows.

The cycle requires a lot of manual work, a lot of it profoundly talented and consequently costly.

Formal verification has become practical today. I believe that the cost is comparable to that of a thorough human audit and that it boosts confidence for both the contract owner and the customers signing the contract.

The field of smart contracts is distinct and specialized. This increases the power of formal verification. Full verification is less expensive because of smart contracts' small size as compared to non-blockchain projects. The domain only contains a few key concepts, making it easy to adapt the tools to it; further lowering costs and enhancing efficiency.

Bug Bounty Program

So, are you sure that your systems will survive cyberattacks? The best way to find out is through a bug bounty program. Before we start any further, I want to emphasize again that security should be the number one priority for you if you are building a blockchain project, because if hackers can see it, they will surely be targeting it.

You must be wondering why we have already covered penetration testing, threat modeling, security auditing, formal verification, and so on. earlier in the book, and where bug bounty fits in the list. These are all good considerations, so let me decipher this by first explaining what bug bounty programs are and how they work.

A blockchain Bug Bounty is a reward program set up by organizations for ethical hackers to identify and exploit blockchain applications in exchange for a reward. There are a few reasons why a blockchain Bug Bounty program is important. First and foremost, they successfully identify and resolve software based on blockchain issues. It is to be noted that as blockchain applications expand more in scope due to their being distributed and decentralized than any other centralized application, the potential attack surface also expands as the ecosystem builds. Such a program can aid in the prevention of potential attacks and safeguard user funds by locating and resolving issues before they go to production.

It also gives non-monetary incentives to hackers, where not only they can enhance the decentralized web's security but also can improve their standing in the community.

It is a three-step process, which starts with security assessment, reporting, and reward distribution.

- **Assessment**: It is requested that ethical hackers evaluate the software's security. The goal of this is to find any potential problems with the software by going over the code, infrastructure, and user interface of the software thoroughly.

- **Reporting**: The ethical hacker is obligated to report any problem they find to the project or business offering the bounty. A thorough explanation of the problem and its potential exploitation ought to be included in the report.
- **Distribution of reward**: A bounty is paid to the ethical hacker if the problem is found and resolved. The amount of the bounty varies based on the severity of the problem. This is because it is necessary to consider the consequences that could result from exploiting the problem.

Pen testing vs Bug Bounty

Now you must be thinking is this another name given to penetration testing. No, it is not true, both are different. It's just that you have expanded the pen testing to a bigger community with no time restrictions. You can do it anytime you feel like it, depending on your organization's risk appetite. It is recommended to do a bug bounty program twice a year.

Another key difference is the company receives a payment for each vulnerability discovered through a bug bounty. The hacker is compensated according to the severity of the vulnerability once a vulnerability report is confirmed to be accurate. Therefore, ethical hackers are compensated for the results of their hunts, and not for the amount of time they spend hunting.

The project is billed for pen testing. The scope, duration, required skills, and number of pen testers, all play a role in determining the project's overall cost. The number of vulnerabilities discovered during the pen test has no bearing on the amount billed to the client organization.

For details on the smart contract audit, please visit **https://www.immunebytes.com/blog/what-is-a-smart-contract-audit/**

For more details on bug bounties, please visit **https://medium.com/immunefi/a-defi-security-standard-the-scaling-bug-bounty-9b83dfdc1ba7**

In addition, there are interesting case studies where the negotiations took place with the hackers in which some portion of the funds are returned. More can be found at **https://www.certik.com/resources/blog/4wDO2hUnaJlHPfAiOTPHdK-a-grey-area-retroactive-bug-bounty-negotiations**

Conclusion

Well done, in making it to the end of this chapter. This chapter covers a complete suite of tools and recommendations on blockchain testing, in particular smart contracts testing. We learned different testing techniques from manual to automated, and then we covered formal verification of smart contracts and looked at case studies and examples. Then, we looked at the independent type of audits, such as bug bounty programs, in which white hackers get involved. With all this information, your blockchain project will be in good hands; you now have enough armory that would make attackers think several times before attempting an attack.

In the next chapter, we will look at the various type of mitigation solutions that you can adopt, from Identity access management to public key infrastructure. We will also discuss infrastructure security measures for various deployment models.

Points to Remember

- Smart contract testing has gained momentum over the years and several tools have been introduced. Remember to start with manual testing, and then adopt automated testing to expedite the process.
- Bugs coming out of the Unit and integration testing should be mitigated. Integration tests evaluate the entire smart contract, whereas unit testing debugs individual contract functions.
- If your contract has a modular architecture or interacts with other on-chain contracts during execution, integration testing is helpful.
- Hardhat, Brownie, and Foundry: Using these tools allow you to expedite your solidity testing. They provide built-in fuzz testing, which means injecting invalid, malformed, or unexpected inputs into a system to reveal software vulnerabilities.
- Formal verification, in contrast to testing, can be used to check that an execution of a smart contract satisfies a formal specification for all executions.

References

- **https://soliditylang.org/**
- **https://ethereum.org/en/**
- **https://runtimeverification.com**
- **https://forum.openzeppelin.com/t/formal-verification-of-open-zeppelin-contracts/3871**

CHAPTER 6
Blockchain Security Solution

Introduction

Who are you on the internet? And how much personal information are you sharing on the web? As more and more of our lives are spent online and the digital world forges stronger connections with the physical world, our electronic identities are becoming as important as who we are in real life. Authenticating who you are and securing access to your personal information on the internet are now critical components of operating in the modern world for both individuals and organizations.

If you think that you have figured out the identity part, think again. What if the identity is spoofed and the request you receive from the trusted IP source has been compromised? What will you do then? If you have a distributed and decentralized network, then establishing trusted identities becomes even more complicated. The only way to control is through the mechanism where trust is established using cryptography and by enabling logging and monitoring within your network.

In this chapter, we will cover blockchain security solutions that can be applied to wallets, smart contracts, and infrastructure components to secure confidentiality, integrity, and repudiation attacks. The examples and use cases will help you understand the concept. This is so fascinating that I cannot wait to take a deep dive straight into it. Let's look at the contents of this chapter.

Structure

We will be covering the following topics in this chapter:

- Zero Knowledge Proof
- Identity and access management
- Public key infrastructure
- Security logging and monitoring

Zero-Knowledge Proof

Giving proof to someone without revealing any information. Does this sound complex to you? In other words, with zero-knowledge proof, you can provide the validity of any claim or statement, without revealing that statement.

To explain, consider how you might prove a claim (for example, *I am a citizen of* X1 *country*) to an airport control agent (for example, a service provider). You would need to provide **evidence** to back up your claim, such as a national passport or driver's license.

So why do we care, even if we must provide the actual statement, like an ID card, to anyone? The problem lies in the handling of such private information. You need to store that information in some database if it's an online portal, and then adopt security measures to protect it, for example, encryption access control, etc. If your storage endpoints are vulnerable, you can expect a hacker to exploit these vulnerabilities. If the leaked information comprises PI data elements, then you must face GDPR compliance issues as well.

To make this all quantifiable and make more sense, consider that 4% of your annual revenue and the trust of your customers are at stake.

Now that you understand the problem, let us see how zero-knowledge proof helps in solving it.

Zero-knowledge proof is a process where the need to share actual information to prove the claims is eliminated. The process uses statements as input to generate proof of validity without revealing information.

The process consists of an algorithm that takes some data and returns some output as true or false. Here is a breakdown of the components that make up this algorithm:

- **Witness**: In a zero-knowledge proof, the person making the claim wants to establish that they know something that is hidden. The hidden information is the *witness* to the proof, and the prover's intended knowledge of the witness sets up a set of questions that can only be answered by someone who knows the information. So, to start the process of proving, the prover picks a question at random, figures out the answer, and sends it to the checker.

- **Challenge:** The checker picks a random question from the set and asks the prover to answer it.
- **Response**: The prover takes the question, figures out the answer, and sends it back to the checker. The prover's answer lets the validator find out if the prover really has access to the witness. The verifier asks more questions to make sure the prover isn't just guessing and getting the right answers by chance. By doing this several times, the chance that the prover may lie about knowing the witness reduces significantly until the checker is satisfied.

Let me explain you this concept with the help of a story.

In the story, Peggy is the person who proves the statement, and Victor is the person who checks the statement.

Peggy has found the magic word that can be used to open a door in a cave. The cave is in the shape of a ring, with the entry on one side and the magic door blocking the other. Victor wants to know if Peggy knows the secret word, but Peggy is very private and doesn't want to share either the secret word or the fact that she knows it with Victor or the rest of the world.

The left and right paths from the door are marked with A and B. First, Victor watches Peggy goes into the cave while he waits outside. Peggy can take either road A or B, but Victor can't see which one she chooses. Then, Victor goes into the cave and shouts the name of the way he wants her to take back, either A or B. If she really does know the magic word, this is easy. If she needs to, she opens the door and goes back the way she came.

But what if she didn't know the word? Then, she could only go back by the named path if Victor told her the name of the same road she had come in on. Victor would pick either A or B at random, so she would have a 50/50 chance of being right.

A side point about third-party observers: Even if Victor is wearing a secret camera that records the whole deal, the camera will only record Victor shouting "A!" and Peggy showing up at A, or Victor shouting "B!" and Peggy showing up at B. A tape like this would be easy for any two people to make. All Peggy and Victor would need to do is agree ahead of time on the order of the A's and B's that Victor will shout. A tape like this will never be believable to anyone but the people who were there at the time. Even someone who was there to watch the original experiment would not be satisfied, because Victor and Peggy might have planned the whole "experiment" from beginning to end.

Alternatively, Peggy could show Victor that she knows the magic word in just one try, without telling him what it is. If Victor and Peggy go to the mouth of the cave together, Victor can watch Peggy go in through A and come out through B. This would show for sure that Peggy knows the magic word, but she wouldn't have to tell Victor what it is. But a proof like that could be seen by a third party or taped by Victor, and that would be enough to convince anyone. In other words, Peggy couldn't get rid of such proof by saying she worked with Victor, and she can't choose who knows what she knows because of that.

Below is a picture of this story. You can think of a million ways that Peggy can prove to Victor that she knows the secret, but she doesn't have to tell him. Other people should believe that she did prove to Victor that she knows the secret.

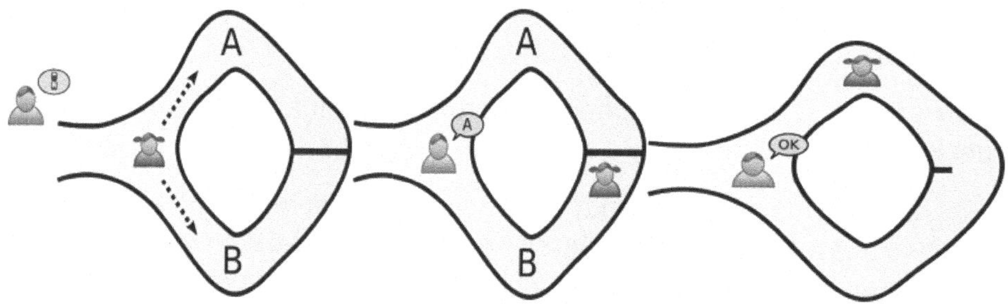

***Figure 6.1**: Conceptual example of zero-knowledge proof (source: Chain-link)*

Now, to explain further, let us understand the different types of Zero-Knowledge proof solutions available.

Types of Zero-Knowledge (ZK) Proof

They can be interactive as well as non-interactive. Interactive proof solutions need the prover and verifier to exchange messages repeatedly and be available. For example, even if a verifier is convinced of a prover's honesty, the proof would be unavailable for independent verification (computing a new proof requires a new set of messages between the prover and verifier).

Another type is non-interactive proof, which requires only one round of communication. In this case, the prover gives the secret information to an algorithm to generate a zero-knowledge proof. This proof is then sent to the validator, who uses a different algorithm to check if the prover knows the secret information.

Non-interactive proving makes ZK-proofs more efficient since both the prover and the checker do not have to talk to each other more frequently. Also, once a proof is made, anyone who has access to the shared key and the verification method can check it. This can be divided into two groups.

ZK-SNARKs

ZK-SNARK stands for Zero-Knowledge Succinct Non-Interactive Argument of Knowledge. The ZK-SNARK algorithm has the following features:

- **Zero-knowledge:** A validator can confirm the truthfulness of a statement without knowing anything else about it. The only thing known to the person doing the checking is whether the statement is true or false.
- **Succinct:** The zero-knowledge proof is smaller than the witness and can be quickly checked.
- **Non-interactive:** The proof is not interactive because the prover and the checker only talk to each other once. Interactive proofs, on the other hand, require more than one round of conversation.
- **Argument:** The proof meets the "soundness" requirement, so cheating is extremely improbable.
- **(Of) Knowledge:** The zero-knowledge proof cannot be made without access to the secret information (the witness). A true zero-knowledge proof is hard, if not impossible, without the presence of the witness.

Note that the shared key that is used in the algorithm to calculate proof should be handled carefully, if the nonce, or the unique value it is made up of, has been taken down, false proof can be calculated.

The key ceremony process, or multi-party computation, is the process that can be adopted to strengthen the parameters. For example, in multi-party computation, the participants in a network each provide an input.

ZK-STARKs

ZK-SNARK stands for Zero-Knowledge Scalable Transparent Argument of Knowledge. ZK-STARKs are similar to ZK-SNARKs, except for the following features:

- **Scalable:** ZK-STARK makes and checks proofs faster than ZK-SNARK when the size of the witness is large. With STARK proofs, the time it takes to prove and verify doesn't change much as the number of witnesses grows. With SNARK proofs, on the other hand, the time it takes to prove and verify grows linearly with the number of witnesses.
- **Transparent:** To create public conditions for proving and verifying, ZK-STARK uses randomness that the general public can check instead of a known context. So, when compared to ZK-SNARKs, they are clearer.

To understand more about the application and to make sense of what we have studied so far, let's look at their use cases.

Use cases for Zero-Knowledge Proofs

There are several use cases where zero-knowledge proofs are useful. Not being able to collect user information can help the platform owners avoid the risk of any potential data compromise. The use cases range from not revealing your driving license, pay stubs, W-2s, and proof of residence all the way to sharing your college transcripts. For me, the best application of ZKP lies in the financial ecosystem due to its complex nature and high regulatory oversight. The second application is in the WEB3 space, especially in the DeFi ecosystem. By decoupling data from layer 2, you can solve the scalability issue on the blockchain.

Decoupling Identity in Payments Infrastructure

Card payments are often visible to multiple parties as part of the payment trail infrastructure, which includes merchants who handle the Point-of-sale terminals (POS), payment gateways and processors like banks and financial intermediaries, and other interested parties (for example, government authorities). All these entities collect user and payment-related information. While financial surveillance has benefits for identifying illegal activity and is part of the standard of cash flow, it has undermined the privacy of ordinary citizens. If those databases come under attack, then it's a different ballgame.

Then, if you look at cryptocurrencies, they were created so that people could make private and peer-to-peer transactions with each other. However, on public blockchains, most of the crypto activities are public and can be seen by anyone if the public key or transaction ID is known. User identities can be established and linked to real-world identities either on purpose (by putting ETH addresses on Twitter or GitHub pages, for example) or by using simple on-chain and off-chain data analysis with the help of forensic firms like CNC intelligence or chain analysis.

It is critical to understand that most crypto transactions get terminated at exchanges, where the users must cash out the cryptocurrency in fiat. All exchanges know the identity of the users, so they end up getting personal information upon registration.

ZK Proof will help individuals and associated parties prove their valid identity to financial entities, without the exchange of personal data. This will also save on the cost of managing and securing the data. This doesn't mean that the financial surveillance would face obstacles; any regulatory entity or platform can request or revoke the validation if the proof conditions are not met.

Improving WEB3 Layer 2 Protocols

Scaling blockchain networks to support the demand is challenging. As demand for block space on layer-1 increases, it leads to network congestion and high transaction costs, which in turn reduces the demand and growth of Web 3. Just to recall, layer-1 is the asset layer, like ethers, and layer 2 is where consensus happens.

A zero-knowledge solution can batch up thousands of transactions and then publish a zero-knowledge proof, like a message hash, validating the correctness of transactions on the underlying layer-1 blockchain. These proofs require far less space than complete transaction data, helping relieve layer-1 network congestion while creating a highly secure environment with high throughput and low transaction costs. An example of such a solution is known as ZK-rollups, which have two versions falling under the ZK-SNARK and STARK categories. There are also a few other protocols. *Figure* 6.2 provides a good view.

**Examples of Zero-Knowledge Layer 2s
Using Different Architecture**

	zk-Rollup	Validium	Volition
zk-SNARK Proofs	Loopring	zkSync 1.0	zkSync 2.0
zk-STARK Proofs	Immutable X	StarkEx	StarkNet

***Figure* 6.2**: *Examples of projects using different zero-knowledge solutions*

Application of Zero-Knowledge Proof

To help solve the identity problem and achieve zero-knowledge proof, we welcome Self-Sovereign Identity (SSID), which enables users to own, control, and present their identity data as needed while enabling service providers to securely validate and trust the identity claim.

So how does this magic happen? Let me explain this concept with the help of the following illustration. It comprises three parties: one is the claim holder, which is the user, the other is the claim verifier, which needs proof; and the last party is the claim issuer, who certifies that the claim is legitimate.

The other important component is the decentralized identity tag, commonly known as the DID, which is stored on the blockchain. The issuer and the holder both sign the DID before storing it on the chain. Any verification needed by the verifier should happen after consent is given by the claim holder. Afterward, the verifier can query the blockchain to check the claim. He will find the digital signature of the claim issuer, allowing them to verify its authenticity. Here, the verifier does not even need an actual copy of the data from the prover. The digital signatures in the claim of the prover and the issuer will be enough to prove that the information he is requesting is accurate.

Below is a picture of SSI design, which shows the different parts of the process. The goal is for the person with the claim to be able to show the checker that the claim is real.

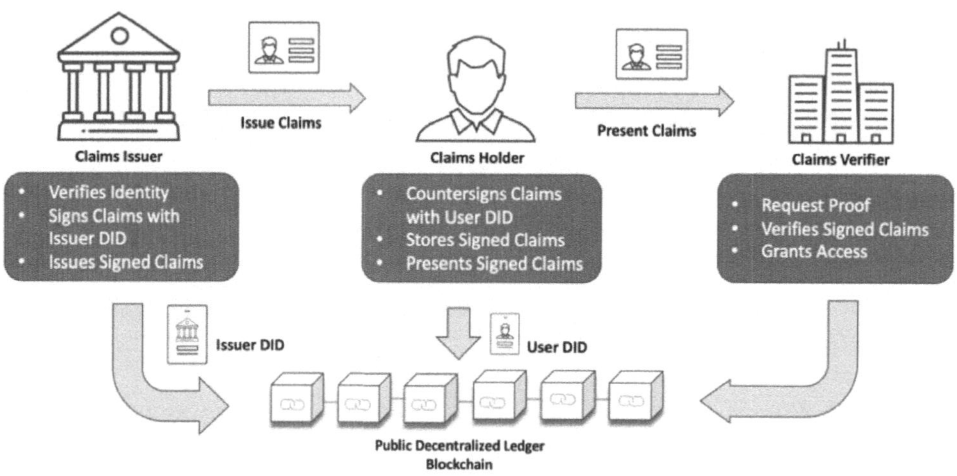

Figure 6.3: *Self Sovereign Identity high-level architecture*

In addition, Zero-knowledge proofs were also implemented in the Zerocoin and Zerocash protocols, which led to the development of the cryptocurrencies Zcoin, which changed its name to Firo and then to and Zcash. Zerocoin has a built-in mixing model that doesn't trust peers or centralized mixing sources to make sure that transactions are anonymous.

Identity and Access Management

Who are you on the internet? And how much personal information are you sharing on the web? As more and more of our lives are spent online and the digital world forges stronger connections with the physical world, our electronic identities are becoming as important as who we are in real life. Authenticating who you are and securing access to your personal information on the internet are now critical components of operating in the modern world for both individuals and organizations.

Indeed, Identity management is an integral part of any network infrastructure, whether you have a public blockchain or a private blockchain. If you have a robust and resilient Identity management solution in place, then most of the cyber-attacks can be mitigated.

In general, it comprises processes, policies, and technologies to ensure that only authorized people have access to technology resources, information, or services. These systems are continuously evolving to improve security and the user experience. A common example is the 'Know your customer' process, in which users register themselves with an application to use its services. First, the user enters their name, email ID, and phone number, which need to be authenticated and validated through a backend process before their credentials are accepted and allocated to them.

There is a lot of content and discussion available on how blockchain plays an important role in identity and access management, with its salient features of immutability, smart contacts, and cryptography. So, just to set the stage and build the context, in this topic, we are taking the opposite side, meaning how a security-hardened access control solution can aid blockchain projects. In other words, how enforcing authentication, authorization, and accounting can power up the blockchain network and help reduce vulnerabilities.

If you look at the blockchain network and the ecosystem, it comprises the technology stack of the protocol, for example, Bitcoin, Ethereum, and Hyperledger, as well as the infrastructure and interworking components like Wallets, APIs, networking nodes, and Layer 1 and Layer 2 protocols. The data assets are distributed across multiple layers with accessibility needs for both human and machine users, as per the data flow and routine operations.

The access use cases can be several, a few of which include:

- A private blockchain network needs to authenticate and authorize validating nodes so that consensus operations can be performed.
- User registration is required by the blockchain mobile or web application.
- Smart contract code that checks whether any calls made to the contract are legitimate or not.
- A backend administrator of a blockchain application is performing troubleshooting for a customer complaint.
- Blockchain developers and quality assurance team to integrate a new feature.
- API Calls are made between oracles to query data on the blockchain.

Now, with all these use cases, if authentication measures are not taken care of, you will not know whether the request is made by a spoofed user or a legitimate user. Whether the person or machine making the request is allowed to query that data or not. Whether we are logging each request query or not, this would help in tracking down repudiation attacks.

Another consideration is that we have different types of blockchains, such as Public and Consortium/private blockchains. Most of the private ones are architected on a public cloud like AWS, whereas access control for Dapps, wallets, the consensus layer, and smart contracts is an integral part of public blockchains. So, let us look at IAM from the perspective of the type of blockchain application.

Identity and Access Management for Public Blockchain

The Internet is a scary place to do business. If you are unaware of who is talking to you or whether a known person is accessing the authorized resources, then you will be in trouble. It is similar to not allowing anyone inside your home and limiting them to whatever they can take.

We tried to illustrate this concept with the help of *Figure* 6.4. As you can see, when the wallet or a decentralized application wants to connect to the network, the request must be authenticated and authorized as it interacts with the blockchain smart contracts.

The Identity and access management server shown in *Figure* 6.4 connects with an active directory server, which authenticates the request and passes it on with the token with the role to the identity and access management server. You can define the policies and roles in the Active Directory, and the same will be applied. The roles will depend on the subjects, resources, and purpose of access. To better secure yourself, you can go as granular as you can.

For example, an administrator developer accessing the smart contract is allowed to make changes to specific functions, whereas a normal wallet user can just submit the transaction on the blockchain network. Other categories of requests from external smart contracts need to be validated.

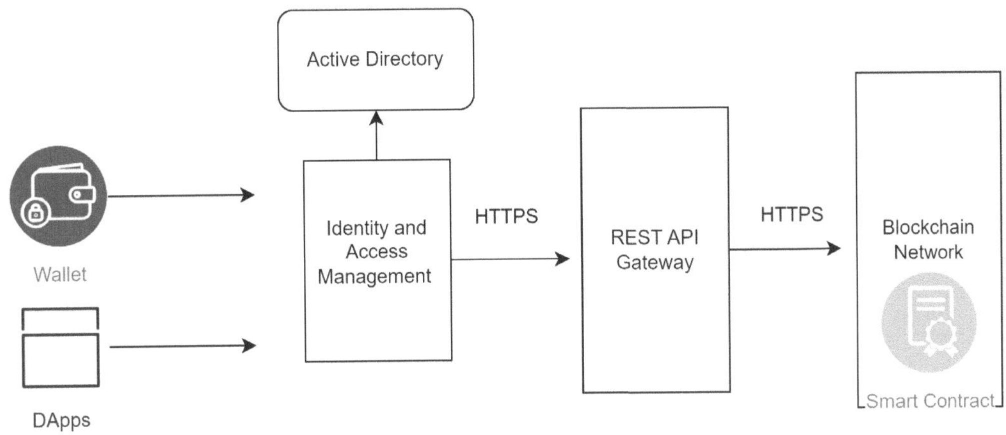

Figure 6.4: *Identity and Access Management Architecture for Blockchain*

In addition, for any registration or sign-ups to Wallet or Daps, it is recommended to use a federated identity mechanism like a Single Sign-On (SSO). It offers two main advantages: first, users do not have to store and memorize the credentials; second, the platform doesn't need to enforce security controls over the datasets, as the information is transparent.

There is a good blog where you can read more details on SSO:

In other words, when you use Single Sign-On, the authentication request is redirected to an identity provider like Google or Facebook. For example, if you are using a Gmail account, then Google is responsible for user authentication. If the request is successfully authenticated, then only you will be allowed to login to the Dapp.

With the authentication and authorization layer, you can secure your Blockchain APIs with industry-standard protocols, including OpenID Connect, OAuth 2.0, and SAML.

You can use either of these protocols in your Single Sign-On solution, and each supports the integration with your enterprise ID registry, including LDAP or Active Directory servers.

Here is a typical example of an OAuth 2.0 Authorization Code flow with Key Cloak running alongside an application backend on a private network.

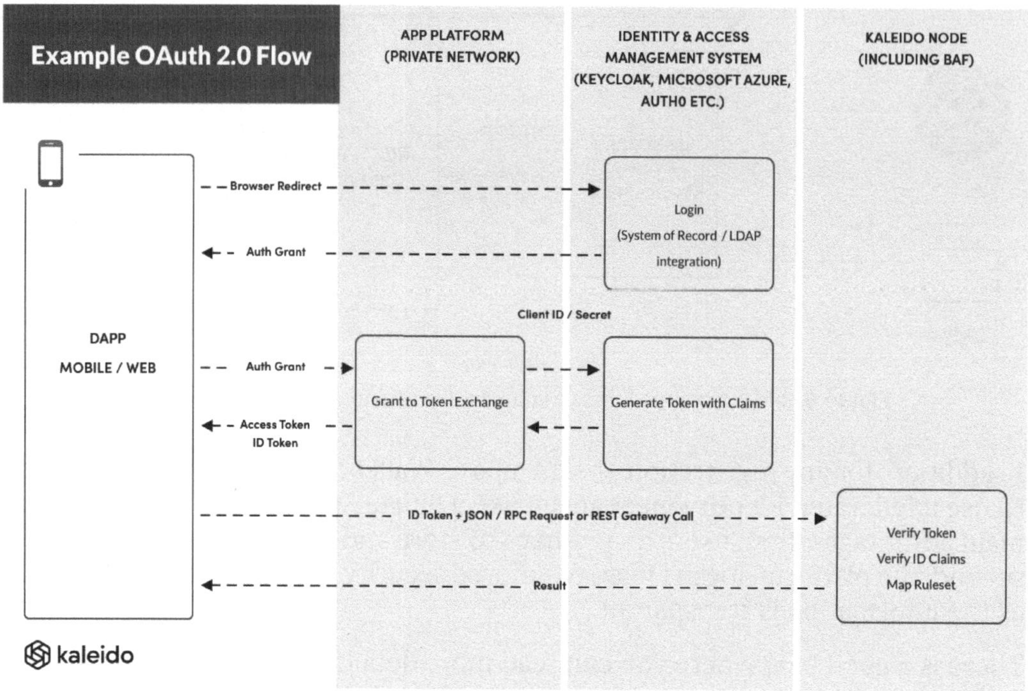

***Figure 6.5**: Single Sign-On flow example of Kaleido*

Kaleido, which is the blockchain solution provider, acts as the OAuth Resource Server. Notice that in this authorization flow, Kaleido never needs to perform outbound communication with either the application or the IAM server, so the IAM can be behind your firewall.

The IAM server has configured Kaleido with the public keys to validate the JWT token.

Key Cloak is used here because it can run behind your firewall and link to your system of record, such as an LDAP server or Microsoft Active Directory.

You could replace Key Cloak with any OAuth 2.0-compliant Authorization Server like Auth0, Cognito, or Azure AD.

How do you track the Bitcoin transaction

Now that you know how to build an Identity and Access Management solution for your blockchain application, let me tell you an interesting story. I fell victim to a fake shopping platform.

I was forced to send the BTC to a fake website that I thought was a real business at first. After two weeks of doing things, I quickly understood that I was part of a scam. Then, I wanted to figure out where my trade went so, I could find out who did it and punish them.

As a rule, if someone is pulling a scam on the internet, they are using bitcoin. As a standard, they all want to use swaps to turn their bitcoin into real money, like US dollars or the currency of their home country. The transaction Hash is the way to keep track of it.

If you look at the picture below, you can see that transaction Hash C1 is sent to address a1, then to address a2, and finally to VASP 1 address a3. VASP stands for **virtual asset service provider**, which is what people usually call **crypto exchanges**.

Dealing with Hash C1 is my transaction, in which I sent Bitcoin to the address that the criminals gave me. Hash C3's last transaction is sent to an exchange wallet address called a3. Legal or customer service of an exchange can be called with the information to find out who owns the wallet address in that exchange. Usually, they won't tell the owner's name unless the cops ask them to.

So, if you think you have been a victim of an online scam involving crypto currency, you should try to find out where your money went through the transaction logs. There are good crypto forensics companies that can give you the information you need once you give them the details of the deal. Lastly, you need to make a police report so that an exchange can tell you who did it and help you take the right steps.

I have copied a picture of a transaction flow from an investigation report below for your reference, so you can know what you can do.

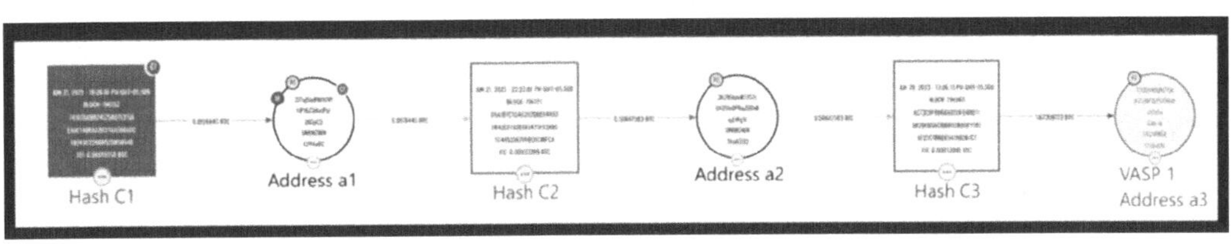

Figure 6.6: *BTC Transaction flow from Crypto wallets to an exchange*

Identity and Access Management for Smart Contracts

In the world of smart contracts, access control—that is, *who is allowed to do what*—is very important. Your contract's access control may say who can create new tokens, vote on ideas, stop trades, and do many other things. Due to this, it is important to know how to implement it and prevent abuse.

Access control in smart contracts is a way to control who is allowed to do certain things in a contract. Most of the time, these are activities that are important for the security and proper operation of the system, like creating new tokens, stopping transfers and withdrawals, or installing upgrades.

There are some functions that are essential to a smart contract's safety. Consider a contract that uses the proxy method to do updates. If access to the upgrade function is never limited, someone with malicious intentions could change the meaning of the contract or run commands that impact performance.

Take the Temple DAO Stax hack as an example. Because there were no access controls, the hacker was able to make new tokens. The attacker took advantage of flaws in the contract. This occurred because people who weren't meant to could call a secret function (migrateStake).

Upgrades are not the only functions that need proper access control. Any function that can have a big impact on how a protocol works needs to be properly protected. For instance, the DeFi protocol Maker DAO uses access control to limit who may submit a price oracle update (so attackers cannot alter the prices of assets in the system).

Although I have covered this topic in more detail in a previous chapter while explaining smart contract security, I am briefing the concepts here again, so that the key takeaways for strengthening smart contract access control can be understood clearly.

Following are some of the best practices you can adopt. In today's smart contracts, two common methods for establishing access control are the **Ownable pattern** and **Role-based permissions**.

Ownable Pattern

This works on the idea that the owner of the contracts holds special privileges, as an administrative function in that contract, although the rights are transferable to other accounts as well.

Under the Ownable pattern, restricted functions have an only Owner modifier that checks the identity of the calling account before executing. If the caller's address fails to match the owner's address stored in the contract storage, the call reverts.

This type of account increases the risk of centralization and single point of compromise, as seen in the recent Ronin hack. In hindsight, giving special account privileges to one account can reduce the risk of mishandling caused by other accounts and reduce management overhead, in case the account needs to be frozen due to a vulnerability or an exploit.

This approach can work during the pre-build phase, but as the contract gets deployed to the main network, role-based permissions should be applied. Let us look at what this looks like.

Role-Based Permissions

Looking at the role access, as the name says, the access is restricted to the role the subject has. The levels of access that employees or a developer have to the network are referred to as roles in RBAC.

This would enable the power to go from one centralized account into multiple accounts, such as a role for token minter, token burner, implementing upgrades, and so on. The individual roles have access to only the functions needed in the contract. It is based on the principle of least privilege, meaning that only the user can perform the assigned duties. Following is a snippet of the code where the RBAC is implemented, for example, only the admin, or *borrow cap guardian*, can call the setBorrowCap function to set new borrowing limits for cToken markets.

```
******************************************
function _setMarketBorrowCaps(DToken[] calldata dTokens, uint[] calldata
newBorrowCaps) external {
        require(msg.sender == admin || msg.sender == borrowCapGuardian,
"only admin or borrow cap guardian can set borrow caps");
***************************************************
```

The complete code can be found at **https://github.com/compound-finance/compound-protocol/blob/master/contracts/Comptroller.sol**

Multi-Signature

A multi-signature account is a special type of account that requires a minimum address signature before contract execution. This will allow the power to be distributed and offer decentralization. This is a technique used by projects like Compound and Balancer.

Another important aspect of having a multi-signature property is the implementation of fault tolerance by adopting an m of n scheme. It simply means that if two out of four are available, then only the function is to be executed. This is an alternative way of controlling access.

Time locks

In a time-locked contract, the state of a smart contract gets locked for a specified period of time, and any state change operation will not be executed until the timer expires. This offers two benefits: first, it delays the contract execution, which means if there is a change coming in the protocol of a contract, users get enough time to react and potentially exit the system.

The other benefit it gives is stalling malicious actions. By adding another layer of security, the blockchain makes it safer to transfer ownership or make new coins. Even if an attacker gets certain powers (by taking over whitelisted accounts or going after features that aren't protected), you still have time to stop them.

The Uniswap Timelock contract is a great example of how timelocks can be used to control routine actions.

Logging audit events in a Smart Contract

Enable event logging in your smart contract layer, such as highlighting different privileged accounts in a smart contract's system with a description of each role. And also, notify administrators if any detail in the access control mechanism changes (for example, via log events).

All these features learned earlier will strengthen your smart contract access control and offer you a defense in depth security posture.

Public Key Infrastructure

In 2020, the SolarWinds Orion platform was compromised when hackers injected malicious code, known as Sunburst, to gain unauthorized access to a plethora of sensitive information belonging to US government agencies like the Treasury and Commerce Department. The culprit behind this major attack compromised public key certificates and went on to exploit public key infrastructure, or PKI. It is one of the highest-profile cyber-attacks in history.

In this topic, we will cover the concepts of PKI, its importance, the challenges, where it fits in the blockchain stack to harden the security, and tools you can use to architect the solutions.

Let us start with the basics.

Public key infrastructure, or PKI, is a catch-all term for everything used to establish and manage public key encryption, which is one of the most common forms of keeping information secure on the internet. It's baked into every web browser in use today to secure traffic across the public internet. For example, when you enable HTTPS in your browser, you can see a lock symbol in the URL, indicating your browser trusts the server you are talking to, and any messages going across it are encrypted.

Now, if you think about security controls and their use cases, they fall into the following categories:

- **Enforcing Confidentiality:** SSL/TLS encryption secures any communication in transit across the blockchain architecture. For example, an HTTPS request from an API gateway going towards blockchain oracles, or the HTTPS communication between the blockchain nodes.
- **Enabling Authentication**: It includes web page authentication, Machine and User authentication, and Two-Factor Authentication. For example, a decentralized web application can only accept requests from trusted sources. Another important entity is the different protocols used in layers 2 and 3 of the blockchain. By enabling authentication, trust can be gained from a spoofed or malicious node, such that a node can only become part of the network if it holds a valid certificate.
- **Data Integrity**: This can enable security at rest; any information sent between two network elements can have a data integrity check enabled. For instance, data values may have a digest that can be easily recognized when it has been altered. You can also enforce data encryption at rest so that data cannot be read through.

Now that we have understood the use cases and how they can help secure your blockchain application, let us look at how it works with its fundamental pillars.

It is essential to return to the fundamentals that established encryption in the first place to comprehend how PKI functions. We should learn more about cryptography methods and digital certificates.

Public Key Cryptography

Cryptographic methods are complex mathematical formulas that are used to hide or encrypt and uncover or decrypt messages. They are also the building blocks for PKI verification. Public key cryptography is essential in blockchain. Think of the use of public and private key pairs in wallets, the hashing algorithm SHA256 in building a block, and the use of digital signatures with the signing of the private key in submitting a transaction. All these use cases are made possible by public key cryptography. It mainly falls into Asymmetric and Symmetric encryption.

Symmetric Encryption

With symmetric encryption, a message written in plain text goes through complex patterns to become encrypted. The encrypted message is difficult to break because the same letter in plain text does not always look the same in encrypted text. For example, the word **XYZ** would not be turned into three of the same letters.

For symmetric encryption, you need the same key to both encrypt and decrypt the message. Without the key, it's very difficult to figure out how to decrypt a message. However, using the same key to secure and decrypt the message is a big risk. This is becausc if the way the key is shared or the key itself gets compromised, the whole purpose and process for sending secure texts are lost.

Asymmetric Encryption

With asymmetric encryption, a message is still encrypted through mathematical formulas, but only the receiver needs to know the private key to decrypt it. Meanwhile, anyone can use the public key to encrypt a message.

Here's an example using the well-known characters Bob and Alice:

- Alice wants to send a secret message to Bob, so she uses Bob's public key to create encrypted ciphertext that only Bob's private key can decode.
- Since only Bob's private key can decrypt the message, Alice can send it knowing that no one else, not even an eavesdropper, can read it, as long as Bob makes sure no one else has his private key.

Asymmetric encryption also lets you do things that are harder to do with symmetric encryption, such as creating digital signatures, which function as follows:

- Bob can send a message to Alice and then use his private key to encrypt a signature at the end of the message.
- When Alice receives the message, she can check two things with Bob's public key:
    - Bob or someone else who had Bob's secret key sent the message.
    - The message was not changed while it was in transit, because if it had, the proof would have failed.

In either case, Alice has not made her own key. With just an exchange of public keys, Alice can send Bob secret messages and check the signatures on papers signed by Bob. Importantly, these things do not work both ways. For Bob to be able to send secret messages to Alice and check her signature, Alice would need to make her own private key and give Bob the public key that goes with it.

Figure 6.7 is an illustration of this concept using different algorithms, and I have also listed the use cases in the box.

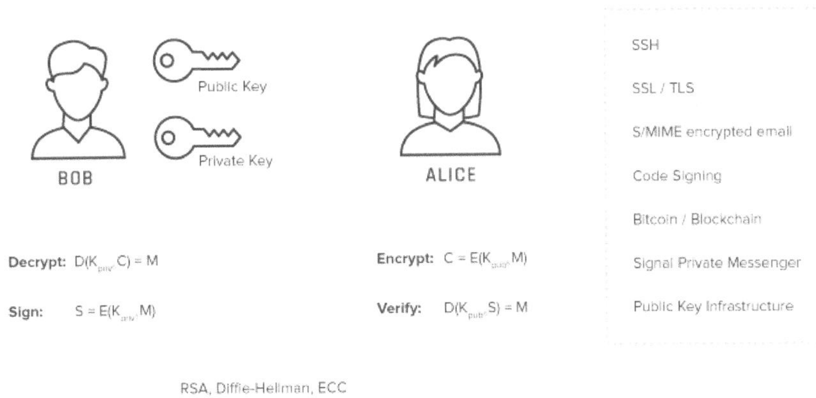

***Figure 6.7**: Asymmetric encryption example with use cases*

Now, how do we generate these keys if only public and private keys are necessary for all encryption, decryption, and digital signatures? Which algorithms do we use?

The answer to this is the RSA, ECC, and Diffie-Hellman algorithms. Each uses a different set of rules to generate encryption keys, but they all rely on the same basic principles as far as the relationship between the public key and the private key is concerned.

As an example, let us look at the RSA encryption scheme. RSA encryption is often used with other types of encryptions or for digital signatures, which can show that a message is real and hasn't been tampered with. A good use case is to use a symmetric key to encrypt the file and then use the RSA key to encrypt the symmetric key, which means that only the RSA private key would be used to decrypt the symmetric key. Several wallet startups have used this strategy. You can implement RSA using open SSL, cryptolib, and other cryptographic libraries.

Another good use case is TLS, which is used to implement secure communication between two entities: Web/VPN clients and Web/VPN Servers. HTTP communication has turned to HTTPS using RSA.

The following steps explain how public and private keys are calculated using RSA:

- Select two large prime numbers, X and Y. Then compute their product, `n=x*y`
- Compute the totient (multiplicative) function, such that $\varphi(n)=(x-1)(y-1)$.
- Select integer f such that f is co-prime to $\phi(n)$ and $1<f<\phi(n)$. The pair (n, f) is the public key.

> **Note**
>
> Two integers are co-prime if the only positive integer that divides them is 1.

- Calculate *e*, such that $e.f = 1 \bmod \phi(n)$

  Note, *e* can be calculated using extended Euclidean formula, the pair (*n*, *e*) is the private key. Following is the sample code to explain the preceding steps in action.

```
int x = 61, int y = 53;
int n = x * y;
// n = 3233.

// compute the totient, phi
int phi = (x-1)*(y-1);
// phi = 3120.

int e = findCoprime(phi);
// find an 'e' which is > 1 and is a co-prime of phi.
// e = 17 satisfies the current values.

// Using the extended euclidean algorithm, find 'd' which sat-
isfies
// this equation:
d = (1 mod (phi))/e;
// d = 2753 for the example values.

public_key = (e=17, n=3233);
private_key = (d=2753, n=3233);

// Given the plaintext P=123, the ciphertext C is :
C = (123^17) % 3233 = 855;
// To decrypt the cypher text C:
P = (855^2753) % 3233 = 123;
```

Sample Code to illustrate RSA function

Now, which algorithm to use and when I should use asymmetric over symmetric in my blockchain application, it is important to understand the relationship between them.

Asymmetric and Symmetric encryption relationship

Asymmetric encryption is much slower than symmetric encryption due to the key length and computation involved, so the two are often used in tandem. For example, someone might protect a message using symmetric encryption and then send the key to decode the message using asymmetric encryption. This would speed up the decryption process because the key is much smaller than the message. *Figure* 6.8 explains this concept where both Symmetric and Asymmetric key encryption are used together.

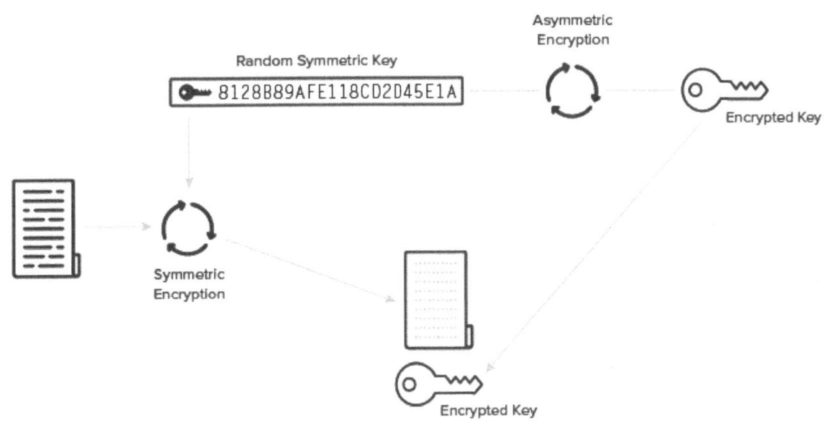

***Figure 6.8**: The application of symmetric and asymmetric encryption*

So, the concept of public and private key encryption powers the PKI and enables what the PKI does.

Both symmetric and asymmetric encryption have one major challenge: How do you know that the public key you received belongs to the person you think it does?

Even with asymmetric encryption, the risk of the *man in the middle*' exists. For example, what if someone intercepted Bob's public key, made his own private key, and then generated a new public key for Alice? In this case, Alice would encrypt messages for Bob, but the man in the middle could decrypt, change, and then re-encrypt the messages, and neither Alice nor Bob would be any wiser.

So, the problem statement is that cryptography is not enough to secure the communication channel between two parties. You need an additional layer of security, which can help establish trust between different parties.

Welcome to PKI as the solution. Here is how it solves our problem.

This problem is solved by PKI, which gives out and manages digital certificates that prove the names of people, devices, or apps that have both private and public keys. In short, PKI gives keys names so that people who use them can be sure who owns them. This confirmation gives users confidence that if they send an encrypted message to that person (or device), the intended recipient will read it and not a *man in the middle.*

As the message reaches any of the parties, it holds the signature of a certified authority, which both parties trust. If you are thinking about how to prevent the spoofing of a certificate signature, this is where the certificate revocation list comes in. In such cases, the certificate authority, also known as Root CA, can send a message to all the parties involved to not trust a particular certificate.

Let me explain this concept by breaking down the components of public key infrastructure.

Components of Public Key Infrastructure

It comprises three major components: X.509 certificates, public and private keys, and certificate authorities, chains, or trust. Let us look at each one.

x.509 Digital Certificates

X.509 is a digital certificate like a driver's license, it is a way for companies and groups to prove who they are online. PKI makes it possible for two machines to talk to each other securely because certificates can be used to check the names of the two parties. *Figure* 6.9 displays what a digital license looks like.

Figure 6.9: *SSL Certificate*

Once you have a digital certificate, it is important to maintain the lifecycle of the certificate, from enrollment and issuance to revocation and renewal.

Public and Private Keys

A public key is a cryptographic key that can be distributed to the public and does not require secure storage. Only the corresponding private key can decrypt messages encrypted by the public key. In the blockchain ecosystem, you are already familiar with the concept of the public key as an identity for the user, but these are also used in a digital signature to encrypt the message.

On the other hand, private Keys are used by the recipient to decrypt a message that is encrypted using a public key. Since the message is encrypted using a given public key, it can only be decrypted by the matching private key. Also, these are used to sign a transaction, similar to their function in the blockchain.

Defining Certificate Authorities and Chain of Trust

Certification Authorities (Cas) are in charge of making digital certificates and owning the policies, practices, and processes for verifying users and giving out certificates.

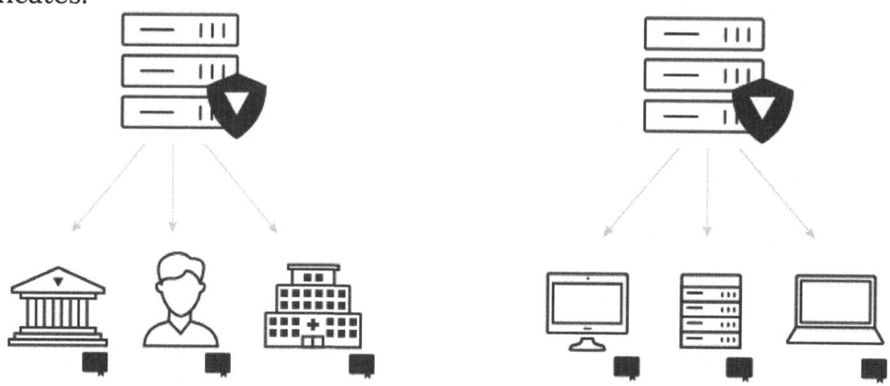

Figure 6.10: *Certificate authorities issuing digital certificates*

Digital identities take the form of cryptographically validated digital certificates that comply with the X.509 standard and are issued by a Certificate Authority (CA). On the other hand, the chain of trust refers to the certificate that links the bank to a trusted certifying authority. For an SSL certificate to be trusted, it must be traceable back to the trusted root from which it was signed, meaning all certificates in the chain server, intermediate, and root need to be properly trusted.

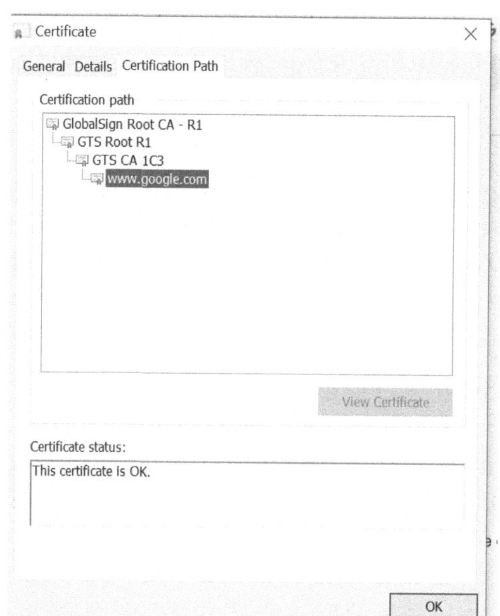

Figure 6.11: *Certificate path to validate trust*

In the preceding figure, we can see that google.com is the server to which we are connected. GTS-CA 1C3 is an intermediate CA. GTS-Root R1 is another intermediate CA. GlobalSign Root CA- R1 is the top root CA. In this way, a chain of trust can be built.

The chain of trust comprises three parts:

- **Root certificate:** A root certificate is a digital certificate that comes from the Certificate Authority that gave it out. Most browsers already have it saved and kept in a "trust store." The Certificate Authorities keep a close eye on the root certificates. For example, *Figure* 6.11 shows that GlobalSign Root CA- R1 is a root CA.

  In an enterprise blockchain network, you can use your own CA as the root.

- **Intermediate CA:** Intermediate certificates branch out from root certificates, like branches of a tree. They act as middlemen between the protected root certificates and the server certificates issued to the public. If you have two departments in an organization where you want to establish a trusted network, you can make two Intermediate CAs, which can be linked back to the Root CA.

- **Server Certificate:** The server certificate is the one issued to the specific domain. For example, *Figure* 6.11 shows that a server certificate is an issue to google.com, which can be any of your DaPPs or a blockchain node in a network.

The question arises: how does all of this apply to blockchain?

PKI Applications to Blockchain

Now, if you think in the context of a private blockchain network, all the infrastructure network components used or the nodes participating in the network can be trusted if digital certificates are issued to them. There can be an argument that blockchain is a trustless system, and trust is achieved with a consensus algorithm and the protocol itself. However, in a private or consortium blockchain network where you want to add an extra layer of security, whenever a node is entered into the chain, it must have a valid certificate.

Moreover, a valid SSL Certificate on your blockchain website helps keep user data safe, proves that you own the site, and stops attackers from making a fake version of the site. Finally, this will also help your people trust you.

Note

If a website asks users to sign in, enter personal information like their credit card numbers, or view sensitive information like health benefits or financial information, it is important to keep the data confidential. SSL certificates help keep internet transactions private and give users confidence that the website is real and safe to share private information.

Now that you have understood the concept of PKI and how it can aid blockchain websites and network infrastructure, we will take a deep dive into verifying its application in Hyperledger Fabric.

We know that a PKI is composed of Certificate Authorities who issue digital certificates to parties (for example, users of a service, service providers), who then use them to authenticate themselves in the messages they exchange in their environment.

This can be seen in *Figure* 6.12, where the principal is requesting a certificate from CA, who is responsible for issuing the certificate.

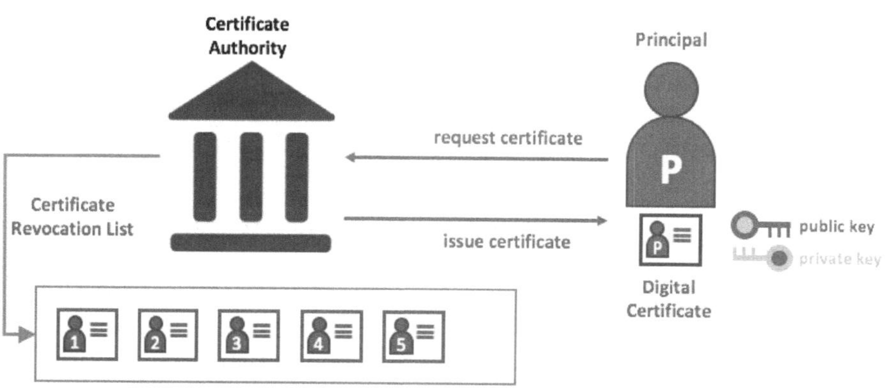

Figure 6.12: *Hyperledger Fabric CA Architecture*

Also, the certificate revocation list is maintained by the CA principals whose identities are compromised or are not qualified to issue the certificates. This is like the concept of an access control list, where you allow specific IPs over another. The Public key, which is maintained by the user, has the signature of a CA. In this way, when the principal communicates with any other users, it can establish the truth.

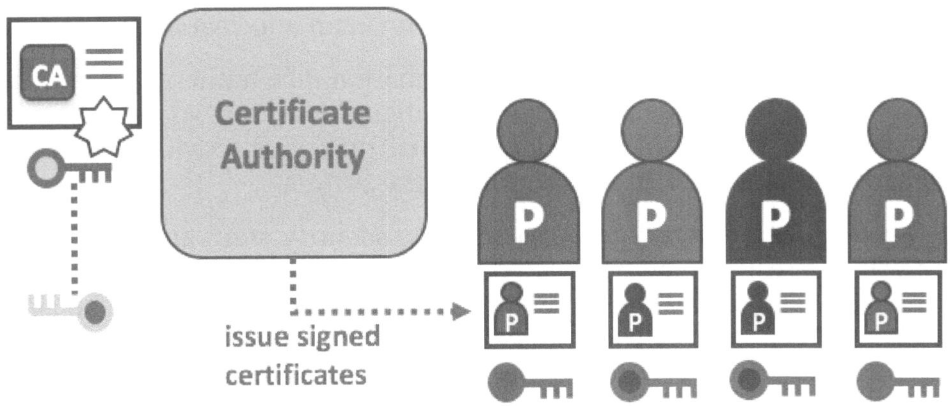

***Figure 6.13**: Issuance of signed certificates to principals*

Figure 6.13 helps us visualize the trust hierarchy, where all principals are verified by the CA, and each holds a signed certificate. Every such principal who wishes to interact must have a validated certificate (public key).

If you are looking for more details about PKI aiding Hyperledger Fabric using DIGI-CERT CA, please visit:

https://www.hyperledger.org/learn/publications/thales-digicert-case-study

Security Logging and Monitoring

We live in an increasingly complex environment where breaches, hacks, and other malicious online activities seem to be in the news all the time. Security systems need to be strong enough to deal with the constant threats that companies face today.

Security professionals have a lot to do identification and authentication, access control, encryption of data in transit and at rest, data integrity, system and data availability, vendor management, incident response, personnel security, vulnerability management, malware defenses, application security, etc. It's important for them to be able to gather, analyze, and report information that helps with all these things, and blockchain is no different. With blockchain, you end up with more ways to get in because the network is spread out.

Why logging is important?

Put simply, a system log is a list of individual records that show specific activity, events, error conditions, flaws, or the general state of an information system or network. These log records have important information that helps system and security managers understand what is going on in an information system.

As many logs contain security-related information (like authentication events, changes in access, changes in system configuration, and so on), they help administrators keep track of potential (or actual) malicious activity on the system or changes that may weaken the security of the system.

If the system does not make logs, managers, security staff, and development teams will not really know what is going on in the system. They won't know if any malicious activities are happening in the system and will not be able to do anything about it. They will not know how a breach happened or where the attacker went after the first break. As long as data is being stolen and their harmful presence is still there, both failed and successful attempts will go unnoticed. Logs are of various types, and they depend upon the underlying infrastructure, the application, and the type of activities involved.

Security Logs Analysis

In a digital world, a log file is information either in the form of events that occur on any digital device or communication information between different users. In simple words, it is an event that took place at a certain time and might have metadata that contextualizes it. Following is an example of a log file:

```
May 14 00:18:04            syslogd[94]: Configuration Notice:
        ASL Module "com.apple.cdscheduler" claims selected messages.
        Those messages may not appear in standard system log files or in the ASL d
May 14 00:18:04            syslogd[94]: Configuration Notice:
        ASL Module "com.apple.install" claims selected messages.
        Those messages may not appear in standard system log files or in the ASL d
May 14 00:18:04            syslogd[94]: Configuration Notice:
        ASL Module "com.apple.callhistory.asl.conf" claims selected messages.
```

Figure 6.14: *Example log file*

In general, they contain timestamp, user, and event information, as shown in *Figure* 6.14.

There are many types of events and signals that you may be able to collect from devices. Monitoring devices should form part of your organization's wider approach to logging and monitoring. Very often, successful intrusion detection requires multiple sources of information.

All the computer systems that are part of the network generate logs, which can be apps, containers, databases, firewalls, endpoints, web services, and smart contracts.

There are hundreds of possible types of log sources in your environment, and choosing which bubbles to the top of your IT consciousness can be difficult. As a rule of thumb, you should be monitoring the following logs in your blockchain network:

- **System Log (syslog):** This is where operating system events are written down. It shows information about starting up, changes to the system, sudden shutdowns, problems and warnings, and other important things. Syslog is made for Windows, Linux, and macOS.
- **Event logs on Ethereum:** When Ethereum smart contracts run, they can send out events. When this happens, the contracts also keep logs that give information about what happened. LOG0, LOG1, LOG2, LOG3, and LOG4 are the five opcodes that the EVM can use to send out event logs.
- **Access logs and authorization:** These logs include a list of the people or bots who accessed certain apps or files. These can be taken from Active Directory, LDAP, or AAA servers.
- **Threat Logs**: They contain information about system, file, or application activity that meets a security rule or a breach. You must install a firewall or a threat detection agent inside your OS for threat logs to appear. A common example of a threat log is a malicious system call generated due to a hacker's intent to perform lateral movements inside the network.

Out of the aforementioned categories, system logs and audit logs are built into the operating system. More granular audit logs can be enabled from the identity and access management platform, whereas threat logs depend upon whether you have any security tools like firewalls, runtime threat detection agents like antivirus software, etc. As most blockchain application development uses Ethereum, clarity on security logging on EVM will give you thorough visibility inside your blockchain architecture and strengthen your defense mechanism.

Ethereum Event logs

Ethereum Virtual Machine (EVM) has five **operation codes** (opcodes) for transmitting Ethereum event logs: LOG0, LOG1, LOG2, LOG3, and LOG4. With such opcodes, Web3 developers can make log records that describe what happened in smart contracts. This can happen, for example, when the owner of an NFT changes or when a coin is transferred.

Topics and data constitute a part of each log record. Topics are 32-byte (256 bit) **words** that explain what's going on in an event. Depending on how many topics need to be in the log record, different opcodes (LOG0–LOG4) are used. For example, LOG1 has only one topic, while LOG4 has four. Because of this, a single log record can only have a maximum of four issues.

These log fields can be seen in the Ethereum yellow paper, as shown in *Figure 6.15*.

a0s: Logging Operations

For all logging operations, the state change is to append an additional log entry on to the substate's log series:

$$A\ 1A'_1 \equiv A_1 \cdot (I_a, \mathbf{t}, \boldsymbol{\mu}_m[\boldsymbol{\mu}_s[0] \dots (\boldsymbol{\mu}_s[0] + \boldsymbol{\mu}_s[1] - 1)])$$

and to update the memory consumption counter:

$\mu'_i \equiv M(\mu_i, \boldsymbol{\mu}_s[0], \boldsymbol{\mu}_s[1])$

The entry's topic series, **t**, differs accordingly:

Value	Mnemonic	δ	α	Description
0xa0	LOG0	2	0	Append log record with no topics. $\mathbf{t} \equiv ()$
0xa1	LOG1	3	0	Append log record with one topic. $\mathbf{t} \equiv (\boldsymbol{\mu}_s[2])$
⋮	⋮	⋮	⋮	⋮
0xa4	LOG4	6	0	Append log record with four topics. $\mathbf{t} \equiv (\boldsymbol{\mu}_s[2], \boldsymbol{\mu}_s[3], \boldsymbol{\mu}_s[4], \boldsymbol{\mu}_s[5])$

***Figure 6.15**: Ethereum yellow paper – Byzantine version*

Topics and Data in Ethereum Log Records

In the first part of a log record, there are several different issues. These things are used to explain what happened. The signature (a keccak256 hash) of the name of the event that happened and the types (uint256, string, and so on) of its inputs are usually the first subjects.

Note that this signature is not always the first subject. One case where it is not is when unnamed events are sent.

Since topics can only hold up to 32 bytes of information, they can't be used to store groups or words. Instead, it should be part of the log record as information, not as a topic.

In the second part of the log record, there is more information. Topics and facts work best together because they both have pros and cons. For example, you can look for ideas, but not for data. Adding facts, on the other hand, is a lot cheaper than adding topics. Topics are also limited to 4 * 32 bytes, but event data is not. This means that event data can include big or complicated data like lists or strings. So, the event data, if there is any, can be thought of as the value.

Storage of Ethereum logs

When a smart contract sends out an event, the log data that goes with it is written down and kept in a transaction report. Every transaction has a receipt that shows the results of the operation, such as the state and event logs. In addition, the transaction logs contain the gas amount used. Let us understand a bit more by looking through the two main use cases.

- **Asynchronous Triggers with Data:** When building daps and other Web3 platforms, you generally set up your projects so that they monitor relevant Ethereum smart contract events. These event logs allow the smart contract to interact with Dapp's frontend.
- **Smart Contract Return Values:** This is to pass along the return value of a contract to a Dapp's frontend, which will enable monitoring of the process flow of your blockchain application.

Here is an example that will help you understand how topics, data, and log records work together.

Token contracts that adhere to ERC20 use the Transfer event, which is what this contract uses:

```
pragma solidity 0.5.3;

contract ExampleContract {
    event Transfer(address indexed _from, address indexed _to, uint256 _value);

    function transfer(address _to, uint256 _value) public {
        emit Transfer(msg.sender, _to, _value);
    }
}
```

Figure 6.16*: Transfer function contract to show events*

Since this is not an anonymous event, the first topic will consist of the event signature:

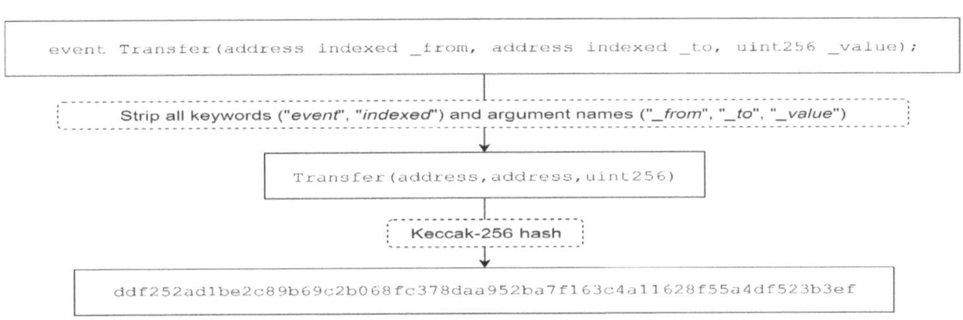

Figure 6.17*: First Topic analysis*

Let's look at the arguments (from, to, value) of this Solidity event:

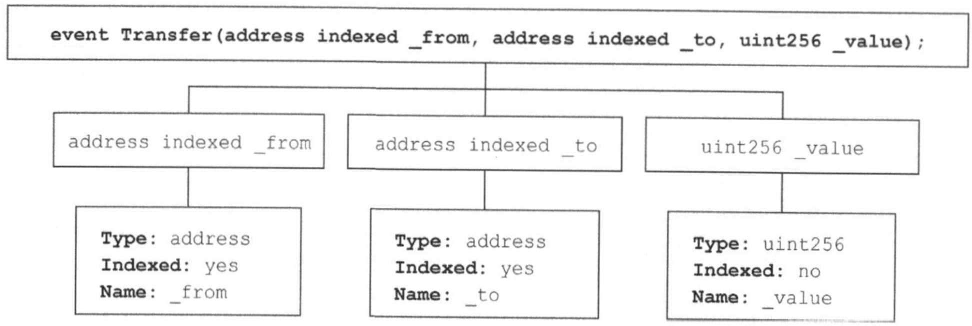

***Figure 6.18**: Solidity event matrix*

Since the first two arguments are stated to be indexed, they are treated as extra topics. Our final argument will not be indexed, meaning that it will be attached as data instead of a different topic. Therefore, we can search for things like "find all Transfer logs from address 0x0000... to address 0x0000". or "find all logs to address 0x0000". but not for things like "find all Transfer logs with value "x"." We know that this event will have three items, so the LOG3 opcode will be used to log it.

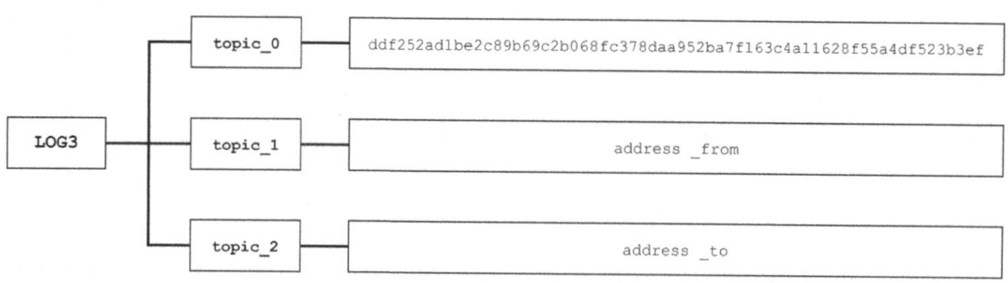

***Figure 6.19**: Log 3 analysis*

LOG3(memoryStart, memoryLength, topic1, topic2, topic3).

Here's how memory is used to read event data:

memory[memoryStart... (memoryStart + memoryLength)]

With higher-level smart contract programming languages like Solidity, Vyper, or Bamboo, they will write event data to memory for us. This implies that you can usually pass data directly as a parameter when producing logs.

Retrieving event logs

The following code sends an alert whenever a new SAI token transfer happens. This can be useful for various purposes. For instance, a wallet display could tell you when your Ethereum address gets coins.

```
const Web3 = require("web3");
const web3 = new Web3("wss://mainnet.infura.io/ws");

web3.eth.subscribe("logs", {
    address: "0x89d24A6b4CcB1B6fAA2625fE562bDD9a23260359",
    topics: [
        web3.utils.sha3("Transfer(address,address,uint256)")
    ]
}, (error, result) => {
    if (error) {
        console.error(error);
    } else {
        console.log(result);
    }
});
```

***Figure 6.20**: Retrieving event logs*

The next step in your logging journey is to understand the high-level architecture, where the logs need to be generated, and how they can be forwarded.

Security logging and monitoring architecture

When your architecture is distributed and decentralized, this task becomes more complex. To better control the risk and prevent repudiation attacks, you need to have a robust logging and monitoring infrastructure for your blockchain network.

To architect a logging and monitoring solution, the first step is to identify the data sources, the interfaces, and the storage elements where the data is parsed and stored. The second step is to ensure that the data sets are marked based on what you want to capture and filter. For example, out of the fields **`Name`**, **`Address`**, **`Phone Number`**, **`Public Key`**, **`Time`**, **`Event`**, you need to extract only the public key and Time fields, as the other fields hold PI information and would not be beneficial, in addition to increasing the overall size.

The last step is to hook up and forward the filtered events into a data lake, where you can get a visual view of the fault management. The architecture of Splunk

Cloud, as shown in *Figure* 6.21, gives a good representation of how to architect a secure logging and monitoring solution for your WEB3 Dapp.

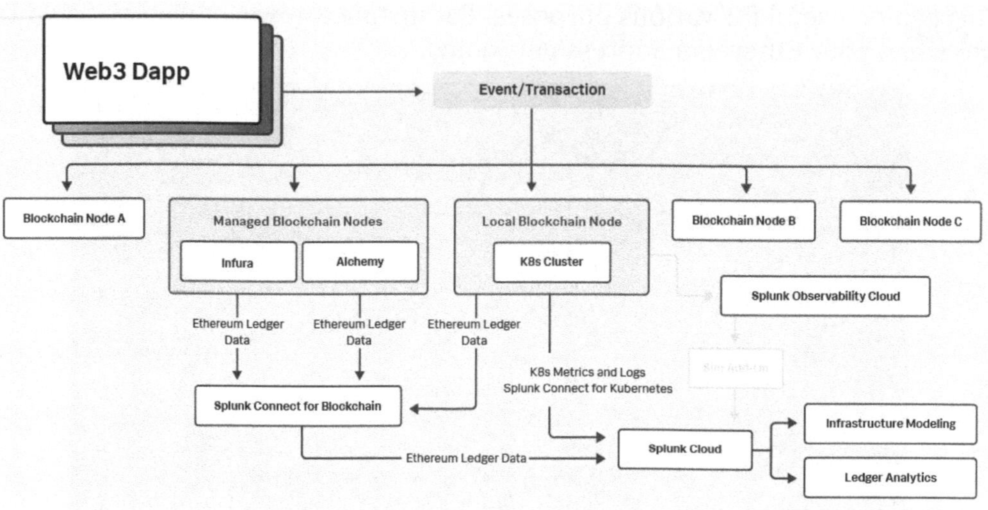

Figure 6.21: *Splunk cloud for blockchain logging and monitoring*

Figure 6.22 displays the anticipated view when the data is injected into the data lake. This offers not only meaningful insights like alarms, health status, faults, and security audit logs but also the ability to understand your user's behavior and performance indicators.

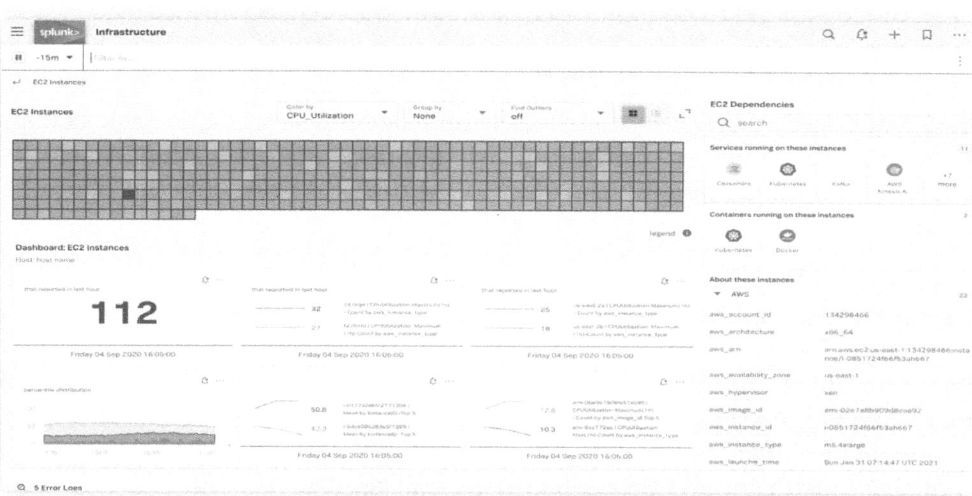

Figure 6.22: *Splunk Cloud – Data insights*

By using these add-ons, you can have good visibility of your blockchain data, thereby reducing risk in your blockchain application. For more information, please visit: **https://lantern.splunk.com/Data_Descriptors/Blockchain_data.**

Conclusion

You made it! Congratulations on reaching the end. This final chapter has covered blockchain security solutions in great detail. We learned zero-knowledge proof concepts and looked at identity and access management and PKI architecture, which will help you enforce security in transit and at rest and make your architecture components trustworthy. We also looked at the security logging architecture and took a deep dive into smart contract logging. All these tools and frameworks will strengthen your defense and allow you to establish trust with your customers.

Now that you have completed the book, you're ready to plan and architect your blockchain solution with confidence.

Points to remember

- With zero-knowledge proof, you can prove to the second party that the information you are sharing is legitimate and proven.
- Identity and access management principles protect the resources from unauthorized access. You can control who is accessing your smart contracts and resources and limit how much they can access.
- The public key infrastructure consists of public and private key pairs, certificate authorities, and digital certificates. It helps you ensure trust in your network and enables authentication and confidentiality in your blockchain network.
- Security logging is the way to filter events in your network to give you meaningful insights that can be used to debug, trace, and monitor suspicious activity in your network.
- Logging infrastructure consists of logging hooks from data processing components and log forwarding agents to consolidate the events in one place and provide a dashboard view.

References

- **https://www.kaleido.io/blockchain-platform/aws-enterprise-single-sign-on**
- **https://hyperledger-fabric.readthedocs.io/en/latest/identity/identity.html**
- **https://ethereum.github.io/yellowpaper/paper.pdf**
- **https://www.splunk.com/en_us/solutions/blockchain.html**

Index

A

B